Vanguards
and
Followers

Vanguards
and
Followers

Youth in the American Tradition

Louis Filler

Nelson-Hall nh Chicago

LIBRARY OF CONGRESS CATALOGING IN PUBLICATION DATA

Filler, Louis,
    Vanguards and followers.

    Bibliography: p.
    Includes index.
    1. Youth—United States.   I.   Title
HQ796.F567   301.43'15'0973   78–5893
ISBN   0–88229–459–8 (*cloth*)
ISBN   0–88229–608–6 (*paper*)

Manufactured in U.S.A.
10 9 8 7 6 5 4 3 2 1

Contents

92287

OTHER WRITINGS IN HISTORY AND LITERATURE BY LOUIS FILLER

BOOKS

Appointment at Armageddon: Muckraking and Progressivism in the American Tradition (1976)
Randolph Bourne (1965 ed.)
The Crusade against Slavery, 1830–1860 (1960 ff.)
A Dictionary of American Social Reform (1963; Greenwood ed., 1970)
The Unknown Edwin Markham (1966)
Muckraking and Progressivism: an Interpretive Bibliography (1976)

EDITED WORKS

The New Stars: Life and Labor in Old Missouri, Manie Morgan (1949)
Mr. Dooley: Now and Forever, Finley Peter Dunne (1954)
American Liberalism of the Late Nineteenth Century (1961), anthology; re-issue, *From Populism to Progressivism* (1978)
The Removal of the Cherokee Nation: Manifest Destiny or National Dishonor? (1977 ed.)
The World of Mr. Dooley (1962)
The Anxious Years (1963), anthology of 1930's literature
Horace Mann and Others, Robert L. Straker (1963)
A History of the People of the United States, John Bach McMaster (1964)
The President Speaks (1964), major twentieth-century addresses
Horace Mann on the Crisis in Education (1965; Spanish translation, 1972)
Wendell Phillips on Civil Rights and Freedom (1965)
The Ballad of the Gallows-Bird, Edwin Markham (1967)
Old Wolfville: the Fiction of A. H. Lewis (1968)
Slavery in the United States of America (1972)
Abolition and Social Justice (1972)

INTRODUCTIONS

Chatterton, Ernest Lacy (1952)
Plantation and Frontier. Ulrich B. Phillips, in new edition, John R. Commons et al., *A Documentary History of American Industrial Society* (1958)
The Acquisition of Political, Social and Industrial Rights of Man in America, John Bach McMaster (1961)
My Autobiography, S. S. McClure (1962)
A Modern Symposium, G. Lowes Dickinson (1963)
A Statistical History of the American Presidential Elections, Svend Petersen (1963)
Samuel Gompers, Bernard Mandel (1963)
The Political Depravity of the Founding Fathers, John Bach McMaster (1964)
Democrats and Republicans, Harry Thurston Peck (1964)
A Political History of Slavery, W. H. Smith (1966)
Georgia and States Rights, Ulrich B. Phillips (1967)
The Pantarch: a Biography of Stephen Pearl Andrews, Madeleine B. Stern (1968)
Forty Years of It, Brand Whitlock (1970)

Preface

Youth as a social phenomenon is a relatively late flowering in our history, but it has been a major force in the twentieth century. Not young people as leaders among leaders, but young people as leaders of youth have demanded and received attention. The manner of their approach and the quality of the attention which followed have helped define changing American conditions.

A key problem is to determine whether there has been a youth *tradition*. What, if anything, connects Randolph Bourne and Abbie Hoffman? Or Vachel Lindsay and Bob Dylan, both minstrels of a sort? John Reed has been recently revived in motion pictures as a heroic figure; but who is his modern equivalent? And the ethnic factor: who *was* the equivalent of Stokely Carmichael fifty years ago, assuming that the ethnic factor is an element in the youth tradition?

It is perhaps a quality of youth that it does not emphasize tradition—even the traditions of youth. The very evanescence of youth would make the building of a tradition difficult. Youth grows older. "Never trust anyone over thirty"—a slogan of the early 1960's—becomes absurd in the early 1970's. A newer youth must create new attitudes which jibe or conflict with those deriving from changed circumstances. The old saw had it that one who was

vii

not a socialist at twenty had no heart; one who was still a socialist at thirty had no head. But in a world which breaks with its past, repudiating older, individualistic ideals, the breakdown of differences betweeen capitalism and socialism compounds confusion, affecting the potentials of the young.

The basic question was and is: what conditions created opportunities for youthful expresson—expression such as the country had not known before? Did those conditions derive from American traditions, or were they the result of particular circumstances which might or might not recur? It appeared in 1977 that such events as were associated with Berkeley, California or Kent, Ohio, or the "family" of Charles Manson would be a long time returning in orbit. But there was no guarantee that new events might not cause a youthful eruption reminiscent of the old. The past tended to take on pizza-like characteristics, being here simmering and tasty, there cold and unappetizing. But seen analytically, it could even recapture some of its old spirit and conviction, and, in any case, suggest ideas for use in the present.

So it is the larger scene, as well as its youthful component, which is here reassessed. The present writing offers little conjecture and as little assertion of sympathies as the shifting situation requires. It believes youth is best honored by candid examination, rather than mere empathy, certainly at the expense of youth's inevitable future as senior citizens.

LOUIS FILLER

Antioch University
March, 1978

1

"Young America"

The American colonies and the nation were founded on youthful premises. John Milton's vision, in his *Areopagitica,* of a "puissant nation . . . mewing [molting] her mighty youth" was often seen by an American people who revered him as referring to themselves.[1] The wilderness and the West presupposed persons of energy and strength, willing to take chances on the unknown, or with ideals or ambitions which drove them to relinquish status, associates, and established ways in favor of hoped-for gains.

Youths permeated the labor system, the value of indentured servants, women, and slaves being largely dependent on the age factor. Thomas Jefferson, in his seasoned correspondence with John Adams, ranked youth and beauty with talent and prestige as influencing opportunities society conferred on individuals.

Assertive agitators and leaders all but became a tradition, North and South, in ways not feasible in Europe, where they could readily have succumbed to prison or the rack. A "bohemian"

---

1. "Methinks I see in my mind a noble and puissant Nation rousing herself like a strong man after sleep and shaking her invincible locks. Methinks I see her as an Eagle muing her mighty youth, and kindling her undazl'd eyes at the full midday beam." For a statement of Milton's hold on the new American imagination, cf. G. F. Sensabaugh, *Milton in Early America* (Princeton, N. J., 1964).

touch was even introduced in the new colonies as early as 1625, when an English businessman, Thomas Morton, set up an Indian trading post at "Merry Mount" (Quincy) in Massachusetts. There he erected a May Pole in recollection of an Old World institution, and with his men disported himself with liquor and Indian "lasses in beaver coats." Following bitter complaints from settlements all the way to Maine (and also from the male Indians of the area) Miles Standish was sent with troops to extinguish the scandal. The May Pole was leveled and Morton sent back to England. He was fortunate to have avoided harsher punishment.

Early Dissident Traditions. The direction taken by early American founders as far as social tolerance was concerned was partially determined by their reluctance to execute or even imprison dissidents for most causes which would have brought cruel punishment in Europe. Prisons cost money, and executions deprived the sparse settlements of valuable human lives. Authorities could and did punish culprits without restraint for acts seen as atrocious, like sodomy. Otherwise they preferred such sentences as flogging or slitting of noses, or banishment. Roger Williams, a young minister who believed in religious freedom, was sent away from the Bay Colony as a heretic. He left to found Rhode Island in 1636. Two years later, Anne Hutchinson was banished for like cause and brought her flock to the new colony of Rhode Island.

The settlers were eager to encourage immigration and willing to endure the presence of independent individuals, eccentrics, women whose indispensability sometimes gave them a self-esteem not common in Europe, and servants who frequently ran away to another colony and passed as free, though they had not completed their terms as bondsmen. They readily found masters who were willing to accept such stories as they offered respecting their past employment.

Nevertheless, the leaders of colonies knew they had to enforce as much law and order as possible if they were to sustain society at all in so loose a formation of settlements as they inhabited surrounded by endless frontier. Children had no rights which did not result from paternal love and piety. The lives of girls were probably more constricted than those of boys. Their adolescence lacked dignity, and their prospects diversity. It has been conjectured that the Salem witchcraft hysteria in 1692, which depended on the testimony of young girls who identified "witches" and told tales of having personally witnessed devilish activities, resulted from their desire to draw attention to themselves and gain some importance in the community.[2]

In such ways American opportunity for young or old was qualified by efforts to control the excesses opportunity created. Significantly, it was a tradition of protest and rebellion which Americans chose to keep green in historical writings and by word of mouth, rather than a tradition of law and order. Protest was identified with attractive personalities, law and order with the gloom associated with the Riot Act, the calling out of militia, the rough dealings at hanging parties and lynching bees.

Bacon's Rebellion. The first great figure in the tradition of dissent was Nathaniel Bacon (a kinsman of Francis Bacon) who came to Jamestown, Virginia, with respectable credentials and settled on its frontier. Young Bacon rated a seat in the Virginia House of Burgesses. He was soon dissatisfied with its limited democracy and its benign attitude toward Indians. Virginians only saw them as traders in peaceful Jamestown. Bacon and his fellow frontiersmen, on the other hand, met Indians who raided their settlements and tried in other ways to keep them from invading their lands.

Bacon appealed vainly to the authorities for aid in fighting Indians. In 1676—a date which took on significance a century later—he moved independently to organize his neighbors and joined in battle with the Indians. Denounced as a traitor and threatened with capital punishment, Bacon had no choice but to set himself up in opposition to the Jamestown government. He projected constitutional reforms and planned to appeal to King Charles II, but died suddenly at age twenty-nine and left demoralized followers who buried him secretly. Then they pleaded for pardon of Governor William Berkeley, an uncompromising conservative who had once voiced the hope there would be no printing press in the New World for a hundred years. Berkeley had them executed without mercy. Said Charles II, "That old fool has

---

2. Marion L. Starkey, *The Devil in Massachusetts* (New York, 1949), 9 ff.

hanged more men in that naked country than I did for the murder
of my father." Bacon's Rebellion was memorialized in "Bacon's
Epitaph, Made by His Man": the first important American poem,
done by an anonymous hand.[3]

Later Crises and Youth. Other actions, uprisings, and provin-
cial differences punctuated settlement and growth before the
American Revolution. These often involved youth, but were not
dominated by it or by ideals distinguishing the young from others.
Bacon had been on the frontier for gain, not glory; and his plantation infringed on Indian land. His ideals, though universal in
theory, served his own people first at the expense of the natives.

Similarly, the later revolutionary crisis drew numerous brilliant young men and many selfless ones, such as Nathan Hale who
died by hanging at age twenty-one in 1776, having uttered immortal words: "I only regret that I have but one life to lose for my
country." The Marquis de Lafayette dedicated himself to the
American war against Great Britain at age twenty. But many of
the young were old in perspective. The later E. P. Whipple put the
matter nicely with respect to Alexander Hamilton's services to the
Revolution, services which began when he was nineteen years old
and writing pamphlets defending the Patriot cause. Whipple found
Hamilton "substantially the same at twenty-five as at forty-five."[4]

The Constitution of the United States, which these partisans
helped create, did nothing for young men and women as such so
far as social privileges, race, sex, education, or the franchise was
concerned. Its glory was that, unlike more glittering documents
drawn up elsewhere in the world, it was set up to endure, and so
gave hope that changing times would do something for the youth
as for others.

"Young America." The slogan "Young America" as such was

---

3. Death why so cruel! What, no other way
   To manifest thy spleene, but thus to slay
   Our hopes of safety, liberty, our all
   Which, through thy tyranny, with him must fall
   To its late chaos?
   The entire poem appears in Thomas Jefferson Wertenbaker, *Torchbearer of
   the Revolution* (Princeton, N.J., 1940), 179–80.
4. "Young Men in History," *Atlantic Monthly,* XVI (July, 1865), 1 ff.

both a political stratagem and a dream: the result of a long, tiring struggle between factions to create loyal attitudes toward the national government. It tried to curb such sectional and separatist implications as could be found in Jefferson's and Madison's Kentucky and Virginia Resolutions (1798). These denied that all acts of Congress had to be obeyed even if they were patently evil. Ideas which also helped create the concept of "Young America" could be found in reactions to the Hartford Resolutions (1815) which all but counseled treason to the country in protest against "Jemmy Madison's War" with Great Britain.

A patriotic, unifying slogan was necessary if the country was to survive such demoralizing tendencies. New voters, new leaders —and first of all Andrew Jackson representing a new, vigorous, democratic voice—expressed pride in their heritage, and declared it their "manifest destiny" to expand westward and turn frontier into civilization. "Young America" was first of all a Democratic Party slogan. It scorned Indians but was affable to new Irish settlers, assuring them that they were welcome and their institutions and religion safe.

Young America, which was a phrase before it became a political faction, was thus a mixture of practical self-interest and idealism: a bitter mixture to harassed Indians, resentful slaves, and aristocrats challenged by discontented workingmen and impatient frontiersmen. But some "Young Americans" expressed their idealism well. George Henry Evans (1805–1855) was seventeen years old when, having emigrated to New York from England, he issued *The Man,* pleading the cause of the workers. Later Evans's *Working Man's Advocate* denounced monopoly, debtor's prisons, and religious authority. He worked for radical political action and did not emphasize youth except as a class oppressed by capitalists.

Emerson. It was a Whig, Ralph Waldo Emerson, who perceived youth as the vehicle of the American future. Over and over again he addressed them on their mission in life. Emerson lectured them at Young Men's Institutes, Young Men's Associations, and Young Men's Unions from Boston and New York to Ohio, Indiana, Illinois, and all the way to frontier Janesville, Wisconsin. In his 1844 lecture on "The Young American," he noted that the cities "drain the country of the best part of its population; the flower of the youth of both sexes go into the towns, and the country is cultivated by a so inferior class."

A similar observation would be made by Randolph Bourne three-quarters of a century later; though, as a spokesman for youth, Bourne had no interest in reversing the trend.

Emerson declared that our society needed a new type of king. He called on young men to "obey your hearts and be the nobility of this land," working for justice and humanity. Leaders in the ordinary sense there must be, but "[w]ho should lead the leaders, but the Young Americans?" Emerson usually seemed to stand on higher ground than politicians. But though they could accuse him of talking rather than doing, any youth movement which can be discerned in pre-Civil War times stems from Emerson's exhortations rather than from any political faction.

Reforms in that period were of unprecedented scope and variety, and they inspired numerous youths to aid in advancing all of them, including the foremost cause: abolition. But the labors of youth could not be distinguished from those of any other group. The cause defined the youth, rather than youth the cause. It was otherwise with the influence wielded by Emerson. To an extent his crusade was conservative. He was proud of his Puritan heritage. He emphasized Self. He had faith in the good purposes of nature.

But it was precisely because Emerson emphasized Selfhood, even at the expense of society, that he could thrill a young man or a young woman and stir their creativity. "Who would be a man, must be a non-conformist," he held, in his essay "Self-Reliance." He would live by his own nature, he said, whatever the consequences. "Every decent and well spoken individual affects and sways me more than is right. I ought to go upright and vital, and speak the rude truth in all ways." Emerson would go further than truth; he would "write on the lintels of the doorpost, *Whim*. I hope it is somewhat better than whim at last, but we cannot spend the day in explanation." And in a burst of chagrin at the temptations of comformity:

> [D]o not tell me, as a good man did to-day, of my obliga-
> tion to put all poor men in good situations. Are they my
> poor? I tell thee, thou foolish philanthropist, that I grudge

the dollar, the dime, the cent I give to such men as do not belong to me and to whom I do not belong. There is a class of persons to whom by all spiritual affinity I am bought and sold; for them I will go to prison if need be; but your miscellaneous popular charities; the education at college of fools; the building of meetinghouses to the vain end to which many now stand; alms to sots, and the thousand-fold Relief Societies; though I confess with shame I sometimes succumb and give the dollar, it is a wicked dollar, which by and by I shall have the manhood to withhold.

Such words seemed to Emerson's critics irresponsible, and likely to release devils in impressionable youth. It is doubtful that much evil could have been traced to Emerson's oratory. It was too firmly surrounded by idealism. The marvel was that it was not offered to a self-righteous intellectual elite, but was freely presented to audiences of representative folk in towns and villages which received Emerson as a lecturer.

Communes. If there was a youth movement within the reform fold, it could be found in such cooperative ventures as Brook Farm outside of Boston, one of many such communes, in which young people conspicuously worked in a conscious effort to create harmony between body and mind. Brook Farm rang with laughter, with the blows of hammers, with shared work on the farm and in the kitchen, with conversations, music, plays, and with an education which left the children with happy and lasting memories.

Nathaniel Hawthorne did not like Brook Farm. It offended the deep solitude his strange youth had created, separating him from others. Henry D. Thoreau was similarly unenamored of the commune. He, too, needed to be alone in many of his mental processes and concerns with nature. His goal, however, was not far different from that of the Brook Farmers. Both they and Thoreau were responding to Emersonian tenets of selfhood, and they proved it by deviating from Emerson's own preferences and ideas.

Republicanism. The "Young America" movement as such was a result of dissatisfaction within Democratic Party ranks with "Old Fogy" control of its program. By 1852 the party was becoming identified with the least attractive aspects of southern political demands. The party could be equated with a Congress stifled by southern suspicions of free speech and civil liberties. It meant un-questioning obedience to slaveholders and acceptance of their view of slavery as permanent and just. As early as 1845 George Henry Evans, no friend of Negroes, but equally no friend of slaveholders, shook off such Democratic thinking as harmful to workingmen. Others, too, sought a new party program which could stir northern and southern patriots, and give hope to the common man.

The year 1848, which set off a round of revolutionary efforts in Europe, saw also the triumph of American arms in Mexico: a war bitterly resented by pacifists and others, but joyously received by loyalists and politicians who expected the victory to curb sec-tional strife and promise a national purpose the world would ad-mire. Their basic idea was that the United States must be an inter-national force. Young Americans also held that the nation must be ready, if necessary by force of arms, to aid the republicans of Europe in their fight for human rights. As one of them put it in 1852, when the nation was welcoming and wining Kossuth, exiled leader of the Hungarian revolution:

> The grand ideas which are most potent in the election are sympathy for the liberals of Europe, the expansion of the American republic southward and westward, and the grasp-ing of the magnificent purse of the commerce of the Pa-cific, in short, the ideas for which the term Young America is the symbol.[5]

The leader of this movement was a picturesque Kentuckian, George N. Sanders, editor of the *Democratic Review*, who brought together major spirits of his party including Stephen A. Douglas of Illinois and Robert J. Walker of Mississippi. Their friends and goals, notably homesteads, identified many of them with the fron-tier spirit, but their overall slogan of "expansion and progress" created a sympathetic bond with easterners as well. Sanders him-self mixed bold appeals to commercial interests with idealistic bombast about a new dawn of freedom in Europe. It would create

5. Merle Curti, "Young America," *American Historical Review*, 32 (Oct. 1926), 45; see essay for these and following details.

mighty markets for American surpluses, he urged. Sanders also hailed new immigrants—Germans, Hungarians, Irish—who fled across the Atlantic as their revolutionary hopes at home dwindled.

Sanders did not permit idealism to blur his own self-interest, and sold at a profit outmoded War Department muskets to European revolutionaries, an activity which did not disillusion them. Young Americans even dreamed of intervening directly in European affairs. When Sanders was appointed consul to London in 1853, his home became the center for plotting revolutions, drawing such guests as Kossuth, Mazzini, Garibaldi, and the French republican Ledru-Rollin. Sanders was refused confirmation by the Senate in 1854, and the exiles mourned their loss. Victor Hugo admired Sanders's "soul elevated and free." Other Young Americans, including August Belmont, New York agent for the Rothschilds, foresaw a great European awakening and thought it America's "sacred duty" to increase its navy in order to help when needed.

Walt Whitman. As compromised with materialism as was the "Young America" movement, it still produced a major bard of youth. Whitman began life as Walter Whitman: a young, attractive, and well-liked Jacksonian journalist. A photograph taken of him in 1840, aged twenty-one, shows a young dandy, sporting modish clothes and a cane. His early writings showed no poetic talent but evinced a sincere concern for progressive education and warm attitudes toward ordinary men and women. His early novel, *Franklin Evans; or The Inebriate* (1842), the one popular success of his lifetime, was conventional and insincere in its attitude toward liquor. Whitman was almost certainly of dual sexual propensities, a fact which made him secretive. Some of his later poems became a bond of sympathy between homosexuals, repressed by society and needing to communicate by indirection.

His emergence as Walt Whitman, poet of the people, came as a result of his sense of the passage of time, his unfulfilled personal wants, and the uplifting oratory of Emerson, who called for free, unfettered poets. A secret inspiration was George Sand's novel, *The Countess of Rudolstadt,* which depicted such a character as Whitman became. Whitman deliberately hid the existence of this book in the lists he drew up of his reading and influences.[6] It helps explain such oddities as Whitman's use of fragments of French, though he had not studied the language, among other curiosities in a style which opened earthy speech to American poetry.

Almost uniquely, he addressed his message to youth, calling on them to be brave and adventurous. As he later wrote:

> The people, especially the young men and women of America, must begin to learn that religion, (like Poetry), is something far, far different from what they supposed. It is, indeed, too important to the power and perpetuity of the New World to be consigned any longer to the churches, old or new, Catholic or Protestant—Saint this, or Saint that. . . . It must be consigned henceforth to Democracy en masse, and to Literature. It must enter into the Poems of the Nation. It must make the Nation.

There is a striking contrast between Whitman and Thoreau, both of whom influenced youth. Whitman seemed to Thoreau too animal-like in his praise of fleshly things, his joy in city life, and regard for people in aggregate. Many came to admire Thoreau's *Walden* as a relief from urban pressures, and to find inspiration in his essay on civil disobedience. Oddly enough, Thoreau, though a total pacifist, was also honored during the radical 1930's for his defense of John Brown. All this, however, was in the future. Thoreau's first fame in post-Civil War eras (he was wholly obscure in his lifetime) was created by nature-lovers, not necessarily young, who enjoyed his observations on the changing seasons.

It was otherwise with Whitman, whose *Leaves of Grass* increasingly stirred young readers. By the 1880's, numerous printings of the book were cherished by would-be poets, labor reformers, socialists, and women's-rights advocates. Whitman himself during his active years was a single, separate person and no joiner of organizations. His friendships were personal, largely nondescript, and sometimes enigmatic. But in his old age in Camden,

---

6. The key work is Esther Shephard, *Walt Whitman's Pose* (1938).

New Jersey, his home became Mecca to young men who came to talk with their revered trailblazer and philosopher.

More complex than as an inspirer of youth was Whitman as a patriot; this quality also separated him from Thoreau. As Whitman wrote in the 1860 edition of *Leaves of Grass* (issued by Thayer and Eldredge, who addressed him "fraternally," and described themselves pridefully as young men):

> I will make a song for These States, that no one
>   State may under any circumstances be subjected
>   to another State,
> And I will make a song that there shall be comity by
>   day and by night between all The States, and
>   between any two of them,
> And I will make a song of the organic bargains of
>   These States—And a shrill song of curses on
>   him who would dissever the Union;
> And I will make a song for the ears of the President,
>   full of weapons with menacing points,
> And behind the weapons countless dissatisfied faces.

Elsewhere he invoked:

> Americanos! Masters!
> Marches humanitarian! Foremost!
> Century marches! Libertad! Masses!
> For you a programme of chants.

Still elsewhere, and in catalogues of names and places which gave rise to numberless parodies, he memorialized the Mississippi country, Iowa, Oregon, California, Alaska, prairie life, mountain life, and the life of teeming cities, including his own beloved Manhattan. "On women fit for conception," he declared, "I start bigger and nimbler babes,/ This day I am jetting the stuff of far more arrogant republics." And for Europe, like another Young American:

> Suddenly out of its stale and drowsy lair, the lair of slaves,
> Like lightning it le'pt forth, half startled at itself,
> Its feet upon the ashes and the rags—its hands tight
>   to the throats of kings.

O hope and faith!
O aching close of exiled patriots' lives!
O many a sickened heart!
Turn back unto this day, and make yourselves afresh....

Liberty! let others despair of you! I never despair of you.

Is the house shut? Is the master away?
Nevertheless be ready—be not weary of watching,
He will soon return—his messengers come anon.

Little wonder that Swinburne, in his *Songs before Sunrise,*
wrote "To Walt Whitman in America," probably aware of muffled
rumors about his private life, but also thrilled by the republicanism
which his verse and nation symbolized:

Send but a song oversea for us,
    Heart of their hearts who are free,
Heart of their singer, to be for us
    More than our singing can be;
Ours, in the tempest at error,
With no light but the twilight of terror;
    Send us a song oversea! . . .

Chains are here, and a prison,
    Kings, and subjects, and shame:
If the God upon you be arisen,
    How shall our songs be the same?
Now in confusion of change,
How shall we sing, in a strange
    Land songs praising his name?

Whitman's love of home did little for his followers. The
Spanish-American War, American intervention in World War I,
and later events seemed to them to give no relevance to his patriotic message. But till then, he was the prophet of youth, and one
of its fulfillments.

2

Outlaws, Bohemians and Libertarians

Edgar Allan Poe, though a great artist, had little insight into his own psychology or society's, and suffered as a result. He accomplished the strange feat of having been a popular author, and yet was unremunerated by the new and enlarged reading audience of his time. The reasons are sadly evident. He was seen as not quite respectable by a new middle class which knew the haunting lines of "The Raven" and the tintinabulation of "The Bells," but which was made uncomfortable by the morbid aspects of his tales and poems, and was privy to the legend that he was a drunkard and drug addict.

Poe did require spirits as a buffer against constant insecurity and need, and he occasionally resorted to drugs which were readily obtainable as medicine or as a cheap opiate for the poor or depraved. But Poe was not an experimenter and he had no taste for a Bohemian life. He kept himself as clean and neat as his meagre funds permitted. He enjoyed formalities, and was happy at a ladies' tea. But he was plagued by compulsions. They drove him to destroy excellent editorial opportunities, such as *Graham's Magazine* in Philadelphia gave him in 1841–1842. His compulsions caused him to be insufferable toward his foster-father, though he hungered for his financial support. And they inspired him to choose as his

13

literary executor his worst enemy, the malicious Rufus W. Griswold.

Poe's life became a series of improvisations marked by false attitudes, but he yet had a profound grasp of the terror and despair which American optimism and reform, distinguished though it was, concealed. As Joseph Wood Krutch later observed, Poe's problem was not that he was misunderstood. His readers understood only too well that Poe's vision was intrinsically atheistic, abnormal, and unrestrained.

Poe was thus inadvertently the originator of an American Bohemia, a tragic one, as compared with that Parisian one which Henri Murger described in his *Scenes of Life in Bohemia*. Poe would in time influence a wide spectrum of nonconformists in America, and even more abroad. It was no accident that he set several of his best tales in Paris, though he had never been there. Intuitively, he realized that his unfortunate destiny better suited the city's permissive ways than his own land. Charles Baudelaire, a Parisian who lacked any spark of his city's gaiety, and whose sick and gloomy intellectual experiments reflected some of its darker aspects, thought he recognized in Poe a fellow-Bohemian, and introduced him to Europe in brilliant translations.[1] As a result, Poe, though without political acumen or social sympathies (as a declassed Virginia gentleman he was partial to slavery) influenced young malcontents and melancholy dissidents as far away as Russia even into the twentieth century. "The life and suicide of [Vladimir] Mayakovsky, the poet of Red Russia, shows him to be a Bohemian of the Poe type."[2]

At home, Poe attracted and repelled many people. But his influence was most noticeable among the true Bohemians who now made their appearance, some of them journalists and litterateurs. In the 1850's New York provided the best available balance of unconventional living and literary work, but Poe (who died by accidental violence in 1849) would not likely have found congenial company there. His roots, such as they were, were sunk too deep

1. See Lois and Francis W. Hyslop, Jr., trans. and eds., *Baudelaire on Poe: Critical Papers* (State College, Pa., 1952).
2. Albert Parry, *Garrets and Pretenders* (New York, 1933), 12.

in middle-class values. His capacity for experiment was within himself, not in outside society.

Pfaff's.

The vault at Pfaff's where the drinkers and laughers
   meet to eat and carouse,
While on the walk immediately overhead pass the
   myriad feet of Broadway.[3]

The writers and characters who visited Pfaff's eating house and saloon in lower New York revered Poe's memory, experimented with liquor and drugs, and drifted toward suicide and violent death. Their leader was Henry Clapp, a New Englander, and editor of the *Saturday Press*. He began by praising Walt Whitman (and giving Whitman space to praise himself) and ended by stirring up a fanfare over Mark Twain, then in California, which began Twain's rise to national fame. Aside from that, the Pfaff regulars contributed little to distinguished literature. Whitman himself was of them rather than with them. He explored their use to him, and then passed on.

What the Bohemians achieved was to help draw a line between conventional expectations in New York and the probings of dissatisfied people like themselves. Thomas Bailey Aldrich, who became a successful stockbroker as well as a successful poet, was offended by Walt Whitman's condescending remark, "Yes, Tom, I like your tinkles; I like them very well." But Whitman's was keen criticism. Bohemians, even the less talented ones, raised questions about life's standards, and they gave a footing to women who would otherwise have had more limited chances for self-expression.

Women in Bohemia. Ada Clare was one of these, famous as "The Queen of Bohemia," during her several years of fame in the pre-Civil War era. Born Jane McElheney in Charleston, South Carolina, in 1836 and in an affluent family, she made her literary debut in New York in 1855, the year *Leaves of Grass* first ap-

---

3. Emory Holloway, ed., *The Uncollected Poetry and Prose of Walt Whitman* (New York, 1921), II, 92.

peared, with verses of little talent, but with a personal assertiveness
unusual among females who were not reformers. As a "Love-
Philosopher" with short, boyish hair and a free, attractive form
and face, Ada reigned at Pfaff's. She took pride in her illegitimate
son by the vain and flourishing musician, Louis Moreau Gott-
schalk, and was downcast only by his subsequent indifference to
her. Ada's day was short. She talked literature at the round tables
of Pfaff's, and scrawled opinions for the press. She imitated Whitman's free verse. Her love affairs were noted and discussed. She
visited Paris. The coming of Civil War chilled Pfaff's and diminished her. Ada visited San Francisco and Hawaii and made con-
quests and literary associations, but none of substance. Back in
New York, she tried the stage unsuccessfully, and her novel, *Only
a Woman's Heart* (1866), was ridiculed. Her later ventures had
no public import.

More notable in creating traditions for young women of spirit
was Adah Isaacs Menken (1835–1868), probably born Adah
Bertha Theodore, of Jewish extraction, though she confused the
record with romantic tales. In 1856 she married Alexander Menken, of a well-to-do Cincinnati Jewish family. He lost his money
the next year in a financial panic and sank into dependence on her
talents. Adah wrote verse and acted. Her stage career was suddenly compromised because of a party given in her honor by the
Dayton (Ohio) Light Guards, a volunteer corps of militia. It probably involved little more than innocent fun, but it was treated as
notorious by malicious tongues and the press.

Adah's marriage having become rocky thanks to her husband's ineptitude and suspicion of her character, she left to make
a career in New York. There she met the new Bohemia, changed
her poetic style to Whitman's (noting, however, that he never
seemed to consort with women), and fell in love with the heavy-
weight prizefighter, John C. Heenan, whom she married in 1859.

Heenan left for England to fight John Morrissey, the heavy-
weight champion. One of the famous ring battles of the time, it was
declared a draw. The event turned Heenan's head and he abandoned Adah, whom he had left with child. Following the baby's
death and her own contemplated suicide, December 29, 1860, she
turned back to despairing verse and the stage. In the spring of

1861 an accidental theatrical idea suddenly rushed her into fame and affluence.

A theater manager had the script of a play based on a florid poem by Byron, *Mazeppa; or the Wild Horse of Tartary.* It concerned a Ukrainian warrior, in love with a Polish noblewoman, who is seized by her father, bound to a wild horse, and set loose to die in the rugged mountains. The play was vaguely based on an actual historic figure.

The idea of having Adah play Mazeppa was not new; women often played men's roles. But having her stripped down to flesh-colored tights, tied to the back of a horse, and set free along a rising run way was one of the theatrical wonders of the time. Adah's role as a pioneer "stripper" was trifling compared to the personality of poet, actress, and adventuress she now unfolded to the world.

Menken and Montez. There were strange parallels between "The Menken," as she was called, and Lola Montez (1818–1861), whose career came to flower more than a decade earlier. Born Maria Gilbert, half Spanish, half English, of a father in the military, she suffered a youth made stormy by family deaths, early marriage, and desperate Continental attempts to establish herself as a dancer. In 1844 she enjoyed a brief affair with Franz Liszt. Her assault on Paris was a theatrical failure, but she was friends with Victor Hugo, Alexandre Dumas the elder, and Alfred de Musset. She did marry a well-esteemed journalist whom she lost by death in a duel which excited Paris. Her greatest conquest was of Louis, King of Bavaria, who made her the Countess of Landsfeld and a figure in society and politics.

The revolutionary uprisings of 1848 cost Louis his crown, and Lola her place. Hectic years of marriage and the theater followed before she left England for New York, New Orleans, and California. There marriage and the theater continued to make her a living legend. She scored a triumph in England as a lecturer, then returned to the United States, dying suddenly, empty-handed and bereft. Undoubtedly, her career stirred many bohemian hearts, and influenced some of the decisions Adah Menken made, with almost equally spectacular results.

Adah took *Mazeppa* and her ambitions to San Francisco. "The Menken wanted to demonstrate her versatility, and the Gold Coast citizens applauded her burlesque of Lola Montez and the rough humor of *An Unprotected Female*. But what they really wanted was nudity."[4] She attracted such young would-be Bohemians as Bret Harte and Joaquin Miller. The latter was an Ohioan who fancied swaggering western garb and flamboyant gestures and verses. Miller made his reputation as a poet in England, where he was viewed as a typical American. His postures gave him unwarranted literary stature at home and abroad. Miller's swagger could be justified, to a degree, because it proved an antidote to an increasingly rigid social establishment.

A curious figure in the San Francisco Bohemia was Charles Warren Stoddard (1843–1909), who later attracted esteem for the style of his travel books. He wrote ecstatically of The Menken, and also of Whitman. His secret, in that era, was that he had a propensity for homosexuality, a fact which later embarrassed his academic career.

The Menken's career proceeded brilliantly. She took *Mazeppa,* her private affairs, and public sensations to London and then Paris. Numerous imitators appeared, but none to match her. A notable detail of her Parisian victory was the pun made on her name: "Dada" for "Adah," *dada* being the French word for hobby-horse, and referring to her famous scene in *Mazeppa*. Her nickname reappeared in the twentieth century as *dadaism*: a protest against formalism in the arts. In France it was known as *surrealism.*

Adah did not marry a king, but she did enchant the aging Alexandre Dumas. Her sincere hunger for literary fame betrayed her. She asked Charles Dickens' aid in publishing her verses under the title of *Infelicia,* but the novelist, though impressed by her magnetism, feared her notoriety and evaded her. Swinburne wrote poems inspired by her, and was vain about her awe of his genius. This final episode in her life was much to her credit, and none to his. She neglected her career to serve the impotent little poet. She endured his peccadilloes, complaining to Dante Rossetti, of the

---

4. Allen Lesser, *Enchanting Rebel* (New York, 1947), 112.

"Pre-Raphaelite" circle, "I can't make [Swinburne] understand that biting's no good."[5] Swinburne, in turn, frightened by newspaper publicity about them and already leaning toward the dull retirement which soon separated him from his past, cravenly repudiated her. Her health ran down. She died in Paris, August 10, 1868, and was buried in the Jewish section of Père Lachaise cemetery, in accordance with her will. Her major bequest to posterity was nudity.[6]

Journalists. The press opened doors for the young not available in other pursuits. Benjamin Franklin at age sixteen contributed essays to his brother's *New England Courant* in Boston in 1722, and he later used writing as his casement to power. Journalism later gave entree to such different young New Englanders as Horace Greeley and William Lloyd Garrison, the first a reformer, the second a radical.

The Civil War changed newspapers. Readers turned first to news of the war, rather than to editorial opinion. The new journalism attracted quasi-Bohemian types who enjoyed the new scene that industry and the burgeoning cities were creating. Some became pessimists, disheartened by the brawls which disfigured capitalist-labor relations, and which seemed living proof of the truth of Charles Darwin's *Origin of Species.* But others were excited by the scene, and were eager to celebrate it in poems or tales, or to encourage reform through vivid accounts of social conditions.

The expanding newspaper press attracted every species of human being, from the old tramp printers, drunk, destitute, but filled with fabulous behind-scenes stories of editors and statesmen, to every type of idealist and swindler. Ross Raymond was one of the latter, a strangely motivated scamp whose talents as a journalist could have netted him any quantity of success. Instead, he perpetrated remarkable but shortsighted frauds which kept him moving between newspaper offices and the penitentiary.[7]

---

5. Rupert Croft-Cooke, *Feasting with Panthers* (New York, 1967), 84.
6. Wrote Anthony Comstock, who became a symbol of censorship, in 1873: "Why is it that every public play must have a naked woman? It is disgusting; and pernicious to the young. It seems as though we were living in an age of lust. Every play... suceed[s] to the extent to which they [sic] cater to the passions and lusts." Lesser, *op. cit.,* 206.
7. Charles Edward Russell, *These Shifting Scenes* (New York, 1914), 62 ff.

Other journalists harbored purposes which ran deeper. They haunted police courts seeking "stories" for their papers, but also tried to understand human impulses and the enigma of justice. They listened to street people—Jews, Negroes, Germans, Irish, Italians—and mastered their dialects. Many dreamed of writing the great American novel and praised each other's news stories as being not journalism, but literature.

Lafcadio Hearn and Stephen Crane. Journalism made room for varied types of artists. Lafcadio Hearn (1850–1904) had the most exotic career among them. Born of Irish-Greek parents and raised in France and England, he emigrated to the United States at age nineteen. He was of morbid disposition because of accidental blindness in one eye. Hearn imagined himself unattractive, and sought relations with women not challenging to his self-esteem. He was incapable of writing forthright journalism. As a newspaperman in Cincinnati and New Orleans, and during a visit to the island of Martinique, he composed colorful, impressionistic essays and tales which contributed to regional writing. In 1890 he visited Japan, where he became a citizen, family man, and professor under the name of Koizumi Yakumo. It was chiefly because of Hearn that Americans acquired deceptive views of Japan's character and industrial potential.

Hearn was conventional in many ways. (His unconventional relations with Negro women while he lived in the United States were accidents of temperament.) But newspaper life tended to attract personalities who helped build Bohemian traditions. Their craft revealed seamy sides of life, and made many of them cynics. Although such great journalists as Ray Stannard Baker, Lincoln Steffens, and Richard Harding Davis disciplined their lives, many of their colleagues slipped into excessive drinking and personal disorder.

Very different from Hearn was Stephen Crane (1871–1900). For the New York *Herald* and the New York *Tribune,* Crane wrote semiliterary accounts of news, while also writing *Maggie: A Girl of the Streets* (1893) and the amazing *Red Badge of Courage* (1895), the latter an arcane tale of the meaning of life. Released from journalism by its success, Crane nevertheless remained a reporter, following wars and attempting to understand what they revealed about people. Crane was not dissolute, as many who followed literary gossip imagined, but his thoughts deviated from current piety and optimism. He was disgusted by those who imagined him to be a drug addict, so much so that he left the United States to die abroad. Yet the gossips were wrong only in details. Many journalists with Crane's point of view, but without his talent, drowned their despair in drugs or drink.

Crane's contemporary, Theodore Dreiser, told of a fellow journalist in St. Louis, competent and imaginative, who veered between stages of strict sobriety and weeks of drunkenness, use of drugs, and stays in brothels. One day Dreiser met the man in the street, weaving, drunk, and boasting of a store of "dope." He opened a white box with some thirty or forty pills.

> *In my astonishment and sympathy and horror I decided to save him if I could, so I struck his hand a sharp blow, knocking the pills all over the sidewalk. Without a word of complaint save a feeble "Zat so?" he dropped to his hands and knees and began crawling here and there after them as fast as he could, picking them up and putting them in his mouth, while I, equally determined, began jumping here and there and crushing them under my heels.*
>
> *"Rody, for God's sake! Aren't you ashamed of yourself? Get up!"*
>
> *"I'll show you!" he cried determinedly, if somewhat recklessly. "I'll eat 'em all! I'll eat 'em all! G—— D—— you!" and he swallowed all that he had thus far been able to collect.*[8]

With the help of a friend, Dreiser got the distracted journalist to a hospital where the morphine was pumped out of him. Yet Dreiser observed that "Rody" was not particularly grateful. "If I was so determined to go you should have let me alone. . . . But— Kismet! Allah is Allah! Let's go and have a drink." Dreiser was later convinced of the unpredictableness in life by seeing his desperate friend become a successful railroad executive.

---

8. Theodore Dreiser, *A Book About Myself* (New York, 1922), 226–227.

Bohemian Circles. Journalists convened to drink, air icono-
clastic views, and often plan or propose literary ventures. One such
famous group in the 1890's was the "Whitechapelers" in Chicago,
It included vibrant spirits of the quality of Finley Peter Dunne, the
cowboy chronicler and Hearst journalist Alfred Henry Lewis,
Brand Whitlock, and the then popular Ben King, an entertainer
whose verses "If I Should Die Tonight" were intended to make an
end of all such sentimentalities. Though these all became famous
names, Chicago's newspaper world also included more eccentric
types. When Dunne decided to settle down, after his "Mr. Dooley"
sketches had made him a celebrity, he moved to New York to
separate himself from them.

The journalists patronized ornate and splendid saloons and
restaurants, but they also attended small, intimate ones. They lived
in unpretentious or quaint neighborhoods where they could save
money or hide unconventional relationships. Such places became
the seedbeds for later Bohemias.

The Yellow Book and the Mauve Decade. New social attitudes at home were helped by new outlooks abroad, especially in
England and France. Russia, under the Czar, produced revolutionaries rather than Bohemians; and its exiles studied languages
and Marxist principles, rather than unconventional gestures.

French dissidents built on earlier generations of Bohemians.
Some, like Prosper Mérimée and J. K. Huysmans, lived conventional lives while toying with exotic or perverse literary themes.
Paul Gaugin created a sensation by leaving his work and family
and (more theatrically than Sherwood Anderson, a generation
later) settling in Tahiti, where he painted its flaming scenes and
people. His sometime companion, Vincent van Gogh, ended his
brief struggle with bourgeois France by suicide.

Symbolic of all the tendencies which troubled Bohemians was
Paul Verlaine (1844–1896), who reacted against the florid romanticism of a previous poetic generation. His clear verse expressed a control not present in his life. Verlaine moved stormily
between married life and homosexuality, notably with the preco-
cious Arthur Rimbaud, all of whose strangely imaginative poems
were written before he was nineteen. Verlaine's was the Vil-

lonesque life of a drunkard and penitent, of a sensualist and Catholic: a legend of Parnassus who wondered whether he had been born too soon or too late.

France was the spiritual homeland of all romantics, and it influenced their art through experimenters with symbolism, impressionism, realism, and surrealism. But English Bohemians had almost as strong an impact on their American sympathizers. "Decadence" in England did not produce the greatest art, but what flourished did so with fierce intensity.

It had its roots not in Bohemia, but in the English universities. Its devotees created a legend of Greek art and amorality which could set up almost bacchanalian overtones at an ordinary tea. The simple practices of Victorian gentlemen in brothels did little for literature. But the advice of Walter Pater, an Oxford don, that one should burn with a gem-like flame, inspired a strong effort to create an art independent of the ordinary world, an art for art's sake. Pater's doctrines were fulfilled in such figures as Aubrey Beardsley, Oscar Wilde, and, on a humbler level, Ernest Dowson.

Of them all, Dowson was the truest Bohemian: a languid young Oxonian who saw no meaning in life. He lived carelessly with no thought of health or a tomorrow, gave himself entirely to an unfruitful love-fixation, and wrote a number of poems which his peers sanctified. His critics saw him as merely Swinburne plus water, and his poems did lack original strength. "They are not long," he wrote, "the weeping and the laughter,/ Love and desire and hate./ I think they have no being in us after/ We pass the gate." He asked the reader to "twine our torn hands, O pray the earth enfold/ Our life-sick hearts, and turn them into dust." And in his most famous poem, "Cynara" (1896), addressed to the very young waitress whom he made the object of his fancy, he wrote lines which would echo in many writings abroad and in the United States. "I have forgot much, Cynara, gone with the wind,/ Thrown roses, roses riotously with the throng,/ Dancing to keep thy pale, lost lilies out of mind." Such sentiments received an amazing respect from journalist-writers who had accustomed themselves to the sordid details of newspaper reports.

Oscar Wilde. The Yellow Book became the symbol of all that the writers of "Decadence" were saying in their protest against middle-class norms, but it rose and fell with the fortunes of Oscar Wilde. A follower of Pater, he was the son of well-known parents, an Irish surgeon and a mother who wrote under the pen name of "Speranza." It is likely that Wilde, at Oxford, not only adopted its esthetic mannerisms, but at least tentatively investigated its homosexual fashions. Wilde was shrewd as well as precious. He was well aware that numerous graduates of Oxford knew Latin and Greek, and yearned to become famous in London: that fame was usually hard-won. His adoption of knee-breeches, velvet jackets, sunflowers, and other symbols of extreme artistic flair was, in effect, a local variation on Joaquin Miller's explosive appearance in London bedecked in cowboy gear. The purpose was, in both cases, to shock or entertain the bourgeoisie.

In a true Bohemia, young Wilde would not have been noticed. In London, he was made famous by Gilbert and Sullivan, whose *Patience* (1881) lampooned him. That year he visited the United States, where he informed customs officials that he had nothing to declare but his genius. Wilde traveled as far as San Francisco, carrying his sunflower, preaching, with more or less seriousness, his gospel of art. He wrote surprisingly little during this time: an indication that it was principles, not achievement, which were at issue.

His period of popularity (1891–1895), in which he wrote his plays and published poems and essays, unfolded over a volcano of social hypocrisy. Wilde socialized with young men of no social standing, as well as with young Lord Alfred Douglas, son of the Marquis of Queensbury, who made a fetish of manliness and was author of the famous Queensbury Rules which guided professional boxing matches. Wilde's confrontation in court with Queensbury, who had accused him of abnormal sexual practices, brought Wilde to Reading Gaol, where he served a two-year sentence while his status in contemporary literature disappeared. After his release, Wilde lived abroad as "Sebastian Melmoth," dying in 1900 at age forty-four in Paris.

Wilde became a symbol for many American litterateurs, Bohemian and otherwise, who felt that Puritan strictures ought not to determine the values of art. Wilde's sins were not clearly understood by all, or known to be malignant. Wilde had been a kindly person and a wit. His *Ballad of Reading Gaol,* published anonymously in 1898, was manifestly one of the great poems of English literature. His *De Profundis* (1905) was a tragic document describing his anguish in prison. His works, published in America in 1907, inaugurated an astounding production of memoirs, critical essays, biographies, and reprints which affirmed the validity of differing views of art and experiences. They helped prepare the way for future generations of youth and Bohemians.

In doing so they doomed the unmoved and unforgiving pillars of the reigning literary establishments, including Alfred Austin and Austin Dobson in England, and Edmund C. Stedman and Thomas Bailey Aldrich in the United States. Even William Dean Howells, though gracious to young experimenters, would be unread as failing to grasp their intentions, which, as in Stephen Crane's case, were pessimistic and antisocial.

Woman and Liberation. There were numerous women in many professions as far back as colonial times, and, in the great movements on the frontier, they shared most tasks with men. They never ceased being indispensable to vital campaigns: for example, serving the abolition movement as lecturers, editors, underground railroad agents, educators, and ministers. Elsewhere, their occupations ranged from mill work to medicine. A curious personality among doctors was Mary Walker (1832–1919), whom an unhappy marriage turned from an attractive young woman into a dogmatic crusader for female rights. Her liberation took the form of wearing men's clothing. When she died, following years of unpleasant agitation and court cases for real or imagined offenses, she was buried in her frock coat and trousers; on her tombstone was simply inscribed the word "Mary."

All such incidents and careers were products of a rural civilization. The advent of the modern city brought large numbers of men and women streaming into its impersonal arteries, seeking status and livelihoods. For the most part the women, like the men, sought to meet conventional expectations of one type or another.

Mary L. Booth, editor of *Harper's Bazaar,* spoke for her class of
females in answering the question: "Do you think women fitted
for journalism?"

> *Eminently so; especially in those departments of newspaper
> discussion which pertain to the family and to the needs of
> their own sex. Their acute and subtle intuition, and habits
> of keen observation, readiness of thought, and refined
> taste, fit them to succeed both as contributors and editors.
> . . . Of course, I speak of those who have had literary train-
> ing, which they need as much as men. . . . Women are espe-
> cially fitted for weekly and evening journals. Night work
> they will necessarily find difficult.*[9]

Such women supplemented the work of men in adapting to
changing industrial and family conditions in post-Civil War decades. Even "Mrs. Frank Leslie" (born Miriam Follin of somewhat exotic background and good education), her path strangely
crossed with that of Lola Montez, who introduced her to theatri-
cals, did little for women's opportunities. She married and unmar-
ried hectically before fully capturing the astute editor of *Frank
Leslie's Illustrated Newspaper,* a kind of early *Life Magazine,*
though less sharp in its social criticism. She survived him to become a major entrepreneur of journalism: "the Queen of Publishers Row," an achievement, but not one in the history of youth
or womanhood. Her most notable feat was to leave her fortune to
the cause of women's suffrage.[10]

Another category of women was more conspicuous and
moved about more freely, without impinging significantly on feminine basic conditions. Elizabeth Cochrane Seaman, as "Nelly Bly,"
did reform and other work for Joseph Pulitzer's New York *World.*
She ferreted out abuses of domestics by heartless mistresses,
probed social and political scandals, and, more significantly, had
herself committed as insane to Blackwell's Island, from which she
emerged to write her account of its shabby treatment of inmates,
Ten Days in a Mad House (1887). Most famous was her tour of

---

9. Charles F. Wingate, ed., *Views and Interviews on Journalism* (New York,
   1875), 253–254.
10. Madeleine B. Stern, *Purple Passage: The Life of Mrs. Frank Leslie* (Norman,
    Okla., 1953).

the world, undertaken to test out the time-span set in Jules Verne's novel, *Around the World in Eighty Days*. (Her own account was entitled *Nelly Bly's Book: Around the World in Seventy-Two Days* [1890].) Her femininity and youth were, indeed, one of the attractions of the event, but they added little to women's prestige as such, and she herself faded rapidly into a wealthy marriage, success in business as a widow, then bankruptcy, and finally anonymity.

The Woodhull. Victoria Woodhull (1838–1927) appeared to her admirers more of a symbol of female emancipation. In fact, she no more than exploited the shaky conventions of her age and left no heritage. With her sister, Tennie C. Claflin, she rose out of a family of tricksters to become herself a "spiritualist" medium with shady associates. She married at age fourteen and again at age twenty-six. She knew Stephen Pearl Andrews, who capped a distinguished early reformist career by founding Modern Times, a town on Long Island dedicated to "free love," as well as cooperation. The brilliant Andrews, who introduced shorthand to the United States as a reform instrument and invented the social scheme he named Pantarchy,[11] provided for Woodhull the philosophic basis for what was essentially a devious, self-serving career.

In 1868 the sisters created a sensation by setting up a brokerage house with money provided by Cornelius Vanderbilt. With Andrews's help, they issued the *Woodhull and Claflin Weekly* (1870–1876), which pretended to socialistic concerns, but pressed hardest and was mostly read for its "free love," birth control, and women's rights materials. Most dedicated suffragists found Woodhull, a fluent lecturer and a strong personality, an embarrassment to their movement; but several adopted her and defended the justice of her crusade.

Her major achievement was exposing the 1872 scandal which brought Henry Ward Beecher and his former protegé Theodore Tilton into court over the alleged adultery committed by Beecher and Tilton's wife Elizabeth. It was the scandal of the century, and one which opened vents rather than windows on unaired Victorian traditions. It is doubtful that the protracted legal proceedings ac-

---

11. Stern, *The Pantarch* (Austin, Tex., 1968).

complished more. Woodhull, "running" impudently for president
of the United States in 1872 for the "Equal Rights Party," with
Frederick Douglass as her vice-presidential candidate (he omitted
this fact in his autobiography), received no votes and spent Election Day in prison for libel of Beecher.

Her "political" effort contrasts well with the effort of Mrs.
Belva Lockwood, who attained a true first as presidential candidate of the National Equal Rights Party of the Pacific Coast in
1884 and 1888. As the first woman lawyer to argue before the
United States Supreme Court, Mrs. Lockwood had helped secure
property and guardianship of children's rights for the women of
the District of Columbia. She had drafted the amendment which
gave the vote to the women of Oklahoma, Arizona, and New
Mexico. As a presidential candidate, she made thoughtful and
well-phrased speeches to her hearers.

Woodhull and Claflin were sensations, rather than, as in Mrs.
Lockwood's case, an inspiration. Their retirement to England with
wealthy husbands lost the suffrage and women's rights movement
nothing. And yet, by youth and brashness, and especially by their
success in exposing the sexual unease in the circles which had
made Beecher and Tilton distinguished, the sisters revealed the
looseness of the American social fabric.

Charlotte Perkins Gilman. Vastly more important to the future of youth was one whose analysis of woman's destiny probed
deeper than the suffrage movement or Bohemianism. Woodhull
shocked and excited her audiences by declaring that her disposal
of her genital organs was her own private affair. Mrs. Perkins, or
Gilman (1860–1935), as she was known at different periods of
her life, asked and sought answers to questions affecting the whole
woman. She was a Progressive, rather than a malcontent or a liber-
tine. She was no longer young when her career got under way in
the 1890's, but her hunger for freedom was one with which youth
would increasingly identify.

A distinguished speaker, she made her entree into public view
with well-received arguments and agitation favoring woman suffrage. Her discontent, however, was individual. She broke up a
happy marriage because it curbed her search for identity. Her first

important book and her masterpiece, *Women and Economics* (1898), made a strong impression at home and abroad. It asked not so much for equal rights as for human respect, an end of false values, and a sense of individual potential which could overcome the clichés which separated the woman's lot from the man's.

She was indeed what she named her magazine: *The Forerunner* (1909–1916). Yet there were facets to her thought which challenged her apparent status as a leader of women. She was concerned for the freedom of children, as well as of women, a fact which circumscribed her sense of what a woman could and could not do. She felt distaste for the Freudism which stirred the younger generation in the 1910's. And she had no enthusiasm for contraception, which she identified with "fruitless indulgence." A woman, to her mind, could and should be feminine but no less responsible to society. Although no one withheld respect for Mrs. Gilman, there was undoubtedly lip service mixed with the admiration some young women gave her. Her last battle was not with flappers, but with cancer. She had long asserted "the right to die." Chloroform ended her sufferings in an era which had completely forgotten her.

Emma Goldman. Charlotte Perkins Gilman was one for the ages. In her time, there was no woman who could hope to span the swiftly changing decades and be an integral part of all of them. The changing status of women, however, was best exemplified by Emma Goldman (1869–1940), whose ethnic origins and feminine needs symbolized much in a nation heretofore dominated by Anglo-Saxon elements. As a Jewish girl in St. Petersburg, Russia, she became aware of the young Russians who attended the university there and of some of their ideals and interests. Married in Rochester, New York, she found the tightly closed Jewish community there oppressive and fled to New York City, where she was introduced to Johann Most's anarchist circle.

She became the lover of another young Russian idealist, Alexander Berkman, and with him plotted anticapitalist deeds. Berkman's attempt in 1892 to assassinate Henry C. Frick, superintendent of the Carnegie Steel Company at Homestead, Pennsylvania, where a desperate strike was in progress, landed him in prison. Thereafter, Goldman, though pilloried and oppressed as an anarchist and sympathetic to all radicals including anarchists, repudiated personal violence. In her lectures and writings she emphasized women's rights, radical literature, and free sexual relations. In effect, she advocated freedom of speech, for which she was harassed by police and immigration officials.

It was, however, a sign of greater social sophistication that, though her thoughts and expressions actually influenced Leon Czolgosz, muddled assassin of President William McKinley, "Red Emma" was not too roughly handled by legal agents in 1901. (Fifteen years earlier, following the explosion of a bomb among officers policing a workers' meeting in Chicago, radicals had been hanged and jailed for having admitted anarchist opinions.) Goldman went on to become one of the fiery voices of women's liberation through her much-read magazine, *Mother Earth,* founded in 1906. Independent to the last, she was a critic of revolutionary Russia when it appeared to her repressive of freedom and a betrayal of the radical dream.

Gentility. For most young women of the post-Civil War era, such excessive programs and commitments were untenable. The big city offered them some leeway and opportunities beyond those possible in tightly structured small towns, but the leeway presented threats to character as well as life. David Graham Phillips, a journalist turned novelist, suggested one dimension of the dangers girls could anticipate in his story of a young female of well-to-do background whose father had been "swept under by a Wall Street tidal wave," and who was attempting to establish herself in business in New York:

> *Emily had expected to find the Theresa of school days developed along the lines that were promising. Instead, she found the Theresa of school days changed chiefly by deterioration. She was undeniably attractive—a handsome, magnetic, shrewd young woman full of animal spirits. But her dress was just beyond the line of good taste, and on inspection revealed tawdriness and lapses; her manners were a little too pronounced in their freedom; her speech barely escaped license. Her effort to show hostility to con-*

*ventions was impudent rather than courageous. Worst of
all, she had lost that finish of refinement which makes
merits shine and dims even serious defects. She had cultivated a shallow cynicism—of the concert hall and the
"society" play. It took all the brightness of her eyes, all
the brilliance of her teeth, all her physical charm to overcome the impression of this glaze of reckless smartness.*[12]

Phillips's standards of womanliness were to be subjected to
serious blows by youth pioneering new freedoms. Such a girl as
Phillips here described had conventional aspirations to status and
amusement. But though she was incapable of the profundity of a
Mrs. Gilman or the courage of an Emma Goldman, she and people
like her had no serious criticism to make of more unconventional
youth. Indeed, they would help make the newer youth conspicuous
by their furtive interest and envy.

More vital to the emergence of a bold, experimental array of
young men and women was the great reform movement of the
1900's. Such women as Rheta Childe Dorr, who wrote *What Eight
Million Women Want* (1910) and such men as Reginald Wright
Kauffman, who wrote *The House of Bondage* (1910), a novel of
prostitution, focused on women's clubs, working women, suf-
fragettes, and the tragic sisterhoods of streetwalkers and others
whom a changing civilization treated with scorn and indifference.
Such exposés and descriptions ripped at the fabric of trite formulas
about women, composed of wishful thinking, ignorance, or malice.
Edward Bok, editor of the *Ladies' Home Journal,* performed many
services for his female readers, but none which ministered to their
deep feelings. In his folkclassic, *The Americanization of Edward
Bok* (1920), he told of having received many letters expressing
sentiments of which he would not speak. Evidently, Bok thought
these sentiments were best hidden and repressed.

The reform movement, though loyal to tradition, did encourage change and free expression, and so opened doors for more
change and freer expression. Also, the reformers were not united
in attitudes toward the virtues they had inherited. Jack London
signed himself at college meetings, "Yours for the Revolution," but

---

12. David Graham Phillips, *A Woman Ventures* (New York, 1902), 49.

accepted animal ethics, fought, drank, and visited brothels. David
Graham Phillips, despite his respect for family and good manners,
did not evade all the female admiration which came the way of his
handsome features and six foot seven inches of height. Lincoln
Steffens, following his wife's death, kept a woman friend in moder-
ate comfort. Some fairly staid reformers drank, occasionally to
great heartiness. As former newspapermen, they were not easy to
shock. The younger people who joined them, or who went beyond
them to newer ideas and associates, built upon much which they
had initiated, though often in ways they had not anticipated and
could not approve.

3

Classic Era:
The Young Idea

We were very tired, we were very merry—
We had all gone back and forth all night on the ferry;
And you ate an apple, and I ate a pear,
From a dozen of each we had bought some where.
           —Edna St. Vincent Millay

The emergence of youth as a separate factor in American life began on a note of fun and confidence in a time filled with social action which persuaded the American public that it was in full control of its destiny. The ingredients for a youth movement were all there: journalists clever in meeting assignments, but with mental reservations about American life; young people, male and female, eager for experience, impatient for reform, and yet clear in their minds that it did not go far enough; radicals determined to push the labor movement in the direction of socialism, pacifism, and international solidarity; restless upper-class men and women who scorned the social merry-go-round which confined them; malcontents generally of all classes who worked, holidayed, read newspapers and magazines, and carried on half-heartedly tepid family and marital duties. And poets. Said John Butler Yeats, father of the poet William Butler Yeats, and for many years resident in New

York, it was as though the fiddles were tuning up all over America.

Indeed, poetry was an element which needed refreshing. The reformers were not overcreative in poetry. Their "dean" was Edwin Markham, whose "The Man with the Hoe" reeking, said William James, with humanity and morality, overshadowed not only his own life but also the refomers's esthetic standards.[1] Edwin Arlington Robinson took the conventional strophes of Markham and others and made of them great poetry. So, a bit later, did Robert Frost. But Edgar Lee Masters, a Chicago lawyer, struggling with his feelings and his goals, could find only conventional phrases and rhythms for his *A Book of Verses* (1898) and *Maximilian* (1902), the latter a blank-verse drama.

The Masses struggled in New York from 1911 to 1913, then settled into a forum for radical-minded poets and other litterateurs. *Poetry: a Magazine of Verse* in 1912 gave Chicago and its poets an international reputation. These two publications were implemented by a host of "little magazines" which ran without advertisements, or even, occasionally, sponsors. Masters was then able to unleash his true feelings in the landmark *Spoon River Anthology* (1915).

Poetry came alive, tempting the veriest amateur to expression. It tempted E. L. Bernays, nephew of Sigmund Freud, who was then driving his way through press agent work toward his 1920's public relations schemes, when he would link art and psychology to selling. Even he joined with three other press agents to produce a book of verse, utilizing the "free verse" which became the hallmark of the time:

> He was a burly Dutch tenor,
> And I patiently trailed him in his waking and sleeping hours
> That I might not lose a story...
> Yearning a coup that would place him on the
> Musical map.
> A coup, such as kissing a Marshal Joffre.[2]

---

1. It overshadowed his own masterpiece, which is yet to be assimilated into the poetic pattern of the time; see Edwin Markham, *The Ballad of the Gallows-Bird* (Georgetown, Calif., 1973 ed.).
2. In *The Broadway Anthology* (1917), quoted in *Biography of an Idea: Memoirs of Public Relations Counsel Edward L. Bernays* (New York, 1965), 94.

Gertrude Stein. Ingredients of the new Bohemianism, one which could hold up its head with that of Paris, were already present and ready to become part of the new American scene. More of spirit than of substance was Gertrude Stein (1874–1946), a true forerunner of the literature to come. Of wealthy parents, she had studied psychology under William James at Radcliffe College and received her medical degree at Johns Hopkins University in 1902. In that year she went abroad. Later she became a friend of such artists as Matisse and Picasso, as well as of American expatriates.

Meanwhile, in 1909, she issued *Three Lives,* requiring a subsidy for publication. It sought the meaning of America in rhythms of language and expression, utilizing repetition and variant phrases in ways which pushed the boldest of previous American writing back into literary history, in terms of technical innovations. Stein directly influenced Sherwood Anderson and Ernest Hemingway; but as early as 1909 her writing did what much writing of the youth-era proper tried but rarely succeeded in doing: to attain an individuality indifferent to status or deportment. In her portrait of "Melanctha," an illiterate Negro girl, Stein founded a democracy of letters which honored vitality more than manners. Carl Van Vechten later put it that the tale was perhaps the first American story (he meant by a white author) "in which the Negro is regarded as a human being and not as an object for condescending compassion or derision."[3]

Ingredients of the "Renaissance." Democratic fraternities assembled in favored streets and drinking and eating places, notably in the environs of San Francisco, Chicago, and, outstandingly, New York. San Francisco's Bohemia was the least fruitful in cultural achievement. It drew from the traditions of roughhouse journalism and the Barbary Coast, with its drunken sailors and adventurers. It was heavily dependent on the reputation of Jack London,

---

3. Introduction to Gertrude Stein, *Three Lives* (Norfolk, Conn., 1933), x. Van Vechten overstated the case. George W. Cable, for example, had drawn distinguished portraits of Negroes in *The Grandissimes* (1880) and other stories. But there was no continuity among white authors, and the youth movement was uninterested in past achievements.

whose prose was far from experimental, and the aging Ambrose Bierce, whose masterpieces threw light on the Civil War more than they did on modern times. George Sterling, Bohemian poet, did have the Dante-like features on which he prided himself. But his verse failed to break out of the lockstep of iambic pentameter, and his drinking habits produced little beyond the lugubrious verses of his "The Man I Might Have Been."

The "Chicago Renaissance" of the 1910's showed more intrinsic power and direction, not only because of the presence of Harriet Monroe's *Poetry,* but thanks to Francis Hackett's *Friday Literary Review,* Ben Hecht's *Chicago Literary Times,* and especially Margaret Anderson's extraordinary *Little Review* which, without fanfare or significant funds, printed so varied an assembly of authors as T. S. Eliot, Sherwood Anderson, Ben Hecht, Ezra Pound, Carl Sandburg, William Carlos Williams, and many others in America and elsewhere. Chicago's Bohemia was impressive for the sense it imparted of a greater future. It could take pride in Carl Sandburg, a journalist, folk singer, and the evident heir of Walt Whitman. Sandburg's *Chicago Poems* (1916) displayed the rugged eloquence and soft byways of his own genius, as well as the power of the city he invoked.

Ben Hecht was journalist, poet, playwright, and one on whom impinged all the sordid and odd phenomena of Chicago. His *1001 Afternoons in Chicago* (1922) would later memorialize the brilliant journalism from which his novels emerged: "an unharnessed talent of nobody knew what enormous powers."[4] Hecht's close friend was Sherwood Anderson, just then seeking to find himself after having fled Ohio and his stifling life as a family man and businessman. Vachel Lindsay, though no true Bohemian, was one of the Chicagoans, having just been made famous by his poem "General Booth Enters into Heaven." Chicago could also claim Maxwell Bodenheim, who mixed Baudelaireian attitudes of careless living and drink with an ironic and fastidious verse ("Death is a black slave with little silver birds/ Perched in a sleeping wreath upon his head") which some sophisticates thought distinguished, but which others despised.

These writers might have made Chicago the Mecca it first

4. Dale Kramer, *Chicago Renaissance* (New York, 1966), 258.

seemed to Sherwood Anderson had it not been for New York's Greenwich Village. This quaint, Old World area of little twisted streets and picturesque houses produced its scores of exciting figures for every one in Chicago. The secret of New York's Bohemia was that though it served as a magnet for youth, it was given body and dimensions by tried figures of maturity and talent. John Sloan was not even intrinsically Bohemian in temperament. He was a serious artist trying to give form and meaning to realism, eking out a living with sketches and cartoons for newspapers and magazines, while studying patience with an alcoholic wife. Numerous artists of his disposition and age (he was forty in 1911) adorned the new age and the New York scene. Among them were Art Young, Robert Minor, George Luks, and Maurice Prendergast, whose combined talents ranged from cartoons to formal art patterns, from the politics of socialism to individualism. Theodore Dreiser, once he cut loose from magazine journalism to satisfy hidden yearnings, took up residence in Greenwich Village.

One of the notable overlaps from the reform-journalistic era was Hutchins Hapgood who, in the 1900's, had worked to create a new species of art, offering detailed accounts of representative human types. Hapgood's masterpiece was *The Spirit of the Ghetto* (1902). The book utilized fine sketches by a New York ghetto youth who in England later became the sculptor Sir Jacob Epstein, Hapgood's other books, including *The Autobiography of a Thief* (1903), *An Anarchist Woman* (1909), and *Types from City Streets* (1910), added up to a challenging vision of American life, difficult, drab, yet exciting in its hope and variety, a vision which a torrent of remarkable journalism partially obscured.

Hapgood, born of a "Victorian" family in the midwest, later intensified his interest in individual fulfillment. He joined other, younger Bohemians in experiments with drink and a search for self. This involved sex as a somewhat pretentious and humorless exploit, requiring introspection and protracted discussion. Sex among the initiates also became a key factor in art. Partisans of the new writing lost much of their respect for the journalism which had nurtured them. Hapgood later imagined that his best book had been the introverted *Story of a Lover* (1919): a study in egotism and self-importance which failed to interest even his own circle.

Youth Leaders. The great bulk of the new youth movement, however, were undoubtedly young, and as varied as the locales which bore them. Floyd Dell recalled:

> [T]here was a boy in Chicago, and a boy in Oshkosh, and a boy in Steubenville . . . and so on [he himself was from Davenport, Iowa]—one here and there, and all very lonely and unhappy. They did not know of each other's existence —they only knew of themselves and the great ugly environment in which they were imprisoned. They were idealists, and lovers of beauty, and aspirants toward freedom; and it seemed to them that the whole world was in a gigantic conspiracy to thwart ideals and trample beauty underfoot and make life merely a kind of life imprisonment.[5]

Dell joined other midwestern pilgrims in Chicago, where his insistence that they write their own views and express their own feelings made him popular with fellow aspirants to emancipation. The Chicago "Renaissance" was weakly grounded in its society, for soon Dell and many of his associates left to take up life in New York. There Dell quickly emerged as a leading Greenwich Villager. His talents were limited, but effective. He ridiculed conventional manners and established writings, asking jocosely who would wish to read Thackeray. He added his voice to those of others who demanded birth control measures as a human, and especially female, right.

More distinctively, and in all seriousness, Dell asked for a simple and naive approach to life. *Were You Ever a Child?* (1919) held that the older generation suppressed joy and creativity. Dell's book was an interesting amateur contribution to progressive education, one of the important social issues of the 1910's. Overall, and surprisingly, in view of Dell's meagre talents, he sustained a high respect among serious youth leaders, as a critic and as an editor of the "radical" *Masses* and its successor *The Liberator.*

More substantial than Dell, and even more a leader in Bohemia, was Max Eastman, who gave up teaching academic logic

---

5. *Liberator, January* 1920, 44.

and "The Principles of Science" at Columbia University to join the rebels downtown. Eastman, prematurely white-haired and vain of his handsome features and lithe frame, drew his radicalism from native American roots. His mother had been a Congregationalist minister of strong personality, and her son found it easy to identify individualism with dissent. But though Eastman edited the *Masses,* lectured on woman suffrage, and hailed the Russian Revolution, he revealed other traits which would ultimately reverse all his positions.

Like Dell, he was impatient of learning, and identified his own preferences with reality. His mother had urged him to seek joy, but she had not had in mind merely personal or sensual enjoyment. Eastman's best-known book, *The Enjoyment of Poetry* (1913), came oddly from an apparent radical and Bohemian, as did his own conventional verses. *Journalism versus Art* (1916) drew a line between his own and earlier generations of writers. Although Eastman identified with Marx, Lenin, and Trotsky, it was possible dimly to see the later *Reader's Digest* editor he became. He would later entitle his autobiography *Love and Revolution* (1964), but in neither field, of love or revolution, did he attain what Matthew Arnold had called "the thrill of a fact." Eastman's genuine eloquence was limited by an overindulged sense of self, a failing of many of his comrades.

John Reed and Upton Sinclair. The youth movement of the 1910's was first and foremost a point of view. Upton Sinclair had been no more than twenty-five years old, and a veteran of ten years of writing for pay, when he published *The Journal of Arthur Sterling* (1903), which was advertised as written by a poet who had committed suicide for lack of public appreciation. The book had, however, been a true account of Sinclair's young anguish, and had included some of his verse. Sinclair's inspirations had been Heine and Shelley, and his dreams those of a better world of spiritual love and poetry.

But Sinclair's outlook was not experimental, either in life-style or art. His first wife, who later ran off with Bohemian Harry Kemp whom Sinclair had befriended, derogated Sinclair as an "essential monogamist," as though, Sinclair added ironically, there

was something wrong in being that. Sinclair's fiction followed traditional narrative patterns, though it ranged from *The Jungle*
(1906) to *Love's Pilgrimage* (1911). But, more importantly, Sinclair's fiction emphasized traditional values of family, duty, hon-
esty. Sinclair's quarrel with society was not with those values, but
with their perversion by businessmen and the law.

Sinclair also lacked a sense of the "irrational" impulses in
people. He appealed to socialist and anticapitalist principles, and
was honored for this by many youth of the time. But their hearts
would often contradict what their lips professed. Thus, Sinclair saw
in Joseph Conrad's "Youth" (1903) nothing more than a blind
defense of industrial greed. It told the story of a boy's first sea-
voyage to the East: his difficulties on an old, rusted, dirty freighter,
which suffered leaks, fire, and an explosion, but which all became, in the seaman's memory, golden with the passing of time and
youth, the best part of life, he thought.

Sinclair thought otherwise. Conrad was obsessed by Nemesis.
He hated Progress. He ignored the avarice of shipowners unwilling
to provide safe ships for their sailor-workers:

> *Every hour the progress of science increases man's control
> over nature, and therefore the safety of travel at sea. If it
> were not for private ownership and the blind race for
> profits, these dangers would be largely a memory, and the
> stealthy Nemesis of Conrad . . . would shrivel up and crum-
> ble and blow away as dust. Would Conrad like that? Or
> would he feel the irritation of an old man who has staked
> his reputation upon a bad guess?*[6]

Well-said, Sinclair's more ardent readers averred. And yet
they continued to read Conrad, certainly more for his art than they
read Sinclair, and, among the youth, responded more empathetically
to Conrad's romanticism than to Sinclair's rational constructions.

Sinclair's contrast with John Reed (1887–1920) was dramatic, especially since Reed came of liberal-minded parents. The
elder Reed had been a western reformer, active in resisting land-
grabbers who despoiled the American public domain. The younger
Reed attended Harvard University along with T. S. Eliot, Walter

---

6. Upton Sinclair, *Mammonart* (Pasadena, 1925), 378.

Lippmann, and others of an outstanding student generation. He then came to New York to be a poet. Lincoln Steffens, his father's friend, got him a job on the muckraking *American Magazine* and urged him to enjoy himself. Reed was in fine mood to do so.

He set up shop in Greenwich Village, then attracting youth at an unprecedented pace. It was made gay and exciting by the publication of manifestoes of every description, flung out by would-be radicals and initiators of "schools" of new poetry and art. Reed interested himself in all of this, and made himself part of it. "Yet we are free," he wrote in 1913 in his privately printed poem, *The Day in Bohemia,* "who live in Washington Square":

> We dare to think as Uptown wouldn't dare,
> Blazing our nights with argument uproarious;
> What care we for a dull old world censorious
> When each is sure he'll fashion something glorious?

Reed proved adept at journalism and published a scattering of articles in the standard magazines. He contributed with greater enthusiasm to the *Masses.* He also formed a liaison with Mabel Dodge, a passionate young woman, friend of Gertrude Stein and an escapee from wealthy circles and family. However, Dodge brought her own money as well as self to the Village festivities. Her funds were of no small importance, since many talented young people were averse to spending their time and energies in commercial byways. Like Robert Edmond Jones (another Harvard man), they lived or visited at her home, while, as in Jones's case, plotting the stage designs which were to make him famous.

Reed took increasingly radical positions, giving his prose first place ahead of his poetry, but his earlier associations were as varied as the Village. Others besides Dodge who brought largesse as well as personality to their circles included Gertrude Vanderbilt Whitney, the daughter and wife of two fortunes, and, unlike Dodge, with more of a passion for art than for love-play. In Whitney's Eighth Avenue Studio radicals mingled with patrons of the art-for-art's-sake variety. There appeared, in those halcyon days, no conflict between wealth and position along the social spectrum. John D. Rockefeller, Jr. subscribed to the *Masses,* which he thought a very interesting publication. Certainly, it offered less of a direct threat to his material interests than had the older muck-raking exposures and attacks.

Reed's Dodge was a radical only in the sense that radical cliques gave her the conditions necessary to the free style of love she fancied. In this dedication she was not alone. Nevertheless, she did participate in such enterprises as the Madison Square Pageant which Reed and others organized to attract aid and sympathy to textile workers on strike in Paterson, New Jersey. Reed, living at high pitch, prowled the streets of New York looking for human interest life stories and finding them in the outcast and rebellious.[7] He reported as a partisan the grim strike of the miners of Ludlow, Colorado, in 1913, when their tents, housing women and children, were set tragically afire by state militia. That same year Reed went south to report the Mexican Revolution for the New York *World* from the standpoint of the peasant insurrectionist Pancho Villa. Here Reed's talent for human interest details and vignettes, and his sense of the drama in revolutionary movements, gave color and excitement to his *Insurgent Mexico* (1914). The book placed him in the first line of American correspondents and won him universal admiration among his Bohemian friends.

The Young Idea. The first youth movement was preeminently dedicated to personal feeling and art; 1910's youth produced nothing significant in the novel. Having given up, in their minds, much of their national heritage, they were in no mood to study its evidently dull and unexciting features. They preferred the tang of art, poetry, drama, the sense of fulfillment which accompanied their highly stimulated senses. For the nation at large, they practiced satire and derogation.

Although the youth movement could seem to claim such a talent as Vachel Lindsay, he was more a Progressive than a Bohemian, and not at the core of the youth program. Lindsay's dream was to bring beauty to "the people," and he actually took walking tours in the countryside, expounding his gospel to farmers and their wives. His experiences and outlook were preserved in his

---

7. Collected after his death in Floyd Dell, ed., *Daughter of the Revolution and Other Stories* (New York, 1920).

Rhymes to Be Traded for Bread (1912) and *Adventures while Preaching the Gospel of Beauty* (1914). Although Lindsay consciously mixed "vaudeville" with clanging rhythms and strong imagery in order to reach the people, his poetry was new only in its sophisticated search for a popular medium.

Dreaming of the vanished buffaloes, recalling the inspiration which William Jennings Bryan had once been to troubled Americans, remembering the late Governor John P. Altgeld of Illinois, whom Lindsay immortalized as the "Eagle Forgotten," Lindsay did all that one man could to be an American bard. His poems "General Booth Enters into Heaven," "The Chinese Nightingale," and "The Congo" seemed to establish him as an unforgettable adornment of democracy, while his standing was bolstered by his public appearances and chanting style. Yet much of what the youth movement intended was pointed in other directions.

The tocsin of the new age was better sounded in the Armory Show of 1913, sponsored by "The Eight," who included John Sloan, William Glackens, A. B. Davies, and others. The show introduced Americans to Fauvism (from the French for "wild beasts"). Cubism, Futurism, and expressionism to puzzle and entertain New Yorkers. The symbol of the Armory Show became Marcel Duchamp's "Nude Descending the Stairs," which provoked endless jokes, parodies, and scorn, as well as ardent defense. Edna St. Vincent Millay, then at Vassar College and not yet part of the New York scene, expressed the viewpoint of many in her response to the exhibition:

> *Went to International Art Exhibition. Impressionistic school, you know, and perfectly unintelligible things done by people they call the "Cubists" because they work in cube-shaped effects. Everything they do looks like piles of shingles. I'll get some postals of the pictures, I think— especially the one called "Nude descending the stairs," and if you can find the figure, outline it in ink and send it back to me.*[8]

---

8. Allan Ross Macdougall, ed., *Letters of Edna St. Vincent Millay* (New York, 1952), 35–36.

The sense of motion and form which the show emphasized raised then-modern questions of the function of postphotographic art which all the wit and irony could not nullify. Less probed was the *relation* between the abstract and semiabstract, and the traditional "representational" art which sought to limn life as it was. In its own way the new art was indicating that a new world was being born. Its connection with the old was even less clear than the art itself. The question was to be raised anew in the 1930's, when naturalism reasserted its values as most necessary to a world in need.

Poetry. In the merrier days preceding World War I poetry enjoyed an unprecedented popularity, especially among the youth. Their greatest achievement was the proliferation of "free verse," which gave every excited or ambitious young person a stake in the new poetry. Its outstanding proponent, Carl Sandburg, was not wholly in the spirit of the time, being (like Lindsay) more rooted in earthy American realities than most of the youth—so many of them fugitives from rural places—preferred. But Sandburg's sense of the poetry in common things expressed well what many lesser poets would have wished to be able to say.

Sandburg seemed part of the intellectual turbulence poetry engendered—a turbulence which mixed egotism with the generous slogans of social change. It was no accident that the *Masses* should have received Sandburg's verses, and also, as naturally, those of Arturo Giovannitti, who became almost a legend to the faithful of the youth movement as a poet who had also been a leader in another of the great strikes of the early 1910's, the Lawrence, Massachusetts textile workers' strike.

For this activity Giovannitti was jailed. Sympathizers of labor and the ardent among the youth were moved by his verses "The Walker," and recalled it as a harbinger of the future when workers would sing as well as strike. Louis Untermeyer, in an early anthology, termed it "a twentieth-century 'Ballad of Reading Gaol,' with an intensity and mystical power of which Wilde was incapable." Although the poem (like so much of the era's verse) did not survive as serious poetry, it suggested in its passion and idealism how real socialist realism seemed to that generation of bards.[9]

A curious leader in the field was Amy Lowell, of the Massachusetts Lowells. She was a total devotee of poetry, a proponent of "Imagism," who studied Japanese verse forms and poured out volumes of her own work which became part of the era's record. The swift disappearance of her verse following her death in 1925 helps indicate how undiscriminating was the poetic wealth of her time. Historically, however, her fame was secure; few did as much as the huge, ungainly Amy Lowell to open publications to the new poetry. The year of her death also saw publication of her *John Keats*, a massive tribute to the English poet.[10]

Ezra Pound, T. S. Eliot, and others of their kind were less conspicuous names on the scene, though they were to inherit much of the future. Eliot, at least, appeared in *Others* (1917), an anthology of verse featuring now forgotten poets, but including Sandburg among others who seemed to sense what the era was driving at. Neither Pound nor Eliot was represented in Lloyd R. Morris's *The Young Idea: an Anthology of Opinion concerning the Spirit and Aims of Contemporary American Literature* (1917), a cheerful compendium of views which weakly discriminated newer impulses from those motivating such traditionists as Joyce Kilmer, Louis Untermeyer, and John Erskine.

Most curious was the appearance in *The Young Idea* of Arthur Davison Ficke and Witter Bynner in their own right as contemporary poets with opinions on their purposes and outlooks, and also as Anne Knish and Emanuel Morgan, who were Ficke

---

9. Louis Untermeyer, *Modern American Poetry* (New York, 1921 ed.), 286–289. For a selection of *Masses* and *Liberator* verse, Genevieve Taggard, comp., *May Days* (New York, 1925).
10. John Peale Bishop cogently observed: "The late Amy Lowell, in her free verse, based on what she called cadence, allowed her logical pauses to coincide with and to supercede [sic] her poetic pauses. As soon as the novelty wore off, it was seen that her verse had absolutely no interest whatsoever" (*Collected Essays of . . . Bishop* [1948]), 365. In fairness to Lowell, it seems proper to cite a typical verse of her own, from "An Aquarium" (*Selected Poems of Amy Lowell* [New York, 1928]) 107:
    Outside,
    A willow-tree flickers
    With little white jerks,
    And long blue waves
    Rise steadily beyond the outer islands.

and Bynner perpetrating their hoax of "Spectrism": a hoax which excited the literary world of 1916–1917. Their purpose in *Spectra* was to ridicule verse without form or substance; both Ficke and Bynner were essentially traditional poets. Doubtless, *Spectra* helped clear the air of some false claims and insincere writings. An oddity of the episode was that it may have produced some interesting verses and made their authors more loose and adventurous than they had previously been.[11]

   Search for an Intellectual Program. The most substantial partisans of the Young Idea, and of the cultural aims it professed, were not editors of the *Masses* or of *Poetry*, and neither from New York nor Chicago. Van Wyck Brooks and Randolph Bourne were both from quiet towns in New Jersey, and both, for different reasons, burned to see alterations in the American way of life. Brooks had glutted himself on great books of the western world, and saw them as life-giving to humanity. American life as he saw it was comparatively arid, with things and competition substituting for uplifting thought. Here and there were lyrics, or passages of prose which could bear rereading, but they were few and immersed in rubble.

   Brooks, working for a publishing house, dreamed of a great American literature and an enduring criticism which would be itself literature. Intellectually active and impressionistic, he concocted startling theories intended to explain American literary defects and invoke the coming new time. He viewed America as psychologically confused and inhibited by Puritanism; its artists made naive and insensitive by dull visions of the frontier. They had, as a result, piled up mountains of poor art and aimless history. Americans had separated the head from the body, harming both; they had divided into "highbrows" and "lowbrows," remote thinkers separated from life, and shallow materialists who feared getting face-wrinkles.

   It was, Brooks thought, the historic task of the younger gen-

11. William Jay Smith, *The Spectra Hoax* (Middletown, Conn., 1961) reproduces the *Spectra* verses. Not uncharacteristic would be a passage from "Emanuel Morgan's" "Opus 88":
    The drunken beast finds epics on the breast-bone of a chicken
    And lyrics under the lettuce.

eration to rid itself of the dross of American life, forge a vital center of perspective, and create a "usable past."[12] Brooks set out to expose the American condition in a series of essays and books which showed American intellectual life as sterile, but about to mature. He made an example of Mark Twain, an artist of great potential (in Brooks's version) turned into a writer of "boys books," of which *The Adventures of Huckleberry Finn* was one, by repressive parents and his wife, and by a crude frontier. In another book, Henry James was seen as evading his duty as an American by cosmopolitan living.[13]

Randolph Bourne. Brooks was a friend of Bourne's but whereas Brooks confined himself strictly to literary associations, there was scarcely a significant intellectual in New York whom Bourne did not meet and impress. Bourne was a cripple who had gone to Columbia College at age twenty-three for lack of any other available outlet for his academic brilliance and idealism. He had won Columbia's most distinguished honor, the Gilder Fellowship for travel abroad. While still at college he achieved publication in the *Atlantic Monthly,* and of a book of essays, *Youth and Life* (1913), which detailed his search for goals and a conviction that the future lay with youth. The young alone had the requisite courage, inspiration, and untainted creativity to build a better world. Bourne enjoyed an enriching trip abroad in 1913–1914, during which he met intellectuals and fervent youth. He witnessed a general strike in Rome and the Kaiser's declaration of war in Berlin. He returned to the United States wearing a beret and, over his hunchback, the cape with which he was identified. Bourne took up life in Greenwich Village.

His position was unique among his peers. He repudiated much of Columbia, its concern for "classics," theses, and aloofness from sweat and strain, but he retained enough contact with its bureaucracy to contribute to the then *a la mode* peace outlook sponsored by its president, Nicholas Murray Butler, and many of

---

12. Compare page 153, where a later generation called for a "new history."
13. *The Ordeal of Mark Twain* (1920), *The Pilgrimage of Henry James* (1925). Brooks's credo, in his first phase, is expressed in *The Wine of the Puritans* (1909), *America's Coming-of-Age* (1915), and *Letters and Leadership* (1918).

its professors. Bourne's articles for *International Conciliation* and his 1916–edited book for the American Association for International Conciliation, *Towards an Enduring Peace,* were humanistic efforts shared by the majority of Americans. Yet Bourne also maintained contact with socialists and others who were suspicious and even contemptuous of the majority, and who expected to dominate it through an alliance of radical-minded workers and intellectuals.

Bourne at this time deemed himself a pragmatist and follower of John Dewey. In his studies and writing about experiments in "progressive education," which was sprouting schools and disciples at this time, Bourne kept his foot in the educational establishment while criticizing it. He also projected himself as a social and cultural critic, urging a new society of all ethnic elements and a literature conscious of social change while also dealing with "the palpitating life of the individuals."[14] Thus Bourne seemed, in those first years of youthful efflorescence, a mediating agent between the world of the reformers and of the youth they had spawned. In reality, his goals were revolutionary. He hailed Dostoevsky for having broken down differences between the firm and the infirm, the normal and the abnormal. He was convinced that only socialism could stem capitalistic war. And he suspected that older Americans were reactionaries, different in kind from his own generation of youth.

Bourne became a "contributing editor" (actually, no more than a contributor) for the *New Republic,* founded by Herbert Croly with funds provided by the businessman and diplomat Willard Straight. The magazine's purpose was to bring together an elite which could run the country, as distinguished from muckraking magazines which aimed to fire up the reading public for action. "The people," Croly thought, could not handle their own affairs. They were too naive, too sentimental, too ignorant, too easily diverted from great national goals. They needed to be led rather than roused. To help him Croly gathered such bright young talents as Walter Lippmann, whose *Drift and Mastery* (1914) showed

---

14. For details, Louis Filler, "Trans-National America," in *Randolph Bourne* (New York, 1966 ed.), 81.

him to agree with Croly precisely. Bourne was not consulted on editorial policy. Croly perceived that Bourne was an elitist, but that he had too many associates among independent artists and radicals to be intimately satisfying to the magazine's *junta*.

Nevertheless, the *New Republic* in its first era seemed not so much a tribune of a coming race of consuls as part of the joy and excitement of an emancipated time. Some Dreiserian pessimism overlapped among the young, and could be found among some college elements which affected cynicism and despair. Despising capitalism, they could toy with alternatives.

> *We [at Columbia College] had begun to develop a cult of failure. One day I overheard Matthew Josephson remonstrating with a friend:*
>
> *"If you keep up this crazy, irregular life, you'll be dead by twenty-five."*
>
> *The friend, who affected sideburns and a moustache which made him look like Edgar Allan Poe, taunted:*
>
> *"And what will you be at twenty-five? A respectable, successful man!"*[15]

One skeptic treated the saga of Greenwich Village with knowing satire, in her mock diary of a small-town girl who moved from belief in the Bible to honest doubt, on to Omar Khayyam, and then to New York. There (her diary continued) she discovered Bernard Shaw, skepticism of all but scientific facts, and contempt for the Average Person. She went on to embrace the new religion of socialism, exalted sincerity, endorsed free love and the rights of man. . . . On she went, losing illusions, joining unions, becoming involved in politics . . . social work . . . clubs and movements:

> *A great weariness. Sick of Action. Sick of Words. Sick of Humanity. No illusions left. Shed everything. Do nothing. Turn to Art. . . . Believe in love. . . . Get married.*[16]

Humanism. Developments among youth did not go unnoticed by conservatives, but they stirred surprisingly little direct

---

15. Joseph Freeman, *An American Testament* (New York, 1936), 82.
16 *New Republic* VI (March 25, 1916), 211–212.

criticism. Antilabor spokesmen made few distinctions between aging militants and younger ones. Patriotic gestures were dominated by survivors of the Grand Army of the Republic, who were fast receding into history. The American armed forces of the 1910's were relatively small and decentralized, and met artists, eccentrics, and their women at almost no point in society.

Bohemians opposed traditional family values, but more in the spirit of good-natured condescension than malice. Ordinary folk, in turn, were more amused than outraged by what they read in the papers about goings-on in Greenwich Village and Chicago, and found few occasions to take them personally. The most formidable challenge to the youth was by those who designated themselves as Humanists, or neo-Humanists: teachers of the classics, of English literature—those to whom Emerson was first of all a moralist and Thoreau a naturalist. They reacted in dismay to what they saw as an abandonment of standards and a lack of regard for the real traditions of civilization.

Their strength lay on the college campuses where they could set standards of critical thinking, literary expression, and moral right. But even there they were forced to become aware of the presence among students and visiting lecturers of socialists, experimenters with democratic themes and language, and critics of the classics. Bourne, for example, argued that it was a waste of time to learn Latin or Greek in order to read Homer or Virgil; excellent translations could save time for the important tasks of life. The Humanists were resentful of such views. They saw Walt Whitman as a dangerous inspiration to new young poets. They saw clearly that what was at stake was not so much one literary tenet rather than another, but a way of life which could change expectations in social behavior.

Two figures emerged from academic ranks to become symbols of the rest. Paul Elmer More was a student of classics, but also believed that no art could endure without a sound, intrinsically moral, base. As a professor and then as editor of the New York *Nation,* he and his contributors condemned the young critics and their friends as without standards and with no way of creating them. More formidable in some ways was Irving Babbitt, a professor of French at Harvard University. It is likely that his poor reputation among the youth later influenced Sinclair Lewis to borrow his name for a character in a novel. Lewis's Babbitt was a crass and unimaginative businessman, but the original was not. Irving Babbitt, born in Dayton, Ohio, had spent an active youth selling newspapers in New York and being a cowboy in Wyoming. His long effort in mastering the classics left him with a conviction that they were the basis of an enduring civilization.

Babbitt saw the enemy as romanticism, which emphasized the individual at the expense of society. In half a dozen carefully wrought books he spelled out what he saw as careless and destructive thinking which went into writings unaware of and indifferent to the experiences of Athens and Rome, and even Elizabethan England. Babbitt's masterpiece was *Rousseau and Romanticism* (1919), which conceded his subject's genius, but argued that only chaos could result from it.

That neo-Humanism could not stem the flow of democratic assertiveness on or off campus could be seen in the development of several careers. T. S. Eliot was of the younger generation, having learned techniques from classic sources, but also from modern French experimenters. His methods and turns of mind insulated him from the democratic impulses working within a Sandburg or a Lindsay. But his poetic derogation of vulgar and banal personalities pleased iconoclasts more than it did genteel traditionalists. They deplored vulgarity, but did not know how to cope with it as a human reality.

Stuart P. Sherman foreshadowed the doom of the New Humanism. He began as a follower of Babbitt and More, but though he insisted on the dignity of man, he rejected their complacency, their tendency to ignore new writers rather than grapple with their styles and goals. Sherman studied earnestly to determine the truth of Dreiser and his fiction. His first conclusions merited Humanist approval:

> *It would make for clearness in our discussions of contemporary fiction if we withheld the title of "realist" from a writer like Mr. Dreiser, and called him, as Zola called himself, a "naturalist." While asserting that all great art in every period intends a representation of reality, I have tried to indicate the basis for a working distinction between*

the realistic novel and the naturalistic novel of the present day. . . . [T]he realistic novel is a representation based upon a theory of human conduct. . . . A naturalistic novel is a representation based upon a theory of animal behavior. Since a theory of animal behavior can never be an adequate basis for a representation of the life of man in contemporary society, such a representation is an artistic blunder. When half the world attempts to assert such a theory, the other half rises in battle. And so one turns with relief from Mr. Dreiser's novels to the morning papers.[17]

Sherman went on to become book editor of the literary supplement of the New York *Herald Tribune,* and to broaden his view of the virtues of current writing. He found himself criticized by former academic colleagues for having "betrayed" the principles of the New Humanism. Sherman received such opprobrium without qualms. He never discovered the virtues of Gertrude Stein, not having struggled with *Three Lives,* and having read her later experiments without guidance from her friends. But he did learn to respect such authors as Sherwood Anderson, Ben Hecht, Don Marquis, and even H. L. Mencken, though Mencken offended his every critical principle.

Sherman's basic change was in agreeing with the literary radicals that judgment ought to be suspended while one was determining what constituted a justifiable way of life. He quoted with pleasure a passage from one of Sherwood Anderson's stories of horse-racing. Wrote Anderson:

Often he would go on talking for an hour maybe, speaking of horses' bodies and of their minds and wills as though they were human beings. "Lord help us, Herman," he would say, grabbing hold of my arm, "don't it get you up in the throat? I say, now, when a good one like that Lumpy Joe I'm swiping, flattens himself at the head of the stretch and he's coming, and you know he's coming, and you know his heart's sound, and he's game, and you know he isn't going to let himself get licked—don't it get you, Herman; don't it get you like the old Harry?"[18]

---

17. Stuart P. Sherman, *On Contemporary Literature* (New York, 1917), 100–101.
18. Sherman, *Critical Woodcuts* (New York, 1926). 17.

Sherman's comment was: "It does me!" Anderson's victory was not only over Sherman; it was over the reading public. And though one or another instructor at a university might work to dampen the enthusiasm a student or a colleague might feel about Anderson or about a score of other talents who expressed youthful ebullience or democratic wants, it was to no avail.

For each American who heard of Sherman or attended to his views, there were ten who knew of H. L. Mencken, a Baltimore journalist who had for years contributed essays to the magazines in scorn of democracy, which he identified with all that was boring and inhibiting in American life. Mencken learned from a number of critics, but his most important association was with George Jean Nathan, a sophisticated young man whose irreverent assessment of plays modernized criticism in the field. Mencken and Nathan made of the magazine they took over, *Smart Set* (1914–1924), a witty publication which youth and discriminating elders enjoyed.

Their target was the "booboisie" and its heritage, which Mencken identified as Puritanism. Here he was at one with Van Wyck Brooks. Brooks, however, took a more sober view of his work, unlike the cynical, atheistic, impressionistic Mencken. Mencken's irony and indifference to principles, other than the right of people to do as they pleased, enabled him to be more or less friendly to a variety of writers, from Upton Sinclair to James Branch Cabell. The latter was a Virginia gentleman and writer of delicate, remote fiction, whose attraction for Mencken would be that it was pessimistic and, in one resounding case—the case of *Jurgen* (1919)—condemned as pornographic.

Mencken's great achievement in the 1910's was his battle on behalf of Dreiser, like himself of German descent and a journalist, though Dreiser's prose was heavy-handed, as compared with Mencken's. Like Dreiser, Mencken believed life was meaningless. Like him, he saw sex and other diversions as human rights. When Dreiser's *The "Genius"* (1915) was attacked as pornography, Mencken fought tirelessly to enlist the literary world in protest of censorship. This battle pioneered many other battles which would instruct successive waves of the *avant-garde*—it is interesting that the very phrase came from France—in principles of social and cultural progress.

4

Classic Era: Youth under Stress

Avant-Garde and Reactionary. The youth who came to the big cities, who lived in cold-water flats and at the Y.M.C.A. and Y.W.C.A., who haunted the new movie houses and dreamed of meeting more available versions of Theda Bara and Douglas Fairbanks—such youth were not vivacious. They appeared less talented than the Bohemian youth, and opposed to them in temperament and goals. Yet the two youthful patterns were as related as the pattern of a crocheted rug and the apparently random cross-stitching underneath the overt design. Although the dissidents were antagonistic to the established order and would have denied their realtionship to conventional youth, both types were critical of the society which had created them. Both found elements of their heritage unreal and unsatisfying.

Their elders of the reform generation imagined they had created an open-ended world capable of filling all rational needs. They failed to realize that their values did not square with actual conditions. Their leader, Woodrow Wilson, spoke eloquently of hearth and home in an increasingly urban world of apartments. He spoke of American traditions, having in mind his elite college background, Anglo-Saxon expectations, family loyalty, and austere religious convictions. His convictions helped his public image. But from the young of whatever intelligence or heritage Wilson's presumptions elicited lip service more than ardor and dedication as they struggled for status and satisfactions in an increasingly impersonal world.

The intellectuals among the youth joyfully flouted Wilson's eloquence in the interests of a freer ethnic democracy, experimentation, and religious skepticism. But though the merry makers of Greenwich Village seemed far away from the youth who worked in shops and business houses, all confronted the problem of how to cope with the emerging world of mass production and service agencies.

Hence, the more radical and bizarre youth found themselves much less alone than might have beeen expected. Bohemians often drifted toward, or came from, the ranks of outcasts and the unemployed. Socialist-minded youth from the poorer classes, students perhaps at the City College of New York which turned out class after class of brilliant graduates, met with workers at rallies and union meetings to argue goals and methods of achieving them. A generous camaraderie created friendships between radicals of nondescript background and exploring sons and daughters of wealthy families.

There was, for example, young Frank Tannenbaum, a boy from the New York ghetto who found the pangs and sorrows of winter among the poor an intolerable affront to human nature. He gathered more than a hundred unemployed men together on a stormy night and led them into a Fifth Avenue church to test its Christian principles. For this, he was arrested, tried, and imprisoned for a year on Blackwell's Island. Tannenbaum came forth from prison white-faced and determined to make his mark.[1] Friendly hands combined to give him a Columbia University education and to help him write and publish books urging prison reform. He gradually matured to become a thoughtful, conservative Columbia professor of Latin American affairs.

Quite different was Lewis Corey, born Luigi Carlo Fraina. Without a high school education, he exhibited boldness, organizing power, and a theoretical grasp of radical principles which made him one of the early founders of the American Communist

---

1. Mabel Dodge Luhan, *Movers and Shakers* (New York, 1936), 96 ff.

Party, ambitious to become the "American Lenin."[2] He was a portent of a new type of youth, one which would proliferate in the 1930's. Corey himself, after obscure travels and changes of perspective in the 1920's, left the radical scene, to reemerge in the 1930's as a student of American business and social history. He became a professor and anticommunist: as firm and challenging in his later views as he had earlier been in his radical phase.

Although radical youths had their temperamental counterparts among conservatives, the latter had fewer prospects for attaining a following. Such organizations as the Ku Klux Klan and vigilante groups emphasized action rather than theory and personality. Their very conservative bias prevented them from mounting campaigns for challenging their elders. Free speech fights, union organizing campaigns, and battles against American intervention in World War I individualized strikers and libertarians in ways not available to their youthful opponents.

The social scene was a welter of causes and crusaders which drew many into its maelstrom who were not seeking violence or the glare of publicity. An unlikely participant in 1910's struggles was young Will Durant, raised in Catholic surroundings and repelled over the years by what he saw as the rigidity of the Church's doctrines and leaders. He may finally have been turned out of the house by his embittered father. Settled in New York, Durant taught at the Freedom Modern School, sponsored by anarchists, knew Alexander Berkman and his comrades, and may have heard plans for bombings discussed; he certainly learned of the philosophy behind them. Durant preached education. A comrade, he wrote, told him he was rotten with books. "One bomb will educate faster than a hundred schools."

A bomb had actually been made: one of a number which terrorized the period. This one was to be used during a strike at Tarrytown by one of several conspirators.[3] Durant's fictional recreation of the climax of the affair captured something of the spirit which pervaded them:

---

2. See Louis C. Fraina, *Revolutionary Socialism: A Study in Socialist Reconstruction* (New York, 1918).
3. For an account of the famous Lexington Avenue bombing, see *New York Times*, July 7, 1914, and following dates.

"Here," he said, *"is the present we have for the old man in Tarrytown. Ladies and gentlemen, let me introduce you to his majesty, Death. With this little black box you solve all your problems. You never have to pay the landlord again, you never have to drag your weary body to the shop again, you find a way to make your wife love you once more. With this you escape the next war, and the hell they call peace. Who will have it?"*

Greb lost some of his taciturnity.

"For God's sake, put that down," he begged.

Carney was not afraid.

"Let's see it," he said quietly.

"If you drop it," said Greb, "we'll be smashed to a thousand pieces."

I watched [Carney] intently. . . . Strange thoughts came to me. "I shall die in a moment," I said to myself. "I shall never have a home, or a child."

"Get away from the window," said Greb to Carney, "and put your clothes on."

Carney surveyed his own nudity, and laughed.

"Isn't it funny," he commented leisurely. "We come into the world naked, and we go out of it naked. I was born naked, and now—"

He raised the bomb over his head, and threw it with all his might upon the floor.[4]

Although all the upper floors of the house were shattered and all the anarchists killed, "Durant" was saved by a bed blown upon him by the blast. He himself went on to discover America, to abjure radicalism, and to begin a career which brought him intellectual eminence. His hectic and all but aborted development was one of many such in an era which juxtaposed old, established ways with newer prospects, insistent on being recognized.

The European War. Ida M. Tarbell observed, while she was collecting memories of Abraham Lincoln, how many people she approached could say precisely what they had been doing when the news came that the president had been assassinated. Similarly,

---

4. Will Durant, *Transition* (New York, 1927), 210–211.

Hutchins Hapgood vividly recalled every detail of the response of his Bohemian friends in 1914 when news came that major war had broken out in Europe. In some ways, this latter identification with history was more remarkable than that relating to Lincoln, since it was not generally realized in 1914 that the United States had a serious stake in European hostilities, which were, after all, three thousand miles away and even more remote in terms of issues.

True, there were Americans who had once called European countries home. But the sheer multiplicity of American ethnic groups made it seemingly impossible that they could band together for any national decision favoring intervention. German-Americans sympathetic to the "Fatherland" wisely sought neutrality, and thus became part of a coast-to-coast peace movement involving millions of people, and uniting workers, radicals, religious pacifists, educators, and housewives. This loose federation of citizens against war made inconceivable a military stance on the part of the United States.

Yet a feeling of restlessness, pessimism, and unease can be discerned under the gaiety of experimental youth and the satisfaction of businessmen and workers who were supplying goods to the embattled British. Some of this unease stemmed from abroad. Although Bohemia was an exciting part of Parisian life, and holiday seasons were reported as joyous from London to Vienna, each year also brought out, all over Europe, new classes of youth being trained in military maneuvers. Some youth in America as well as abroad expressed feelings of doubt respecting the future.

Socialists and pacifists anticipated war as a byproduct of imperialist actions by competing powers. But deeper and more illuminating than their dogma were more subtle expressions of pessimism and imminent doom, as spelled out by poets and others of sensibility. As one of them, a young Englishman who committed suicide, wrote in intuitive anticipation of the coming military slaughter:

> I am only a dream that sings
> In a strange, large place,
> And beats with impotent wings
> Against God's face.

The Darkness is all about,
    It hides the blue;
But I conquer it with my shout,
    And pierce it through. . . .

But the sound of my shouting dies,
    And the shadows fall,
For Death is upon the skies
    And upon us all.

The shadows fall and the still,
    I am loath to sing;
I have wondered and kissed my fill
    On the lips of spring.

But the golden cities are gone
    And the stars are fled,
And I know that I am alone,
    And I am dead.[5]

The scene at Provincetown, Massachusetts, the day after England declared war on Germany, as recalled by Hutchins Hapgood, helps indicate the clash of lifestyles between his friends and the America around them, and the unreadiness of the Bohemians for the world crisis which was about to inundate them. Provincetown, then relatively unsullied by vacationers, was a haven for Greenwich Villagers. Present at one of their gatherings that day were Hapgood and several members of the revolutionary Industrial Workers of the World, one of them, Fred Boyd, just released on bail for preaching sabotage. Also present was Bayard Boyesen, a Columbia University instructor and director of the progressive Ferrer School, the name honoring a revered Spanish anarchist and educator executed for his allegedly treasonable ideas. Included in the company were Max Eastman; Hippolyte Havel, a philosophic anarchist and *Masses* editor; Mary Heaton Vorse, a radical writer; and Polly Holliday, who kept a well-patronized restaurant for Greenwich Villagers.

They drank much and consorted with one another on various personal and ideological levels, and were excited by liquor and

5. Richard Middleton, *Poems and Songs* (Toronto, 1912), 98–99.

individual tensions when news of the war was reported to them. "Fred was seized by the conviction that we should stop the conflict at its beginning. He had been drinking, to be sure, but I believe that the whisky had no important influence on the grandeur of his thought—it was his faith in reason that dominated him. Don Quixote had the same faith." [6]

Boyd proposed "an immediate conference of the intellects of Provincetown." His reasoning was that by "a fortunate accident . . . we happen to have here assembled the brains of America." He wanted a statement drawn up to the working classes of the world explaining the true economic causes of the war. It was clear to him that workers would not kill one another for the sake of a few privileged persons or groups. Unfortunately, the conferees could not agree on resolutions, and ended "immersed in whisky and wisdom."

A variety of scenes ensued. O'Carroll, a poet, tried to recite verses filled with feeling for workers; later he rushed nude to the water, apparently attempting suicide, but was rescued. There was a nude beach party. Boyd fell from the veranda to the beach, a gesture, Hapgood thought, "of immense significance." Polly Holliday appeared on the veranda, her clothes wet. "I wanted to die," she said, "but the water was so cold."

Boyd later attempted to cable what he imagined were his friends' resolutions to the German Kaiser; Edward Grey, British Foreign Secretary; the President of the French Republic; the Czar; and the Emperor of Austria. The telegraphers humored Boyd, pretending to send the messages. Boyd returned to create further alarm by seizing a revolver which he brandished before children and the cook. Even the dogs were disturbed, two of them fighting until Eastman threw pepper in their eyes. The story reached the Village that he had flung it in the eyes of Hapgood and O'Carroll.

Others of the youth movement reacted more rationally to the coming of war in Europe, but no more effectively. The years from 1914 to 1917 belonged more and more to those who yearned for personal involvement or national intervention. Alan Seeger, along

---

6. Hutchins Hapgood, *A Victorian in the Modern World* (New York, 1939), 385 ff., for this and later quotations.

with some forty or fifty young Americans then in France, enlisted
promptly in the Foreign Legion of the French Army. Seeger
(1888–1916) who, had he lived, would have been the uncle of
folk singer, Pete Seeger, was almost the exact American counterpart of the English poet Rupert Brooke: both handsome and
romantic, and Byronesque in outlook. Brooke died in the British
service on the Greek island of Skyros, having cut his name into
English letters with the sonnet which began, "If I should die, think
only this of me." Seeger did the same with a poem beginning, "I
have a rendezvous with Death/ At some disputed barricade."

Ernest Hemingway, then a very young reporter, also enlisted,
first to join a volunteer ambulance unit in France, then, later, in
pursuit of his personal vision, to transfer to the Italian infantry and
suffer wounds.

Pacifists and Interventionists. The war violently shook the
younger generation. At first it appeared that only radicals and
Bohemians would be adversely affected by its blasts. The *New
Republic* joined the "Great Crusade" in order to make the League
of Nations a reality. It turned cool to Randolph Bourne's pacifism,
and reduced him to writing meagre book reviews. John Reed broke
with the Socialists, and, though harassed by government agents,
worked to build the new Communist Party. Both Bourne and Reed
were soon to die of war-induced diseases. The editors of the *Masses* (and subsequent *Liberator*) were literally brought into court
on charges of treason.

A curious hero of the young was Frank Harris, a swash-
buckling English-Irish litterateur who spent time in the United
States and whose truculence and notoriety with women had
brought him disrepute at home. He now emerged as editor of the
formerly muckraking *Pearson's Magazine* and a vengeful anti-
British voice. His social views and attitudes bridged the gap between Bohemianism and radicalism, and made him admired by
both groups beyond his deserts.[7]

---

7. Frank Harris, *England or Germany?* (New York, 1915) was a pro-German
   memento of what was his second American period. See also A. I. Tobin and
   Elmer Gertz, *Frank Harris: A Study in Black and White* (Chicago, 1931).

The rough and even bloody work of local vigilantes throughout the country, and of the so-called 100 Percenters (supposedly indicating one hundred percent Americans) quelled dissent everywhere. A new meaning was given to patriotism. Once, it had been the reformers who had been esteemed as patriots, concerned for their country's health and good repute as mere profiteers were not. As a result of war propaganda and the stifling of malcontents and radicals, patriots were now publicly defined as those who asked no questions of government and who discouraged those who did.[8]

The hand of wartime feelings, however, fell not only on unbridled Bohemians and would-be revolutionaries, but also on citizens who because of their ethnic background, religious convictions, or pacifist sentiments offended dedicated prowar partisans or malicious neighbors. Ben Hecht icily recalled the spirit of the time:

> *A time of singing. Songs on the lips of crowds. Lights in their eyes. High-pitched, garbled words, brass bands, flags, speeches . . . Mine eyes have seen the coming of the glory of the Lord but we don't want the Bacon, All we want is a piece of the Rhine(d). . . . A brass monkey playing "Nearer, My God, to Thee" on a red banjo. . . . Allons les enfants . . . le jour de gloire est arrivé! You tell 'em kid! Store fronts, cabarets, hotel lobbies, sign-boards, office buildings all became shining citadels of righteousness beleaguered by the powers of darkness. . . . A bonfire of flags above the streets.*
>
> *Boom, boom! . . . societies for the relief of martyred Belgium. Societies for Rolling Cigarettes, Bandages, Exterminating Hun Spies, Exterminating Yellow Dogs and Slackers. . . . A slacker is a dirty dog who does what I wanna do but am afraid to do. Who lies down. Who won't stand up on his hind legs and cheer when he's supposed to. . . . Societies . . . with an obbligato by the Avon Comedy Four—I'm a Jazz Baby. . . .*
>
> *A mighty nation had gone to war.*[9]

---

8. Upton Sinclair, *100%: The Story of a Patriot* (Pasadena, 1920), is a fictionalized version of the change in social temper, with a factual appendix.
9. Ben Hecht, *Erik Dorn* (New York, 1921), 175–176.

This spirit was unleashed at Russian Jews in New York, and citizens of German and Scandinavian descent in Minnesota. It blighted the career of Charles A. Lindbergh, Sr. (1859–1924), a congressman and Progressive who opposed intervention and drew the wrath of anti-German and political opponents. The torment and Lynch Law their elders endured from coast to coast were observed by such children as John Steinbeck in California, himself of part-German derivation, who arrived at somewhat less than patriotic conclusions from the scenes of arson and humiliation. Older dissident youth were required to submit themselves to the rigors of prison camps. One of them, a conscientious objector, noted:

> In the storm we found each other. A handful of students. A poet-professor of English, of old Yankee stock. An instructor of philosophy, a Jew. A professor of mathematics, a Hollander. a professor of physiology, a Canadian. . . .
> In the storm we clung together. We clung, also, to a few great names—[Bertrand] Russell . . . [Romain] Rolland . . . Randolph Bourne. Even with these we were still so few.[10]

Some sensitive young intellectuals sought to resolve their dilemmas of loyalty and distaste for war by volunteering for service with the ambulance corps. John Dos Passos, e. e. cummings (as he became in his nonconformist later period), and Malcolm Cowley were among many who made choices enabling them to ride the whirlwind; Cowley thought their services "were college extension courses for a generation of writers."[11] They came forth from the war period resentful of what they saw as wasteful, inhumane carnage, the reverse of the democracy the war was supposed to foster. The youth movement, born in an atmosphere of freedom and hope, ended in an era of repression. It was to reappear in post-War years as irreverent, disdainful of tradition, and impatient with reform.

Wrote R. L. Duffus, an author and *New York Times* editor, to the present author:

---

10. Ernest L. Meyer, "Hey! Yellowback!" (New York, 1920), 5. See also Norman Thomas, *The Conscientious Objector in America* (New York, 1923).
11. Malcolm Cowley, *Exile's Return* (New York, 1951), 38.

[A]ll of us who shared the beliefs of the pre-1917 peace movement must always feel a certain nostalgia. We were fundamentally right. No good and decent person or nation, none of the millions of families on this earth who just want to earn a living, raise their children and have an occasional good time with their neighbors, can gain by any war. . . . [I]f there had only been enough Bournes—not only here but in Britain, France, Germany and Russia, in 1914–18!

Yet it is striking to observe how little of a political nature would remain of the youth's first crusade. The 1910's were without question a seedtime artistically; almost all the authors who emerged as popular or influential in 1920's began their careers in the earlier decades.

Their heritage as social leaders is more debatable. They had despised reform and reformers as makers of half-measures, as sentimentalists who sought to win the "people" rather than to direct them. Upton Sinclair seemed to them no artist, and foolish in his belief in monogamy, a principle that, much later, would be termed "square." And yet they somehow expected the reformers to stand at their posts, holding the line for reform, while they themselves probed their own individualistic potentials and wove millennarian slogans. They were horrified when the reformers joined Woodrow Wilson in his wartime crusade, and won the nation to it; for it is not conceivable that the war could have been fought without the eloquence, the insight into popular psychology, the prestige of the reformers. As one of the youth wrote of Charles Edward Russell, socialist and muckraker, whom he termed "A Lost Leader":

I saw him once,
In a great, hushed hall,
Where thousands held their breath to hear him. . . .
His bold frank face shone under his gray hair,
Like the face of some warrior saint.

He who was the seven-fold trumpet blast,
Around the Jericho of Greed—
Now that the walls are crumbling,

> Now that the city is ours—
> Deserting our hosts in the battle;
> Crowning our triumph with shame;—
> This is a great defeat![12]

Yet strangely, the youth, while denouncing reformers, were also aware that there were much less agreeable types to choose from than reformers. Max Eastman drew the portrait of a wealthy businessman and associate of the youth movement out of his memories. His character, Forbes, expressed contempt for the unthinking masses (whom the youth somehow distinguished from the middle classes they despised), and he looked forward to what would in time be called fascism. Forbes was scornful of what he termed "fog breathers": futile people with philanthropic impulses who would not recognize that life meant ruling, or being ruled. Forbes esteemed himself an "engineer of history." He would mold humanity to his purposes, using their greed, dreams, and ignorance as materials. He predicted America's intervention when it was still a European War:

> *Wilson! ... What the hell has Wilson got to do with it? Jo, you're incurably filled up to the gills with fog. I tell you we're going to war and we're going. It doesn't make the slightest difference to us whether Wilson writes the declaration [of war] or [Charles Evans] Hughes. Not the slightest.*[13]

Forbes was disappointed but not wholly surprised, when Eastman's alter ego responded that he opposed war, and was for the "working class." "Don't deceive yourself," Forbes answered. "You're not a revolutionist. Nobody will ever take the trouble to hang you. You're a fog-breather. You'll never break through."

The youth movement of the 1910's, shattered by prowar forces, broke into two main streams of social energy. One of them continued the Bohemian tradition, notably in New York and Paris, living the life Ernest Hemingway and Henry Miller were to chronicle in *The Sun Also Rises* (1926) and *Tropic of Capricorn*

---

12. Alter Brody, *A Family Album and Other Poems* (New York, 1918), 128–29.
13. Max Eastman, *Venture* (New York, 1927), 388–89, for this and following quotation.

(1935), the latter in the midst of economic depression. Swarms of experimenters produced much less than these authors, but left varied accounts of their passages by way of fetes, liaisons, suicides, and hundreds of "little magazines" which disdained advertisers and were suspicious of verse which could be readily understood. Robert Clairmont, a wealthy young man who subsidized many of their exploits and was ruined by the great stock market crash of 1929, commented acidly: "It cost me just $800,000 to learn that the only art which mattered vitally to those apostles of esthetics was the art of getting dollars for nothing."[14]

The second stream of the old youth movement, less consequential in the United States than abroad, went political. It consisted of those who committed themselves to radical tenets, and those (Lenin called them "fellow travelers") who were sympathetic to their purposes, but held on to aspects of individualism or social status. Robert Minor was a talented cartoonist whose appreciation of socialist objectives made him one of the most admired of *Masses* contributors. He ended as a dray-horse of the Communist Party, prepared to say or do anything that was asked of him. Typical of the second class was John Dos Passos, who voted for the Communist Party presidential candidate of 1924, but whose prose and verse expressed ideals of love and personality which ultimately turned him against the Communists as dehumanizing in their goals and practices.

The war marked an era not only for the younger generation, but for their elders who conducted the war with more or less conviction of righteousness. All who were left at the end were uncertain of what they had won or lost. A friend of one of the famous pacifists, who had himself become a Washington bureaucrat during the war, confided to the present author that if he had truly believed in the validity of the "Crusade for Democracy," he should have enlisted for action on the fighting front. The belief that only by entering into a dangerous physical situation could one prove that his cause was just may be debatable. It does, however, suggest that some of the patriots during the war were uncertain of their own virtue and harbored guilty consciences.

---

14. Parry, *op. cit.*, 319.

Stuart P. Sherman, reviewing a collection of *Memoirs of the Harvard Dead in the War against Germany,* noticed that there was "a diffusion among us of mordant skepticism regarding 'military glory.' " He felt compelled to take less satisfaction in what the dead American soldiers had achieved than in "the fine gallantry and unselfishness which they exhibited." Sherman reported that one of them had seen the war as a religious crusade. Others had taken their own deaths with jests on their lips. They had written letters which were thoughtful, homesick, eager. A twenty-year-old lad who had died had earlier brought down five German planes in one day, and gaily noted that he had got one "boche" in the evening.

But Osric Mills Watkins, an Indiana boy who died at age twenty-one, had prepared letters against that exigency which Sherman found himself too filled with emotion to quote. One letter which he did cull passages from suggested to Sherman "more poignantly than any other page in these five volumes . . . the incalculable costs of war." Watkins's letter had concluded with the thought that, death being imminent, he would be proud to have died for America.

> *It was very obliging of these boys* [commented Sherman] *to die for us. But after a careful study of these three hundred and seventy-three personal records, I must say that it strikes me as rather a florid figure of speech on our part to declare that death was "the crown of life"—for them.*[15]

---

15. Sherman, *Critical Woodcuts,* 348.

5

Youth in Boom Times and in Depression

> *The trouble is that mass production involves a change in the commodities produced that hasn't been worked out yet.... Certainly eighty percent of the inhabitants of the United States must read a column of print a day, if it's only in the tabloids and the Sears Roebuck catalogue. Somehow, just as machinemade shoes aren't as good as handmade shoes, the enormous quantity produced has resulted in diminished power in books. We're not men enough to run the machines we've made.*[1]

The optimism engendered by a victorious war for democracy would have seemed capable of unleashing new youthful energies everywhere. But though youth was vocally honored or recognized in many lands, the form in which its qualities were acknowledged varied widely. Thus young arms and energies were eagerly sought, first in Italy, where they were called to a new *Risorgimento* (resurgence) intended to revive the pride in Italian birth to which Julius Caesar and Garibaldi had once appealed. The young, black-shirted Fascists whom Benito Mussolini, formerly a Socialist leader, now addressed were not intellectuals. They sought action,

---

1. John Dos Passos, *Three Soldiers* (New York, 1932 ed.), vi, introduction.

self-esteem, and results, as did soon after the young brown-shirted Nazis whom Adolf Hitler mobilized to overthrow the new German Republic.

Their nationalism theoretically distinguished the young of Germany and Italy from the youth who organized or were organized in branches of the Young Communist League throughout the numerous "republics" of the Soviet Union, from the Ukraine to far Siberia. The latter youth presumably identified themselves with young Communists everywhere. In actuality, the Soviet youth had no individualizing qualities of the kind which have been previously noted, and those who exhibited such qualities found themselves liable to social rejection, if not worse.

It is possible that there was a somewhat larger component of intellectual curiosity among Soviet youth, at least in its Leninist period (1917–1924), than among Fascist youth, but this had little effect on young Communist potential for independent action. Leon Trotsky's *Literature and Revolution* (1925) was as cerebral and esthetic a work as any revolutionary leader proved capable of writing. But it totally denigrated art as no more than furthering or impeding the program he perceived as necessary to humanity's advance. Democratic leaders in the West were often limited in their grasp of artistic goals, but they did not necessarily put obstacles in the way of pretenders to excellence.

In the United States the dispersed youth movement did not pick up immediately, but manifested its presence in a series of little related actions. Many of the prewar young had been quelled by the war's demands. Some were embittered by the 1919 Steel Strike, which broke the unity forged by such leaders as Samuel Gompers of the American Federation of Labor and such leaders of industry as Elisha Lee of the Pennsylvania Railroad and Bernard Baruch, the financier. Some American youth were disheartened by their government's unwillingness to enter the League of Nations, and by the nation's overwhelming endorsement of the amiable but unidealistic Warren G. Harding for President. But most of the younger generation were caught up in the sense of prosperity which soon succeeded the postwar economic depression.

Randolph Bourne had foreseen a sharp, satiric literature which would expose the shallow aspects of American affluence and self-satisfaction. A considerable amount of such writing emerged. Young John Dos Passos's *Three Soldiers* (1921) told a poignant and disillusioned tale of young men in war, and his friend, e. e. cummings, did the same the next year in *The Enormous Room.* But Sinclair Lewis, at age thirty-five, was even better able to catch his countrymen's attention in 1920 with *Main Street,* a novel which looked askance at small-town values. The general public was willing to read works critical of itself by both younger and older scribes.

The war had made absurd some of the phrases and attitudes of American elders, to which they themselves were no longer willing to give more than lip service. They patronized, rather than helped prosecute, the new, brutal rum-runners and bootleggers who made a mockery of the Volstead Law. They were unbridled in their hunger for the things mass production and the installment plan made available. Despite the versifier Ella Wheeler Wilcox's plea to the American Expeditionary Forces to "come back clean," it was evident that times had changed. "How you gonna keep them down on the farm," a popular song had asked, "after they've seen Paree?" There was no way in which their movement toward the city—and toward city ways—could be stopped.

Nor was there a general desire to stop them. If anything, there was a will toward joining them. Gertrude Atherton, at more than sixty years of age, and following distinguished literary work and associations, published *Black Oxen* (1923), a novel of youthful rejuvenation. Joseph Hergesheimer, dedicated to fine writing and dignified living, scored with readers who responded to his *Cytherea* (1922), a novel of passion which was its own excuse for being. Ben Hecht, emerged from his cocoon of journalism and elitist prose as an important 1920's novelist, preached the gospel of futility to an interested readership in his *Erik Dorn* (1921) and *Humpty Dumpty* (1924). He also augmented his contemporary fame with skillful Broadway plays and motion-picture scripts.

Flapper-Philosopher.

> Beer, Beer for old Dover High,
> You drink the whiskey, I'll take the rye.

> Send the freshmen out for gin,
> But don't let a sober sophomore in.
> My honey, we never stumble, we never fall,
> We sober up on wood alcohol.
> When we yell we yell like hell
> For the glory of Dover High.
>   —Football Song

The major evidence that youth had become a national pre-occupation, independent of its virtues or program, was the triumph of F. Scott Fitzgerald's *This Side of Paradise* (1920), written by a young man whose experiences encompassed little more than life in the schools, notably Princeton University, and several years beyond. It is doubtful that the novel would have interested Woodrow Wilson, though he had once been the most popular and admired of Princeton professors. Yet Fitzgerald's novel went into printing after printing for the delectation of readers who were paying less and less attention to the now-stricken president whose eloquence had awed them only two years before.

Fitzgerald could hardly be blamed for writing of what he knew. The wonder was that his sophisticated tone and romantic hungers should have seemed momentous to a public which had recently been following the battle of Verdun and the war on the eastern front:

> *Amory saw girls doing things that even in his memory would have been impossible: eating three-o'clock, after-dance suppers in impossible cafés, talking of every side of life with an air half of earnestness, half of mockery, yet with a furtive excitement that Amory considered stood for a real moral let-down. But he never realized how wide-spread it was until he saw the cities between New York and Chicago as one vast juvenile intrigue.*[2]

What Fitzgerald saw—or, at least, reported—was not particularly lurid. It did give evidence that the young, girls as well as boys, questioned values and were not notably respectful of their elders. Amory Blaine, Fitzgerald's youthful protagonist, in the last

---

2. F. Scott Fitzgerald, *This Side of Paradise* (New York, 1920), 65.

of his responses to friends, family, professors, and others, patronized a wealthy man of affairs for his belief that one must be har-
nessed to his job, for his complacencies about "human nature,"
and his skepticism about the realities of change. Amory ranted
against the "great middle class" as lost in confusion, and declared
himself "a product of a versatile mind in a restless generation—
with every reason to throw my mind and pen in with the radicals."

> *Even if, deep in my heart, I thought we were all blind*
> *atoms in a world as limited as a stroke of a pendulum, I*
> *and my sort would struggle against tradition; try, at least, to*
> *displace old cants with new ones. I've thought I was right*
> *about life at various times, but faith is difficult. One thing*
> *I know. If living isn't a seeking for the grail it may be a*
> *damned amusing game.*[3]

Jazz Age. Fitzgerald's greatest impression in his first phase
was made not through his young men, but his young women. He
had discovered the "flapper," made conspicuous by the war, and
now the focus of all eyes for what she might represent.[4]

The emancipated mood spread to wide circles of young and
older females, emphasizing such obvious symbols as short skirts,
rolled stockings, tight-fitting brassieres intended to create "boyish"
lines. None of this had any necessarily intellectual ingredient. In
Fitzgerald, as in the commonest "flapper," it meant an indifference
to older opinion, appreciation of jazz and attendant dances, a willingness to smoke cigarettes, drink hard liquor, and experiment
sexually, from "petting" to "going the whole way."

None of this was novel. What was novel was the effort of
participants to function in the open and without loss of social effectiveness or status. Accordingly, they attracted more attention

---

3. *Ibid.*, 299–300.
4. *Flapper* originated in England, decades before the Great War, apparently deriving from reference to a fledgling partridge or wild duck. The word thus
indicated a "very young harlot." It expanded its meaning to take in the more
numerous "soldiers' delight." It came to the United States, and continued in
England, designating a bold, bobbed-haired, or generally unconventional
young woman. Interestingly, it persisted in use in America longer than in
Great Britain; Eric Partridge, *A Dictionary of Slang and Unconventional
English* (New York, 1950 ed.), 282.

than ever before, from outstanding authors like George Santayana and William Lyon Phelps to the veriest scribbler who pandered to public curiosity and disturbed feelings. Commentators deplored moral dangers attending possession of an automobile and saw youth as disappointing or as meriting a chance to prove itself. One author saw youthful demands as irresistible. Another thought he discerned a religious impulse in flapperism. Edgar A. Guest, who wrote verse, averred that "My Youngsters Don't Worry Me." Others frankly worried, or, in the case of the humorist George Ade, were amazed by the new crop of "eighteen-year-old roués and nineteen-year-old vamps." Will Payne, another of an older generation of writers asked whether persons who reached sixty years of age ought to be chloroformed. Still another of the prewar writers, Samuel Hopkins Adams, who had won honors as a muck-raker, gave a name to the era with a novel named *Flaming Youth* (1923) published under the pseudonym of "Warner Fabian." For all the book's lack of esthetic quality, it helped make clear that a crisis in social relations faced Americans: a crisis which affluence obscured but did not negate, and which an old-fashioned reformer of Adams's stamp could not handle.

His problem was also that of succeeding generations: he did not understand that the "new youth" were not merely enjoying prerogatives as a result of the weakness and uncertainties of their elders, but were determined to build up an ethic of their own. Thus Joseph Freeman, then bemused by a desire to serve both art and "the revolution," and working in Europe for the highly unrevolutionary Chicago *Tribune,* was surprised to receive a letter from one of his best friends, who followed philosophical and other remarks with the casual information that he had attempted to seduce Freeman's "lady," but was unsuccessful because it was "the wrong time of the month, and therefore her sexual passion was very low." However, he promised to try again when temporal conditions were in better order.

Freemen's reception of the letter was "correct" according to the era. His friend was right to attempt the seduction, and to tell him of it. Freeman was correct not to manifest jealousy, though he was disappointed in himself to feel it. Jealousy was a primitive and philistine passion. Writing as a revolutionary, on the other hand, he analyzed the letter as bourgeois in deeming the lady private property and as belonging to anyone. Finally, he and his friend continued their relationship for many years. "I never rebuked him for his conduct; I was in style."[5]

Companionate Marriage. Nevertheless, it was another reformer with older credentials who created one of the sensations of the era by suggesting, as a solution to the uncertainties of family and youth-elders relations, the program of "companionate marriage." Ben Lindsey's previous reputation had been won in Denver, Colorado, where he had shone as "the kids' judge," one of the founders of the juvenile court system. Now he stood once again clearly in the public eye, condemned or defended for having argued that iron-clad marriage sanctions could only further discredit marital traditions, and further weaken society's chances to stabilize itself.

For such suggestions Lindsey was reprobated as approving fornication, extra-marital affairs, and a host of other evils. Yet Lindsey's plan was extremely moral and responsible, and ingeniously constructed. Lindsey insisted on marriage. He simply faced the fact that many marriages were likely to dissolve, unless they were sincerely pursued and not dependent on harsh laws impeding divorce. He wanted society to face these facts, provide psychological counseling, disseminate information respecting sex, and permit birth control until such time as the companionate couple felt confident that they were indeed ready to commit themselves to full marriage responsibilities. Lindsey's *The Companionate Marriage* (1927), written with one of his collaborators, Wainwright Evans, tried to find a mean between older sanctions and the heady freedoms which threatened more harm than good to brash youth. The enduring worth of the companionate marriage idea lay in its insistence on character in the people involved, its potential for exposing fraud in the pieties of elders, and in the young themselves.

A Tide of Criticism. In such an atmosphere of experiment,

---

5. Freeman, *op. cit.*, 176.

the revaluation of American life, which in the 1910's had involved
coteries, expanded to take in many other groups. Floyd Dell observed, in his lightweight *Love in Greenwich Village* (1926), that
the Village had become "commercialized." He could not perceive
that he had himself become commercialized. His autobiographical
novel *Moon-Calf* (1920) sold better than it deserved. His *Intellectual Vagabondage* (1926) played over, in essay form, his earlier
themes of youthful expression, dilettante radicalism, and love to
a receptive audience.

   Youth, published in Chicago in 1922, touched off a rash of
"little magazines" which featured prose and verse writings, much
of it richer than before the war, but also sharper in derogation of
native life and resources. The symbol of such a viewpoint, and a
bible to the young, was Mencken's *American Mercury,* founded
in 1924, and bringing together ironists and iconoclasts of various
sorts. Mencken himself culled from periodicals choice selections
intended to reveal the emptiness and stupidity of editors, ministers,
educators in the "Bible Belt" and elsewhere. They vilified Menck-
en as evil and indecent. Mencken cheerfully collected their opinions and published them in a *Schimpflexicon* (Dictionary of
Abuse, 1928).

   The *New Masses,* begun in 1926, sought to revive the left-
wing spirit of 1910's radicalism. It mixed faith in the potential for
a militant labor movement with reverence for the Soviet Union and
gave political tone to the disillusionment of some intellectuals.
American Caravan was an annual publication, first issued in 1927,
and edited by, among others, Lewis Mumford, one of whose clos-
est associates was Van Wyck Brooks. Although it contained af-
firmative writings, it also featured satire and cultural alternatives.
Alter Brody, once a poet and idealist, contributed "Lowing in the
Night," which treated with disrespect his immigrant progenitors.
Michael Gold, editor of the *New Masses,* published his "Hoboken
Blues," an impressionistic play in jazz rhythms which condemned
American racism. William Ellery Leonard, poet-professor at the
University of Wisconsin, issued hitherto unpublished sonnets from
his famous *Two Lives,* descriptive of his personal tragedy and the
persecution he suffered. As he wrote, "they make . . . a sonnet-
sequence, with the background of events in the shadows. . . . the

insanity and suicide of the wife . . . the grief and the calumny for the husband. . . . all in this contemporary prosperous America of ours."

Individualism. A second major theme of the time, and one not unrelated to the protest aspects of the youth impulse, was individualism. Mencken despised socialism, but he despised even more what he saw as the crass conformity of American life: its Rotary Clubs, its American Legion, and other agents of fraternalism. He therefore found himself at one with people who opposed him, when they thought of it, for his superman hatred of the masses. Mencken was cordial to Upton Sinclair and even toward Edwin Markham, whose "Ballad of the Gallows-Bird" he first published.

Individualists were of various types, and interwove according to their preferences. Robinson Jeffers, living with a certain austerity on an independent income in California, fashioned poetry which linked primeval impulses to the human. He was helped in his career by James Rorty, a 1910's poet-radical, who now in the Twenties divided his time between verse, advertising, and editorial work for the *New Masses*. When he left the publication, Robinson commented: "It is pleasing to learn that Rorty isn't editor of the Masses any more. I like and admire him, besides owing him a lot. . . . I think that ostentatiously proletarian atmosphere is too slipshod to be good for anybody, at least in this country.[6]

Jeffers sought a deeper normality than life ordinarily offered. Hart Crane, by contrast, was a disturbed child of divorced parents, indulged himself as a homosexual while dividing himself still further between advertising and abstruse poetry which won the regard of leading experimenters and funds-granting foundations. Homosexuality then not being generally accepted, he suffered guilt and confusion, as in his denunciation of the poet Sara Teasdale, whom he accused, probably unfairly, of having prevented him from attaining more normal sexual self-expression. Crane also feared psychiatric treatment, which he thought might destroy his

---

6. Robinson to George Sterling, October 9, 1926, in Ann H. Ridgeway, ed., *The Selected Letters of Robinson Jeffers, 1897–1962* (Baltimore, 1968), 90.

"genius."[7] Despite Crane's tormented and often debased life, he was a friend of Allen Tate, one of the southern "Agrarian" poets, who revered Jefferson Davis and Stonewall Jackson, and idealized life as they imagined it to have been lived on antebellum southern plantations.

All of the above figures overtly despised American business-men, industrialists, and technicians, though, as indicated, not a few worked intimately with them or derived profit from them. e. e. cummings was aware of the threat which business, education, and advertising posed, especially to artists exposed to their lures and subtleties. cummings consciously resisted them in his poetry, con-trasting the innocence of love and joy in nature with the unattrac-tive and humorless aspects of conventional life. His eccentric po-etic lines and punctuation, his contempt for every patriotism, and his devastating "Poem, or Beauty Hurts Mr. [Harold] Vinal," a fling at a conventional poet of the time, were all triumphantly in-tended to assert the values of personality, freedom, and free choice. That cummings was no mere American-hater became clear when he protested the conventionalization of radical thought, as in his *EIMI* (1933), an account of a trip to Soviet Russia.

It is significant that although cummings's friend John Dos Passos advanced esthetically in the 1920's, he became more con-spicuous for his antiwar *Three Soldiers* than for his *Manhattan Transfer* (1925), the latter a novel which grappled at least as strongly with the meaning of American life of the time as did Fitzgerald's *The Great Gatsby,* published that same year. Appar-ently readers were interested in the phenomenon of flappers, the antics of Bohemians, and in Sinclair Lewis's Babbitts and Elmer Gantrys. But the young people who predominated in *Manhattan Transfer* struggled between the new freedoms of a permissive so-ciety and old sanctions of loyalty and sincerity, and were thus not sufficiently stereotyped to represent anticipated types. The John Dos Passos of the 1920's was sensitive, poetic, and impressionable. He grimly identified with the anarchists Nicola Sacco and Barto-

---

7. There was, however, considerable opinion which favored respect for valid persons of deviant temperament. It expressed itself in such an international success as Radclyffe Hall's *The Well of Loneliness* (1928). See also Una, Lady Troubridge, *The Life of Radclyffe Hall* (New York, 1963).

lomeo Vanzetti, whom he saw as hounded by Massachusetts law and victims of its conspiratorial forces. Their death by electrocution in 1927 for complicity in a payroll robbery and murder in 1920 seemed to Dos Passos the death of old America, with its hopes and opportunities.[8] The hard, impersonal prose of his trilogy *U.S.A.* (1930–1936) memorialized that fact, as he saw it, and gained him a fame in the 1930's such as he had not quite achieved before.

The values of tradition and social continuity were thus downgraded in an era which fulfilled Van Wyck Brooks's appeal for an intellectual repudiation of rubbish, an uncovering of a "usable past," though the process of discriminating usable from unusable materials was not spelled out. "Debunking" of the past was a vogue in the Twenties, and one not only adopted by youth, but by many of their elders. W. E. Woodward and Rupert Hughes were only two among many of the older generation who went after George Washington in order, as they thought, to reduce him to more human proportions and so clear the way for new ideas and fresh enthusiasms. Stephen Vincent Benét's *John Brown's Body* (1928) was almost unique among notable poems by younger writers in seeking inspiration from past heroics, and it was not indicative of a trend.

Thomas Wolfe came on the scene at the end of the Twenties with his *Look Homeward, Angel,* expressing the era's spirit of loss and hunger and its passion for self-expression. Wolfe's stature in the troubled time which followed suggests that individualism was not so much lost as a result of depressed economics as transformed into an inquiry into American values. As a southerner, Wolfe was critical of New Yorkers. But his youthful exuberance and egotism seemed too precious to give up, even to the most doctrinaire young of the 1930's, while Wolfe's unseasonable vanity, antisemitism, and other traits were more easily tolerated in "good times."

Expatriates. The crusade in Europe had introduced to Parisian life numerous men who might not otherwise have savored it. Some stayed on in France after the war and were joined by others

---

8. John Dos Passos, *Facing the Chair* (Boston, 1927).

in the States who, between 1920's prosperity and the inflated franc and other European currencies, were able to live abroad on little money, on money from home, or on generous friends. Travel was democratized; young people disported themselves in Paris streets and houses who would not have been seen there in earlier times.

The war had unleashed a spirit of personal adventure and immediate living which, in Paris especially, moved expatriate Americans. There was, of course, a conventional French establishment as well as a licentious one. Hence, "dirty" books could be published in English in Paris which were not tolerated by French authorities in their own language. The situation on that level was not totally different in America. French texts of daring color could be readily obtained there, and conservative literary criticism accepted tales about foreign women of easy virtue (Madame Bovary, for example) which caused literary quarrels and legal entanglements when identified with American-born women.[9]

France's economic needs helped the French to practice patience with the excesses of some American Bohemians who made of Paris "a moveable feast," and they endured the antics of American females abroad which would have scandalized them in decent girls of French nationality.

American youth abroad pursued various purposes. Few failed to give some attention to jazz, amours, liquor, and other amenities. But not a few made of their "exile" a crusade. Harold Stearns, who, as a young editor of the *Dial,* had suffered wartime censorship, was a leader in the migration abroad. He had already, in *Liberalism in America* (1919), savagely arraigned liberalism as a "doctrine of impotence"—of high-sounding ideals and actual abasement before race hatred, narrow morality, and persecution. In *America and the Young Intellectual* (1921) Stearns committed himself to flat hatred of American civilization. He was not alone in his attitude. Henry Miller later imagined himself as spraying machine-gun fire at the complacent crowds in Manhattan's busy center. Numerous expatriates saw their country with Ezra Pound's eyes, as "an old bitch gone in the teeth, . . . a botched civilization."

---

9. Irene and Allen Cleaton, *Books & Battles* (New York, 1937).

By contrast, they saw Paris and the French countryside as varied, welcoming and nourishing such exciting artists as James Joyce and Pablo Picasso, and mind-expanding movements like "Dadaism"—bizarre and defending meaninglessness.

Many visiting Americans came to see Gertrude Stein, who reminded Samuel Putnam (then a Bohemian, later a distinguished translator) of Amy Lowell, no doubt because of the way she held court for her admirers. Glenway Wescott was one of her favorites at the time. He had begun his writing career as a sensitive interpreter of the Midwest. *Goodbye, Wisconsin* (1928) signaled his abandonment of America, his assuming an expatriate stance which largely ended his creative life.

The expatriate phase of Bohemia had its substantial aspect of introducing foreign styles and art to Americans and creating a species of cosmopolite. Henry James had known little, and would have cared less, about such cultural phenomena as poets who scored their verses on music sheets and artists who glued materials together, to say nothing of the drunkards and roisterers who sought moods and sensations in the several centers of Bohemia. Typical of many such as A. Lincoln Gillespie, a Philadelphia high school teacher who suffered a head injury in an automobile accident and thereafter "made Joyce at his most Joycean appear disconcertingly pellucid."[10] Typical of Gillespieese was his definition of art as a "dynamomentous sculpforth wroughtsmithing." Some of his friends thought him Joyce's superior as a craftsman. Gillespie attained publication in the avant-garde magazine *transition,* and was exultant, his wife depressed. She informed their friends that she and "Linc" were separating: "He says I'm not his intellectual equal any more."

So the youth struggled for identity and for justification. The distinction between the conventional and the unconventional was not always obvious. Ernest Boyd did not respect the experimenters though he was himself an Irish freebooter who lived in the United States and translated writings from half a dozen and more languages and contributed to the wit and impudence of the time. In

10. Samuel Putnam, *Paris Was Our Mistress* (New York, 1947), 77.

Appreciations and Depreciations (1918) and *Literary Blasphemies* (1927), he did not hesitate to conclude that William Shakespeare was overrated. No essay of Boyd's attracted such attention as did his imaginary study of "Aesthete: Model 1924," which originally appeared in the first issue of the *American Mercury.*

The sensation caused by the article revealed like nothing else the uncertain, intuitive nature of the new youth efflorescence. Boyd drew the portrait of a conventional young man who had been attracted to poetry because it suggested free living and female opportunities, and who mixed clique enthusiasms with "little magazine" editorial thunders made up of wind and ignorance.

That young Malcolm Cowley should have fancied this was an arrow directed at him indicated a touch of paranoia, but also a set of expectations which had bloomed under loose Parisian skies, feelings of self-importance, and Dadaism. Cowley had in Paris hit a restaurateur because he intuitively felt he was evil. Burton Rascoe, influential literary columnist of the New York *Herald Tribune,* quoted Boyd as vowing he had never heard of Cowley. This was certainly true since the latter had just recently arrived in New York and begun the avant-garde *Broom.* But Boyd's ironic and patronizing portrait did inadvertently touch aspects of numerous young litterateurs. Cowley, like Boyd's antihero, had attended Harvard, and had "evaded" military service, as service with the ambulance corps could have been interpreted. He had become an enthusiast for the new poetry, had enjoyed a Bohemian phase in Paris, and was now in New York to concoct experiments shocking to the "Babbitts."

Cowley later confessed that he and his associates on *Broom* had a sense of persecution. "Crowds, whistles, skidding taxicabs, all the discomforts of the city were a personal affront. . . . I had nightmares in which I suffered from the malice directed against contemporary art."[11] That he should therefore have harassed Boyd with telephoned threats and telegrams, and with his friends picketed Boyd's hotel, not only made them all ridiculous, but also

---

11. Malcolm Cowley, *Exile's Return* (New York, 1951 ed.), 190 ff.; compare Ernest Boyd, *Portraits Real and Imaginary* (New York, 1924), 11 ff., 153 ff.

compromised free speech. Yet they also served notice that Bohemian activities, even when light-minded, had a serious base and could produce serious results.

Hemingway.

> *The scum of Greenwich Village, New York, has been skimmed off and deposited in large ladlesful on that section of Paris adjacent to the Cafe Rotonde. New scum, of course, has risen to take the place of the old, but the oldest scum, the thickest scum and the scummiest scum has come across the ocean, somehow, and with its afternoon and evening levees has made the Rotonde the leading Latin Quarter show place for tourists in search of atmosphere.*[12]

Hemingway was to emerge as the finest flower of the expatriate experience, though how much he would rate in the future as artist and as personality became uncertain following his death. *High on the Wild with Hemingway* by Lloyd R. Arnold (1968) had nothing to do with his literary stature; it was an account of his hunting experiences in the West. Whether *For Whom the Bell Tolls* (1940) was read for its art or for its Spanish Republican sympathies was undetermined. And so with other of his works. *Death in the Afternoon* (1932) was probably at least as much a traditional introduction to bullfighting as it was a capturing of Spanish character, and it patently contradicted Hemingway's later pro-Republican journalism. In addition, Hemingway had a curious streak of sentimentality hidden beneath his "hard-boiled" surface which enabled him to transmute several of his works into popular motion pictures. It was not entirely accidental that one of his most popular novels should have inspired a seasonal tune entitled "Farewell to Arms that Caressed Me," or that a posthumous collection of his writings should have been copyrighted as by "Ernest Hemingway, Inc."

All this, however, was part of an international success for which he was not entirely responsible or prepared. In the 1920's he was legitimately one of the two outstanding writers of the youth

---

12. "American Bohemians in Paris," *Toronto Star Weekly*, March 25, 1922, in William White, ed., *By-Line: Ernest Hemingway* (New York, 1967), 23.

movement: the expatriate counterpart of F. Scott Fitzgerald. During the 1920's, they were not closely identified with one another. The fact that they both came from the Midwest did not strike anyone as important. They were both Jazz Age products. But Fitzgerald was of the college crowd. Hemingway, like Ben Hecht, had learned his trade on newspapers. Fitzgerald's contact with the war had been remote. Hemingway sought it out and suffered wounds at the war front. Fitzgerald strove for sensitive writing, appreciative of individual feelings, and he practiced a kind of disillusioned patriotism; his name was, after all, Francis Scott Key Fitzgerald. Hemingway's clipped, unfeeling words and sentences tried to get down to the stark realities of life, to strip it of its familial, patriotic, and religious rubbish. His protagonist in *The Sun Also Rises* (1926) has been made impotent by war wounds (this theme sparked rumors about Hemingway which he was at pains to refute); what was there in life for him but drift and forgetfulness?

But Hemingway did more than express futility and despair for youthful dissidents and malcontents. Especially in his fine short stories and sketches—Hemingway lacked the fine novelist's grasp of character—he was able to glorify courage, individual dignity, primitive passion, and ritualistic violence.

What explains Hemingway's continued and expanding influence? Fitzgerald's reputation disappeared in the 1930's, and only revived following World War II, when he was joined in the "Hemingway-Fitzgerald" syndrome. Hemingway, on the other hand, stayed abreast of events in the 1930's, taking on a tinge of "social significance," and continued on as an international man of letters. A curiosity of his career was that it depended so much on violence and hunting—qualities for which Theodore Roosevelt was increasingly scorned by the young and some of their elders. Quite evidently, it was not violence as such which was here downgraded, but Roosevelt's identification with patriotism and family virtues. These enabled his detractors to make their points against him in a social atmosphere of cynicism and cultural change.

Not until the 1970's did a spokesman for youth turn on Hemingway, and by indirection deride him as a brainless man of violence.[13] But by then events had given new meanings to peace and war and forced revisions of doctrines of art and philosophic despair.

"He Who has the Youth has the Future."

All right we are two nations[14]

The economic crisis of 1929 put a quick end to the merry japes of the era. It hurled expatriates homeward as Europeans impatiently shrugged them aside, while those on the American scene hastily reorganized for bread and butter projects. Radicals of the right, but even more, radicals of the left, mobilized for what they expected to be a desperate assault on decayed capitalism. Persistent radicals like Joseph Freeman, who dreamed of "proletarian art," found themselves in the Promised Land, able to voice authoritarian sentiments and to have them respected.

A remarkable case involved Scott Nearing. Born and raised an individualist, he topped a brilliant career in Philadelphia as a student with one as a teacher of economics at the University of Pennsylvania and as a writer and lecturer on such topics as child labor and women in industry: subjects which should have, in the Reform Era, created no problems. In 1915, mainly because of Nearing's insistence on his right as a citizen to participate in public forums, he lost his contract with the university. The affair made national headlines, and advanced the cause of tenure for teachers. Nearing then taught at the University of Toledo, in Ohio, a connection which terminated when he took an antiwar stand. He next published *The Great Madness*: *A Victory for the American Plutocracy* (1917), a book which brought him a much-publicized trial and acquittal. Nearing went on to indict American imperialism in terms which brought him closer and closer to the Communists; one of his books, *Dollar Diplomacy* (1925), was prepared with Joseph Freeman as collaborator.

In 1927 Nearing applied for membership in the Communist

---

13. Kurt Vonnegut, Jr., *Happy Birthday, Wanda June* (New York, 1971).
14. John Dos Passos, *The Big Money* (New York, 1936), 462.

Party, and was informed that the party needed to know if its members could control their petit-bourgeois impulses sufficiently to accept party discipline. Wrote Nearing, in response:

> *You ask whether I am willing to accept Party control over my writings and educational activities. I understand this question to mean that the discipline of the Party extends to the writings and utterances of its members who are held accountable for the expression of opinion on public questions. I believe that this is a* sound policy and would accept and support it.[15]

Nearing later offended party functionaries by publishing opinions on imperialism which transgressed doctrine set down by V. I. Lenin in his own book on the subject. So Nearing resumed his political wanderings in 1930: a friend of radicalism, rather than an obedient follower. But his willingness to accept a "discipline" which was far more rigid than any offered him in previous commitments helps indicate the strong pull which ideals and examples of revolution offered in the 1930's.

The reason for this was a combination of the impasse facing youth and their mentors in a stalled industry, with the urgent cries for world-wide insurrection voiced by Communists everywhere. Stilled by death was Lenin's bitter rhetoric forged during World War I in opposition to capitalist "vultures," sharks," robbers," and their Social Democratic 'lackeys." But rhetoric such as Lenin's had in 1930 become a tradition among his followers.[16] Though relatively few in number, they were able to impress many of their peers who envied or admired their "boldness" in flouting

---

15. Freeman, *op. cit.*, 343–344. Italics in original. Compare Scott Nearing, *The Making of a Radical* (New York, 1972), 146 ff.
16. An example of Lenin's analyses, germane to American experience, helps indicate his research and manner of reasoning. In the following passage, written in 1918, he is justifying his willingness to make any kind of agreement which he feels will advance the world proletarian revolution, even though it may require concessions to "bourgeois governments" and even demand cooperation with them:
     "The American people resorted to these tactics long ago to the advantage of their revolution. When they waged their great war of liberation against the British oppressors, they had also against them the French and the Spanish oppressors who owned a part of what is now the United States of North America. In their arduous war for freedom, the American people also entered

their teachers, defying fathers who had been unmanned by economic troubles, and learning a revolutionary jargon which carried with it intimations of drama.[17]

The New Deal and Youth. The rousing victory of Franklin D. Roosevelt in 1932, with his promise of experimental government and his call to a new crusade against fear, marshalled some youthful forces in distinctive pattern. Youth was one of the problems faced by the New Deal. It set up a National Youth Administration to acquire data on the subject and administered funds in its behalf.

Most impressive of New Deal achievements here was the Civilian Conservation Corps—a literal materialization of William James's old (1910) call for a "moral equivalent of war"—a war against antagonistic nature, rather than people. The C.C.C. drew hundreds of thousands of young men off the city streets where they smoldered in resentment and set them working on mountains and in drought-plagued farm territory. It organized them into work camps where they received status, found friends, and were paid not much but something by a society which indicated that it cared.[18]

C.C.C. was implemented by a host of other youth-centered organizations such as the National Student Federation of America, scout organizations, religious organizations, and the National Recreation Association. Yet all the programs together were less conspicuous than those of a few, highly organized political groups, committees, and leagues. Membership in other agencies was too diffuse for highest social effectiveness, and their purposes too

---

into 'agreements' with some oppressors against others for the purpose of weakening the oppressors and strengthening those who were fighting in a revolutionary manner against oppression, for the purpose of serving the interests of the oppressed *people*. The American people took advantage of the strife between the French, the Spanish and the British; sometimes they even fought side by side with the forces of the French and Spanish oppressors; first they defeated the British and then freed themselves (partly by ransom) from the French and the Spanish." (V. I. Lenin, "Letter to American Workers," in *Collected Works,* volume 28 [Moscow, 1965], 68.)

17. For an example of one such youthful career, Milton Hindus, "Politics," in Filler, ed., *The Anxious Years* (New York, 1963), 268 ff.
18. Kenneth Holland and Frank Ernest Hill, *Youth in the CCC* (Washington, D.C., 1942).

widely spread to crystallize around the key issues of the time: un-
employment and fear of war.

The "debunking" of the affluent Twenties had done its work
well. The "Great Crusade" of 1917–1918 was thoroughly deflated. Conservatives and radicals were oddly at one in believing
that the United States had been gulled into sacrifice of youth and
treasure during the past war to aid one alliance of imperialists
against another. United States Senator Gerald P. Nye of North
Dakota expressed midwestern isolationist feelings in 1934–1936
in public hearings which persuaded newspaper readers that munitions manufacturers—"merchants of death"—had helped drag the
country into war. *Idiot's Delight* (1936), a shallow play by Robert
Sherwood, exploited the theme and received the Pulitzer Prize.
Sherwood himself later served as director of overseas operations
of the Office of War Information.

"[A]ll right we are two nations," John Dos Passos's deadly
challenge, went further than Disraeli had intended in his novel
Sybil (1845). Disraeli had pointed to two nations, indeed, "between whom there is no intercourse and no sympathy; who are ignorant of each other's habits, thoughts, and feelings . . . and . . . not
governed by the same laws." Disraeli had the rich and poor in
mind, and projected in his mind a government which would curb
the one and minister to the other. Dos Passos, instead, drew a line
between two civilizations, which could only settle their differences
by revolution.

Such views dovetailed with those of radicals who held that
capitalist overlords had a stake in international wars, that the poor
suffered by them, and that there was a direct relationship between
capitalist-created economic depression and the threat of war. To
such issues conservative youth organizations could not address
themselves. Groups centering on youth employment and antiwar
measures became foci of attention from both the "right" and the
"left."

Individualism in the 1930's. The times acted severely on
some reputations. James Branch Cabell, whose ironic fantasies had
been treated as classic only the day before, found himself entirely

forgotten. Mencken, because of his frank contempt for socialism, was demoted to semihistorical status. F. Scott Fitzgerald's *Tender Is the Night* (1934), promising a new maturity, came and went as a novel of the season, as he himself struggled with alcoholism and despair.

Some of the finest proponents of self-expression were abashed by the pervasive stark distress and anxiety and made efforts to re-tool for new tasks. Matthew Josephson, expatriate author of *Portrait of the Artist as American* (1930), now wrote *The Robber Barons* (1934), explaining American capitalism in uncomplimentary terms. But soon, thanks to family background, he became a stockbroker. Even Ezra Pound explained the world's troubles by way of cconomics, finding answers in usury and semitic conspiracies. It was evidence of the hold art and Bohemianism continued to have on youth that many of his most foolish opinions were treated with respect, not only by his friends, but by moneyless young would-be writers who dreamed of socialism while clinging to memories of idiosyncratic good times.

Nathanael West (1903–1940) wrote modestly received, but well-remembered fiction, notably *Miss Lonelyhearts* (1933), while working as a scriptwriter in Hollywood. His hatred of the town and his interpretation of it made West a legend among writers, as did his sudden death along with his wife in a car accident, an incident made famous by Ruth McKenney's *My Sister Eileen*. More important, and a moderating influence during the 1930's, was Edmund Wilson, a college mate of Fitzgerald's and a Twenties esthete, whose *The American Jitters: A Year of the Slump* (1932) was unqualifiedly personal. During the 1930's, he persisted in treating fiction, Marxism, the Soviet Union, and other themes from an individual perspective which annoyed dogmatists.

Kenneth Fearing came from Ernest Hemingway's home town of Oak Park, Illinois, a generation later. No goals materializing for him, he wrote pulp stories and became passive and critical toward society, drinking when he could and finding friends among the New York left-wing youth who hoped he would see the social light as they had. Fearing developed a style satirizing American success symbols, as many did, but added to it a jazz rhythm and personal style. His verses circulated among his friends, and were finally published by subscription as *Poems* (1935), one of the few such successful collections of the era. Fearing's talents were real but limited, and he turned to writing mystery stories when his brief inspiration passed.[19]

Old Youth Movement and New. The essence of the youth movement since the 1910's had been disaffection. But to youth's general alienation was now added an international component which made it different in important respects. It was doctrinaire to such an extent that Max Lerner, a left-wing intellectual who had been an aide to Alvin Johnson in preparation of the landmark *Encyclopedia of the Social Sciences* (1930–1935), could believe Marxism was unique in explaining the world as it was. Harold Rosenberg, who esteemed himself an esthete, believed that "putting aside the fetishism with which the mediums of fiction and poetry are still received in some quarters, no poem or novel of the past few years can equal as a literary expression of modern human consciousness the Communist Manifesto or Marx's Eighteenth Brumaire."[20]

The new youth were gaining a species of elder statesmen whose experience could help them combat traditional feelings, and enable them to work up a "usable past" which would be subservient to the present and future. James Rorty, having been poet and radical in the 1920's, emphasized the latter strand in his thinking. His *Your Master's Voice* (1934) resourcefully attacked the advertising world which had fed him, and others like him. *Where Life Is Better* (1936)—an ironic title—described California as ridden with vigilantes and other repressive forces. Strikingly, it was criticized in the Communist press as too "individualistic," though Rorty had thought that personal feelings and experiences added color and weight to social analyses. Rorty went on to attempt a kind of muckraking in criticisms of the American Medical Association and food manufacturers. The new youth welcomed

---

19. Albert Halper, *Union Square* (New York, 1933) portrayed Fearing in fiction as the author perceived him.
20. *New Masses*, March 23, 1957, 18.

derogation of American activities in all fields and eras, though also claiming such classic names as Thomas Jefferson and Abraham Lincoln.

The former youths found themselves serving the younger in esthetics. In social politics, however, it was the mature radicals who called the tune. Louis Adamic set down the case of Granville Hicks, who had begun as a religious-minded student looking forward to academic work. His first book was *Seven Ways of Looking at Christianity* (1926). Adamic recalled him at a literary party in 1932, where also was present Jay Lovestone, recently head of the American Communist Party, now in disfavor with Moscow but still recognized as a Communist leader:

> *Hicks knew only that Lovestone was a Communist; ... he sank upon the floor at Lovestone's feet and, looking up at him, inquired what he as a Communist should do. Lovestone ... smiled at the flushed boyish face with the blazing eyes and said there was probably not much he (Hicks) could do right away, but he might study Marx, keep informed on world and domestic affairs, and speak to likely people on Communism.[21]*

Hicks soon became a "high priest" of official Communist literary opinion, and in that role contributed to raising and demeaning reputations among readers.

The influence of this tide in the affairs of Americans has been debated. The "underground" nature of Communist activities has been scrutinized, its "subversive" quality argued. The Communist Earl Browder's phrase, that Communism was twentieth-century Americanism, was popularized by his adherents. Those who opposed investigations of Communists asked not only for the defense of civil rights, but demanded also to know where Communist influence could be discerned. Hollywood motion-pictures, exposed to millions of eyes, showed little but the vaguest appeal to world cordiality. The numbers of Communist Party members were manifestly small.

Many statements qualifying such arguments were offered, but

---

21. Louis Adamic, *My America 1928–1938* (New York, 1938), 95.

one of the most challenging was that by Murray Kempton, who
had himself once been touched by the spirit of the times: The
Communists were a tiny fragment of the whole, but they were a
majority of the committed."[22]

As such, were they able to carry any weight? Vast sections
of the country were relatively untouched by the ardor of the committed. But in such strategic centers as New York, Washington,
and Hollywood, it was possible for dedicated persons to accom-
plish much more than their numbers would indicate. A much
larger number of individuals were touched by their fire or argument, and could not only proliferate as "fellow travelers," but
work more freely and effectively than others who had exposed
themselves to public view.

All this touched the youth deeply; as Kempton noted:

> *If one was young in the middle thirties and felt compelled
> to dream revolution, there was no temple for it long ex-
> cept with the Yipsels, as the Young Socialists were called,
> or with the Young Trotskyites. The idea of force and vio-
> lence may have stuck in the back of the heads of the
> Young Communists . . . but in practice . . . [t]hey enjoyed
> the sense of being in the stream of great events, and some
> of them toyed with unfounded theories that Mrs. Roosevelt
> or Harold Ickes must be "one of us."[23]*

The Student Movement. During the years of unremitting depression, millions of children passed through grammar schools and
high schools with no goals in sight. Over a million students en-
rolled in public and private colleges and universities wondered
what was to become of them once their degrees had been granted.
The schools were a wide field for radical agitation, but not a fer-
tile one. Limited funds for public schools and controlled funds for
private schools made for constricted conditions for rebels.

Almost all the activity took place in cities of the North.
Limited though it was, student action created slogans and occasionally headlines. Student militants were Puritanic, decrying

22. Murray Kempton, *Part of Our Time* (New York, 1955), 320–321.
23. *Ibid.,* 321–322.

campus highjinks and excessive sports, and expressing disgust over tales of drinking and sexual exploits. Reed Harris's *King Football* (1932) was an inchoate catalogue of complaints regarding Columbia University affairs, but it imparted a sense of frustration which many students felt who were not secure either in conventional purposes or radical dogma.

A major force in the student movement was City College of New York, the "Harvard of city colleges," which had incubated generations of humanists and scientists on its impeccable campus. Now it produced an army of competent militants who challenged the first study-as-usual administration headed by the college's president Frederick B. Robinson. They made him notorious for his irascible response to their demonstration against a parade and review of the military corps on campus in 1933. Dr. Robinson had wielded an umbrella against the protesters, and subsequently suspended or expelled a number of them.

In April 1934 the Student League for Industrial Democracy and the National Student League sponsored a strike against war. Though it was largely a New York affair, it attracted wide attention, and encouraged organization of student chapters across the country. It also produced a number of leaders, notably Joseph P. Lash of C.C.N.Y., and James A. Wechsler of Columbia. Both proved impressive spokesmen for what promised to be a widening program for youth membership drives.

Lash spelled out some of the history of the socialist youth movement in his *The Campus Strikes against War* (1935), published by the Student LID, a pamphlet introduced by John Cripps of the University Labor Federation of England. Lash expressed pride in the great student turnout of April 12, 1935, which had brought out 175,000 students for an hour, not only in New York, but also in Boston, Chicago, Los Angeles, and elsewhere. Four thousand students had struck in Berkeley, California. "Schools Not Battleships," their signs had declared. They demanded the abolition of the Reserve Officers Training Corps (ROTC). To the question of whether the United States had to fight in Asia, they had answered with a ringing NO! Student militants had circulated the Oxford Pledge, "Not to support King or Country in the event

of war." In this United States it had become: "This House will
not support the government in any war it may undertake." Lash
underscored that he made no distinction between offensive or defensive war, since propaganda made them one and the same.

Wechsler, who was the better journalist of the two, and had
been editor of the Columbia *Spectator,* that year published his
Revolt on the Campus. It established his expertise as a writer. He
and Lash collaborated on a work issued by International Publishers which demonstrated their increasing skill as formulators
of programs. Their book was introduced by Bruce Bliven of the
New Republic. Bliven could not see why a nation like the United
States, so uniquely isolated from the clash of imperialisms, needed
defensive preparations beyond its continental borders. The two
young crusaders covered a wide field of national and international
history. They discussed M-Day, the ominous-sounding word employed by the War Department to signal the first day of mobilization. They reviewed what they saw as the tragedy of Wilsonian
idealism, cited statistics which told of profits by munitions manufacturers, indicated parallels between American military personnel
and fascists abroad, and charted dangers to peace posed by vigilantes and propagandists. They proudly reviewed the student
strikes:

> [N]o gesture more accurately reflects the temper of the
> student peace movement, no other enterprise more clearly
> distinguishes it from its fumbling predecessors of 1917. . . .
> Out of these demonstrations have arisen an accredited na-
> tional leadership, commanding allegience among all under-
> graduate groups. . . . out of them we can discern the shat-
> tering of old restraints, which made men prey to inertia.[24]

The Cultural Component.

> The New Masses disappointed me; or it would have had I
> honestly hoped anything fresh and kicking to come from
> the particular group that's running it. . . . The difference
> between the old-fashioned revolutionist and . . . us . . . is

---

24 Joseph P. Lash and James A. Wechsler, *War Our Heritage* (New York, 1936),
117.

*that they, essentially were contented with ... [a] transfer
[of] power from one class to another, whereas we want
... [to] displace a mean and inferior kind of life with a
completely different kind.*[25]

As perplexing as the question of the Communist political influence upon the young was that of the impact of radical arts.
Norman Thomas, Socialist leader, was quoted as having admitted
that the Communists had captured the "cultural front." They
themselves did not hesitate to predict the rise of a "proletarian
literature." Whether it developed at all, and in what sense (they
later hailed as "proletarian" the then universally admired *Grapes
of Wrath* by John Steinbeck), it was certain that some erstwhile
literary and other notables were shelved, and that others who
showed traces of "social significance" received excessive attention.

Cultural rebels appeared on campus, decrying effete literature and honoring writings which promised action. It was a sign
of social health that Tess Slesinger's *The Unpossessed* (1934)
satirized their humorless, dogmatic views which saw all writing as
directly or indirectly propaganda for or against "revolution," their
abasement before Soviet culture, and their mechanistic view of sex.
Instructors, too, fostered such views; Mary McCarthy's *The
Groves of Academe* (1951) later made fun of campus debates inspired by the firing of an instructor for incompetence, which he
triumphantly resisted by pretending that his political "opinions"
had been the issue.

The *New Masses* inherited all such sound and fury. It had
struggled with dogma and anticapitalist views through the 1920's,
attracting some sympathy from such broader-ranged authors as
Dreiser and Dos Passos. It now found itself in an excellent position,
offering firm opinions on government, foreign affairs, artists, the
popular arts, and every other topic, and being read by eager youths
whom it lionized as arrows to the future.

A formidable array of editors and contributors was calculated
to persuade readers they were at the front line of vital events and
on the correct side. New editors proved themselves on review and

25. Lewis Mumford (1925), in Robert E. Spiller, ed., *The Van Wyck Brooks-
Lewis Mumford Letters* (New York, 1970), 35.

feature pages, then joined older Communist Party wheelhorses as
editors; writers of the quality of Isador Schneider, Ruth McKenney, M. R. Bendiner, and Richard H. Rovere; and, among the
cartoonists, Crockett Johnson, later for a while famous as the
creator of "Barnaby." Marc Blitzstein, Alexander Kendrick, M.
B. Schnapper, Anton Refregier, Theodore Draper, Dale Kramer,
and Alter Brody represented a combination of older and newer
talents in cultural and public affairs, as did such women as Elizabeth Gurley Flynn, Eleanor Flexner, Anna Louise Strong, and
Elizabeth Lawson. There was a continuous alertness to new talent,
though one letter-writer complained that

> *There is a great need today for the wide-open welcome of
> Jack Conroy's old Anvil. Maybe some of the stuff in the
> early revolutionary magazines was rotten, but the un-
> known writers were published and had an opportunity to
> develop.*[26]

William Saroyan was given space in the *New Masses*, following the success of his *The Daring Young Man on the Flying Trapeze*
(1934), but his unbridled individuality offended the magazine and
it dropped him. Few young authors in the orbit of social concern
took similarly bold, principled stands opposing the *New Masses*
"line." This premised devoutness toward the Soviet Union, contempt for "Trotskyism," due reference to the poor and unemployed at home and, more vaguely, the "workers and peasants"
abroad. Realistic art with naturalistic touches was in vogue, as was
an awareness of the political nature of all sentiments. Alfred
Hayes, then a "revolutionary" poet, told Mike Gold, whose *Jews
without Money* (1930) had made him the "dean" of revolutionary
writers, that "Down Tools for May Day!" was a perfect line of
poetry.

The dream of a "proletarian" literature never lagged in the
New Masses through the 1930's: it was one of Trotsky's heresies
that he believed proletarian literature a contradiction in terms. A
constant stream of stories, verses, and especially plays was interpreted as advancing the creation of such a literature. *Waiting for*

---

26. Dee Brown in *New Masses*, May 12, 1936, 23.

Lefty (1935) by Clifford Odets was a forthright Communist "agit-prop" (agitational-propaganda) play, contrived so as to involve the audience in its unfolding. It was considered evidence of the validity of the proletarian concept. Even skeptics had to take into account the fact that it was produced with outstanding success from one end of the country to the other. *Bury the Dead* (1936), a moving antiwar play by Irwin Shaw, was accorded similar honors and attention.[27]

The *New Masses* and its numerous associates in literary, political, and other fields gained not only by the flood of talent in the Newspaperman's Guild, the Congress of American Revolutionary Writers, the American League against War and Fascism (later named the American League for Peace and Democracy), and affiliates of the American Communist Party; it could also call upon a host of distinguished independents of the quality of Ernest Hemingway, Thomas Wolfe, William Carlos Williams, and Corliss Lamont (son of the financier Thomas W. Lamont) who, in one issue of the *New Masses,* explained "Why Members of the Upper Class Go Left." And it could call upon numerous names from abroad to endorse the validity of its works, such names as Henri Barbusse, Maxim Gorky, Federico García Lorca, Thomas Mann, and, among younger conspicuous figures, Stephen Spender, John Strachey, Diego Rivera, Andre Malraux, Ignazio Silone, Ludwig Renn, and other famous personages from the Communist insurgents of China to those of the Soviet Union.

The *New Masses* never ceased claiming a heritage from the past, feeling free, for example, to quote the recently deceased Lincoln Steffens as being an "ex-liberal" who had learned the only solution to America's problems was Communism. But its main emphasis was on peace and antidepression measures, as well as the spectre of Fascism, perceived as growing in all sectors of American society and government. The New Deal first impressed the *New Masses* editors as imitating Mussolini's Italian system, then Hitler's. The president was caricatured as heavy-jawed, and with his

---

27. So effective was Shaw's play that, following American intervention in World War II, he determined that it ought not to be shown, and removed it from the public domain.

Seal of Office overhead adorned with a "Blue Buzzard." Communist leaders first anticipated a "revolutionary situation," and dissuaded their followers from seeking emergency government jobs. But the hunger for work soon overcame this program, as young and old applied for jobs with the Works Progress Administration, the Federal Arts Projects, and the National Youth Administration.

This last became the special target of youth leaders. "A Generation Is Stirring," Wechsler declared, in the March 31, 1936, issue of *New Masses*. He was in Washington, covering a youth gathering seeking a more comprehensive Youth Act, and urging congressmen to grant education, vocational training, and job funds. He wrote coldly of the president who, he thought, was "once again making his peace with Wall Street." He honored Edwin Mitchell, a nineteen-year-old leader of the Southern Tenant-Farmers' Union, and Gil Green, head of the Young Communist League.

Popular Front. World events were invoked to rouse the youth. There was the Republican political victory in Spain, and a Falangist uprising against it, headed by Generalissimo Franco. The Rhineland was reoccupied by the Nazis. In Japan, military extremists attempted to seize the government. In Moscow there were trials intended to prove that Trotsky and others were treasonably associated with Fascist governments. Wechsler, reporting for the *New Masses* the meeting of the American Student Union, an organization founded in 1935, anxiously echoed its call for a People's Front among students as among natoins. He was critical of the slow growth of the union; it had no more than some 10,000 paid members. He singled out Trotskyites among the youth as splitters of the unity he deemed necessary.

Thereafter, youth commentators followed foreign developments with particular closeness. Numerous youth enlisted in an Abraham Lincoln Brigade, for service with the Popular Front government in Madrid. Their "Republican" sympathizers deplored the Neutrality Act of 1935 which limited aid to Spain. Joseph Lash, momentarily leaving his role as youth leader, reported for the *New Masses* readers the progress of Spanish arms, declaring that "Time Works for Us." He resigned from the Socialist Party, reporting for the American Student Union, "We can no longer sub-scribe to the Oxford pledge . . . with the Fascists brandishing their torches of war." Franklin D. Roosevelt in a 1937 Chicago speech declared for collective security and a quarantine of aggressors: a sentiment Lash and the *New Masses* embraced. Lash now repro-bated pacifists, Trotskyites, Lovestoneites, Socialists, "and a few liberals" whom he discerned among the membership of the Ameri-can Student Union, as impeding "action for peace."[28]

A curious victim of such unfoldings was John Dewey, once one of the great names among radicals and radicalized liberals. As an idol of experimental education, he had been forgiven his ac-ceptance of the necessity for supporting American intervention in World War I and had resumed his position as an elder statesman of dissident educators and youth. When, however, he undertook to chair an independent committee to investigate the truth of charges that Trotsky had been a paid agent of Fascists plotting to destroy the Soviet Union, his reputation among radical admirers began a descent which ultimately affected their view of experi-mentalism as an instrument of bourgeois decadence.

The youth movement showed apparent signs of continuing health in its identification with the World Youth Congress, which met at Poughkeepsie, New York, in August 1938. It linked the American delegation with representatives of such politically in-nocuous organizations as the League of Nations Association and the American Youth Hostel Association, and joined with them in endorsing the "quarantining" of aggressors and mutual assistance pacts. But the disintegration of the Madrid government and Franco's triumphant entrance into the capital in the spring of 1939 began a series of actions which increasingly isolated the left-wing youth.

Central to these developments was the Soviet Union, now looking for friends in a Europe increasingly in the hands of Fas-cists. Its friends in America appear to have had no inkling of the bombshell which Soviet diplomats were preparing. As late as May 23, 1939, the *New Masses* published as evidence of the foolishness

---

28. Key issues of the *New Masses* include December 29, 1936, February 23 and October 19, 1937, and January 11, 1938.

of a former Communist, Ludwig Lore, columnist for the New York *Post,* that he had written: "It looks now as though Joseph Stalin were ready to come to terms with the Reich."

In August of that year, Stalin bound the Soviets to a nonaggression agreement with Germany, pledging no war between the two nations for ten years. Although the Communist press outdid itself in explaining how Stalin had taken giant strides for peace,[29] the deed disintegrated numerous Communist-related organizations. Shock was added to shock when Reich troops and Soviet troops marched west and east to dismember Poland. Disillusionment grew more intense as the Russians seized the little Baltic nations of Lithuania, Estonia, and Latvia, then attacked Finland. All official Communist explanations of having liberated Poland and resisted military attacks by the Finns were coldly received by the American public.

The youth movement, as represented by the American Youth Congress, fought on to the end. American International Brigade veterans sought to refurbish their old Spanish slogan of "No Pasaron" (They Shall Not Pass), originally directed against the Franco armies but now intended to resist American efforts to intervene in European developments. Despite the Nazi-Soviet Pact, considerable youth opinion still held to nonintervention. The AYC now rigidly adhered to the Neutrality Pact. Joseph P. Lash had become a friend of Eleanor Roosevelt, and, persuaded by her program of aid to Great Britain, was replaced as chairman of the AYC by a more isolationist leader. AYC adherents convened in Washington in 1940, where they sang "No, Major! No, Major! No" to the tune of "Oh Johnny." They also interpreted concern with foreign affairs as an evasion of domestic needs.

Randolph Bourne's old pleas against intervention and John Reed's old phrase, "This is not our war" were revived to underscore the inconsequence of the German-Allied "phony" war of the winter of 1939–1940. Churchill was correct, said the *New Masses,* in declaring that he had nothing to offer but blood, toil, tears, and sweat. "Instinctively in this tragic moment our sympathy goes out

29. See, for example, Richard H. Rovere, "What Every Appeaser Should Know," *New Masses,* September 8, 1939, 5.

to the peoples on both sides of the battle."[30] This publication thought it "sad and sickening" that the *New Republic* took the lesson of devastated Norway to be that the United States continue to supply the Allies and even to attack Germany to rescue the Allied fleet. The *New Masses* was far from isolated, even though it had lost some editors and subscribers. In June, a Gallup Poll found that Americans opposed by 13 to 1 entrance into the war.

While the military forces mobilized, the AYC planned an Emergency Peace Mobilization for Labor Day, 1940, in Chicago. But although Paul Robeson, highly regarded Negro singer, performed, and Joseph Curran of the militant Seamen's Union attended, it was the swan song of the youth movement.

On June 22, 1941, Germany invaded the Soviet Union. The *New Masses,* well aware that it was accused of "flip-flops" in policy, immediately turned its attention to the ignominy of Nazism. On July 8, it featured the article, "Why This Is Our War."

---

30. *New Masses,* May 21, 1940, 4.

6

The Times
They Are A-Changin'

The war against Fascism put an end to the youth movement. Its former partisans, with the exception of conscientious objectors, accepted without protest or qualification draft status or one of the numerous well-paying jobs now available.

Many of the old "militants" were completely forgotten in succeeding years, but others took on new personalities which sometimes became the opposite of their earlier ones. Thus, Richard Rovere emerged as a well-esteemed social commentator who expressed contempt for Communists as unesthetic and without influence. Granville Hicks entered a period of silence, punctuated by his modestly titled *I Like America* (1938) and an apologia, *Where We Came Out* (1954), after which he wrote literary criticism for the *Saturday Review*. John Dos Passos, wholly disillusioned by Communist maneuvers and executions of dissident Communists during the Spanish Civil War indicted them in his *Adventures of a Young Man* (1939). He turned not only his outlook but his fiction into conservative channels. Others of his generation also ceased looking to the youth as leaders or as followers.

Arguments for an expanded Youth Act had become obsolete, as did most of the programs and emotional images which had been identified with youth. The general prosperity gave a new start to all ages and classes of the population.

There were patent domestic injustices even under the war-emergency full employment conditions. The herding of Japanese-Americans into concentration camps later was made notorious by scholars and public figures. The careless attracting to the mainland of Puerto Ricans as servants to take the place of others working in shipyards, military installations, and elsewhere was accomplished without regard to the well-being of the uprooted Puerto Ricans, bewildered by New York and unable to cope with it.

Aged persons, unable to enter on equal terms into war prosperity; multiple-amputees of the last war, abandoned by their relatives in Veterans Administration Centers; children all but abandoned by parents eager to work at one or even two jobs; and other categories were either forgotten or processed by social workers who in many cases brought perfunctory attitudes to their work. A notorious case became symbolic of a new social laxness: it was discovered that a welfare recipient was being serviced in a New York hotel, and that she was the owner of a then-esteemed mink coat. So there were social problems to be unraveled. But they did not demand attention and did not particularly involve youth.

The war ended on a high note of triumph. Germany's disgrace as a land of gas chambers and mass murders was a marked contrast to heightened American self-esteem. The ensuing "cold war" diminished the positive Soviet image indulged during the war, when Leon Trotsky's antagonistic manuscript life of Joseph Stalin had been shelved by publishers in order not to offend the Russian leader. Revelations of the atrocious murders by Soviet troops of great numbers of Poles, prisoners in the Katyn Forest, were not permitted to embarrass the "Grand Alliance." Now it was possible to "expose" such excesses, further enhancing the image of the democratic powers.

There were war heroes to admire in plenty, including such youths as Audie Murphy, winner of the Congressional Medal of Honor. Although the war crisis overlapped a continuing international crisis made ominous by the explosion of atom bombs over Hiroshima and Nagasaki, those in the heroic mold did not grow in national consciousness. The fame of Generals Marshall, Patton,

MacArthur, and others rested on solid bottom, but they provided no dynamic for reconstruction following the war. Even Dwight D. Eisenhower assumed the presidency as a "father image," rather than as the standard-bearer of contemporary ideals. A demobilized nation looked elsewhere for men and women to emulate.

"War Babies." The largest contemporary fact was neither Russia, Korea, nor even the atom bomb, but a surging and triumphant prosperity. A nation which had "tightened its belt" for victory in World War I had learned how to carry on production needs for both peace and war during World War II. The conversion to a combined peacetime and "cold war" economy was carried out with little pain. "Deficit spending" became a catchword for numerous stipendiaries who had never heard of John M. Keynes. Families raising "war babies," and recalling their own deprivation during the Thirties, looked about for means to enjoy their new-gotten gains. Men formerly organized by the military services were now organized by expanded corporations and moved from locale to locale as industrial "parks" proliferated.

New communities appeared overnight in the suburbs, based not at all on tradition, natural resources, community characteristics, or other human features, but on government and other contracts which could have motivated building anywhere. The new towns drew their inhabitants mainly from the cities, and featured lawns, transportation facilities, and labor-saving devices. Civic affairs were minimal and emphasized efficiency first and human relations second. The latter took on new forms which in later years would come under critical scrutiny: the "soft sell" of insincere friendship, conspicuous consumption, social envy and emulation, and the mindless intensity of diversions which were seen as mechanical rather than congenial and capable of binding people only to crass goals.[1]

---

1. William H. Whyte, Jr.'s *The Organization Man* (New York, 1956) was not intended as satire, but as a criticism by one who had lived with and believed in the businessmen's creed and social validity, but who was appalled by their latest permutations. A charming footnote to this best-seller was the fact that Whyte, made affluent by his book, turned from business to pioneer concern for environment, propagandizing for intelligent control of public lands for conservation and beauty.

"Fun" took on a priority such as responsible America had never previously acknowledged. Liquor was now adopted by the middle classes with unprecedented gusto, creating attitudes and conditions with which they would have to deal as their children got older.

Little was heard of those children during the 1940's except in their adoration of Frank Sinatra and other singers and entertainers. A few radical-minded youth turned to unions for careers, rather than to industry; but with labor firmly established in law and economics, in many cases such youth did no more than choose one job over another.

Radicals and the children of radicals there were, but they faded for the moment into insignificance. They lacked sympathizers, funds, or the binding force of new theater, music, and situations to bring them together. A radical could still express devout belief in the purposes of the Soviet Union, and contempt for those who referred to "Iron Curtain" countries and Soviet oppression. He could be critical of President Truman for approving the Loyalty Order of 1947 calling for investigations of federal employees as possibly engaged in treason. But he could take solace from Truman's veto of the McCarran Act (1951) which would have registered Communist and "Communist front" organizations, even though the act was passed over the president's veto.

Yet the number of persons willing to stand fast with the Communists in their plight was small. Conservative fury and alarm against dissidents was heightened when the Soviet Union attained explosive atomic power of its own, probably with the aid of Americans on salary in American military installations. Although this event and the sweep of Red Chinese forces in 1949 to power on the mainland could give an American radical sympathizer a sense of being part of large historical forces, he could not too publicly express his joy. Venice, California became a center for radicals and malcontents; Communists, once austere in their attitude toward sex, accepted the sympathy and companionship of homosexuals who had made the seaside place one of their resorts.

Such malcontents, carrying memories of the Thirties, with psychological commitments to the USSR or to deviant impulses for which the American temper made no provisions, were remote from American concerns. But they had reservoirs of support waiting for them in the form of youth, many of whom were unaware of the sources of their dissatisfaction in the increasingly run-down cities as well as in the antiseptic suburbs. Here children were being raised with an affluence they took for granted, and which tended to obscure wants which were not even articulated.

One disturbed observer saw the problem of the new youth as occasioned by "Mother," who dominated the household while her bemused spouse went off to the city to earn an inordinately high salary. The apocryphal story which haunted him was of a lady in mink who visited an expensive Miami hotel, gave her bags to be delivered to her room, and her thirteen-year-old son to be carried there.

"But, Madam," said the doorman, "can't the child walk?"

The woman answered: "Of course, but isn't it nice that he doesn't have to?"[2]

The critic told tales of children pressured to make high grades in school, to be conspicuous in its affairs, to seek material rewards, and all with no idea of a real world outside with poor people and ethnic minorities. He then asked:

> *Will their "filtered vision" and "horizontal experience" leave them permanently incapable of coming to terms with the world at large? Will their fathers' absenteeism turn the boys into emasculated neuters who can "bake a fine cake" but lack the essential attributes of manliness? Will the girls be bossy Amazons? Will their coddling mothers mold both sexes into a race of weak-kneed hypochondriacs? Will they wind up as naive, frenetic snobs unable to face adult responsibilities?*[3]

Although perhaps no actual thirteen-year-olds were carried to their rooms, there were a sufficient number of youth, endowed beyond their deserts, to give force to such questions. A new youth movement evolved in part out of such unpromising materials, aided by factors upon which Americans were barely able to con-

---

2. Peter Wyden, *Suburbia's Coddled Kids* (New York, 1962), 32.
3. *Ibid.*, 116.

centrate. One of them involved the forgotten cities. Wrote one
journalist:

> *Many Americans have a comfortable feeling that city*
> *slums are a thing of the past. Slums are something we as-*
> *sociate with the Triangle Shirtwaist fire, the "melting pot,"*
> *the crowded and colorful life of the lower East Side at the*
> *turn of the century.*[4]

The facts of juvenile delinquency told him otherwise. It revealed
a story of squalor, recklessness, contempt for authority, teen-age
gangs, sex, liquor, theft and killings, many unmotivated and with
no discernible purpose. The antisocial impulse affected girls as well
as boys. They were not interested in sewing classes. Clubs on traditional models of play and good-natured fun lacked attendance.
Parents could and did do little to combat the slide of the less affluent—yet far from "deprived"—youth into surliness, apathy, and
malicious mischief.

The gangs were mostly city gangs. They made trouble, but
none which disturbed the public seriously. Negro youth in the new
ghetto of Bedford-Stuyvesant in Brooklyn "bopped" with other
Negro gangs; whites with whites. They rarely impinged on the
suburbs. The police made no serious efforts to quell them:

> *"We don't want no trouble around here," a police sergeant*
> *said. "We try to discourage them from filing complaints.*
> *This is a quiet community and we aim to keep it that way.*
> *We have some fine people here. Of course, sometimes, the*
> *kids get a little wild. But we try to keep things in the*
> *family you might say."*[5]

But what about a report that a gang of Negro boys had driven
down one of the main streets of town recently, firing shots in the
air, and stopping to beat up two boys who had been walking home
from the railroad station? The policeman admitted this had occurred. "But those 'hoods' better not try it again. They'd get what
they had coming." He didn't think the Negroes were from New

---

4. Harrison E. Salisbury, *The Shook-Up Generation* (New York, 1958), 61.
5. *Ibid.*, 86.

York. Probably from Newport, a nearby suburban town with several factories and a small Negro population.

The reporter, a Pulitzer Prize winner, was conscientious about balancing causes and effects. The key fact was that he saw the disorderly situation as challenging the older generation, rather than threatening it. It was an age which glorified violence; small wonder the "kids" practiced it. Elders drank themselves into insensibility, but asked the youth to avoid liquor. Churches ran Bingo games. It ought not be a surprise that salacious motion pictures and tabloid newspapers stirred and excited the "kids." New York Police Commissioner Stephen P. Kennedy was an honest cop, but he was warring against a sea of dishonest policemen.

Power of the Establishment. Disheartening to would-be youthful dissenters was the overwhelming might of government and the military. Armed with sophisticated weapons of every size and type, they seemed impervious to opposition of the active type. Indeed, by way of Congressional and other investigations they carried the fight to those suspected of being "un-American." In the process, thousand-dollar-a-week writers could lose their place; others became frightened or bewildered. Albert Halper, betrayed into a false position by a Soviet agent he had believed to be a friend, found himself confronted by FBI men who knew him as a writer for the *New Masses.* As he tried to explain:

> *"I contributed to the* New Masses *during the thirties along with Hemingway, Thomas Mann, Granville Hicks, Edmund Wilson, Sherwood Anderson, and a lot of other writers."* My heart was pounding harder. *"It was a time when the literary and social climate was different than it is today. It was during the Depression, when artists and writers were concerned. . . ."* I stopped talking . . . From the studied, impassive looks on their faces I knew they didn't know what the hell I was talking about.[6]

---

6. Albert Halper, *Goodbye, Union Square* (Chicago, 1970), 247–248.

Halper felt "like an animal caught in a trap." Neither he nor
his friends could have imagined their earlier outlook and opinions
could bring them to such a pass. The new young did not have to
cope with this sense of nightmare. Few of them were rebels in
politics. There did not appear to be much to rebel about, with jobs
abundant for the fit, and the unfit shunted off on welfare or whatever arrangements they could manage. The new young expressed
bravado in relatively innocuous ways. They wore "zoot suits," the
coats long, the pants with high waists and narrow cuffs, baggy at
the ankles. A few Mexican-American youth in zoot suits in Los
Angeles quarreled and attracted the attention of the police. But
most youth seeking a consequential self-image tried zoot suits and
gave them up. Conspicuous were girls who borrowed their brothers' shirts, and the couples who tired themselves with long juke
box sessions, doing the "Lindy Hop." Their idols as late as 1950
were still not only curiously traditional, but well-divided into males
and females. Franklin D. Roosevelt, Abraham Lincoln, Roy
Rogers, Joe DiMaggio, Douglas Fairbanks, and Babe Ruth represented a spectrum of men; but at least several of the women—
Louisa May Alcott, Doris Day, Clara Barton, Sister Elizabeth
Kenny, Vera-Ellen, and Florence Nightingale—were destined for
temporary oblivion.[7]

Beats.

*"So that," began Pavel Petrovitch, "so that's what our
young men of this generation are! They are like that—our
successors!"*

*"Our successors!" repeated Nikolai Petrovitch, with a
dejected smile. He had been sitting on thorns, all through
the argument, and had done nothing but glance stealthily,
with a sore heart, at Arkady. Do you know what I was
reminded of, brother? I once had a dispute with our poor
mother; she stormed, and wouldn't listen to me. At last I
said to her, 'Of course, you can't understand me; we belong,'I said, 'to two different generations.' She was dread-
fully offended, while I thought, 'There's no help for it. It's*

---

7. *This Fabulous Century, 1940–1950,* V (New York, 1969), 44–45.

a bitter pill, but she has to swallow it.' You see, now, our
turn has come, and our successors can say to us, 'You are
not of our generation; swallow your pill.' "

Turgenev, Fathers and Sons

"Generations" now began to appear in almost frenzied pro-
fusion, each "generation" claiming its moment of reality. The
"Beat" generation, the "Angry" generation, the adorers of "Elvis,"
and of The Beatles, the 'Drug Cult" generation, the "Love" generation, and, most formidably, that of the civil rights crusade and the
"New Left" stood across the path of American affairs demanding
attention.

Mere firecrackers from abroad, of the sort which busy execu-
tives could afford to ignore, once more jarred loose the stalled
wheels of youthful action. No display seemed more innocuous than
that by Kingsley Amis, in his comic novel, *Lucky Jim* (1953). In
it he told of an unprepossessing assistant in a British university
department, kept anxious by an exploiting chairman who covered
his small-mindedness and shoddy scholarship with feigned heartiness and a taste for the ancient music of "Merrie England." Jim's
search for dignity among pompous collegiate frauds, his resentment over having his research boldly stolen by the professor, his
boredom with the research itself, and his efforts to disentangle
himself from a false alliance with a neurotic woman were all told
with sharp humor which left a sense of significant things bared.
The novel was a success in both Great Britain and the United
States: a crack in the wall of established education which was to
multiply many times before it became clear that the whole body
of education and its practice was under fire, from within as well
as without.

Even more sensational, and made influential by repeated
stage performances first in England then in the United States, was
John Osborne's *Look Back in Anger* (1957), a play with a protagonist who would soon be termed an "antihero": a university
man of "working class" origins who not only lacked respect for
education, but for the entire social pattern against which he directed endless harangues. He despised graciousness, loyalty, cour-

age, reverence. Implicit in his unbridled scorn was a hatred of capitalism and its supporters as the creator of misery and injustice. As he informed one of his women:

> I suppose you're going over that side [of religion] as well. Well, why don't you? Helena will help to make it pay off for you. She's an expert in the New Economics—the Economics of the Supernatural. . . . Sell out everything you've got; all those stocks in the old, free inquiry. . . . Tell me, what could be more gilt-edged than the next world! It's a capital gain, and it's all yours.[8]

Such sentiments, including rough repudiation of his wife's pregnancy as not meriting compassion, circulated on and off campuses and thrilled more spectators and auditors than they revolted. They contained some evident dangers: giving status and respect to persons who would take such sentiments literally as representing new truth and morality, and who could justify cruelty and emptyheartedness as positive qualities. But they also seemed to express legitimate resentment against an artificial world and to open ways for answering its sophistries.

The United States contributed its own philosophers of youth. The resounding success in the 1950's was Jack Kerouac, a Lowell, Massachusetts boy who had played football at Columbia University, served in the Marines, and traveled about from New York to San Francisco, from New Orleans to Mexico, and who published his findings in *On the Road* (1955). His paperback publisher put its contents with fair accuracy:

> Wild drives across America . . . buying cars, wrecking cars, stealing cars, dumping cars, picking up girls, making love, all-night drinking bouts, jazz joints, wild parties, hot spots. . . . This is the odyssey of the Beat Generation, the frenetic young men and their women restlessly racing . . . in a frantic search—for Kicks and Truth.

This summary failed to indicate Kerouac's sense of character, good ear for language, and other literary qualities. It did not note

---

8. John Osborne, *Look Back in Anger* (New York, 1957), 55–56.

the variety of his experiences and those of his friends. Most important, it glided over their genuine hope that their efforts would unfold new realities: "Somewhere along the line I knew there'd be girls, visions, everything; somewhere along the line the pearl would be handed to me." His prose leaped over the Thirties and made circuitous contact with things Thomas Wolfe had once worked over. But Wolfe had made epics of the university crowd, the literary crowd, and of himself and his family. Kerouac composed his saga indiscriminately of drifters, floaters, totally lost drug addicts, Bohemians, and of women they met accidentally rather than by design.

They sought experiences and made no distinction between the cultured and the uncultured, the stable and the unstable. Kerouac was candid in describing their meetings and drew pictures of places and people thousands of youth would seek out. Outstanding was Kerouac's utter lack of interest in the world of war, politics, and society. His emphasis—and that of his segment of the Fifties crowd—was wholly on self, on euphoria, and on "mystic" experiences which might be attained through sexual contact, liquor, and drugs. These were his people's answer to the overbearing power of government and industry: they would not clash because they would not meet.

Kerouac offered a full picture that could be especially verified in San Francisco by visits to Bohemian hangouts, notably in the Coexistence Bagel Shop. One of hundreds of such cafes and bars, this became famous as a meeting place for young, apathetic dropouts from society, shoddily dressed, talking little, and in the argot of their street, worker, and Negro circles. Their vernacular featured such words as "chick," "bread," "dig," as well as a variety of casual obscenity. Later the obscenity would become a cause, savagely thrown at all opponents, and so uniting the literate with the illiterate, the well-intentioned with the cruel and impotent.

Meanwhile, they were occasionally stirred to listening by someone dressed like themselves, in odds and ends of clothing, who carried a guitar and offered old songs and new concerning drifters, love, Negro blues, oppression of one sort or another: all the themes of rock, pop, folk songs, and with new verses added, new styles imitated. During the "Beat" period as such, roughly 1950–1957, the musical beat was "cool," on one plane of modulation. As the youth movement gathered momentum, it became more "funky": heavy, primitive, strident, and aggressive.

On one subject they were rigidly unanimous: the discrimination of people by color. And though they made little of domestic or world affairs, their lives flowed freely into mixed and deviate alliances, casual or entangled.

Kerouac was Pied Piper to many youth who threw away their books and left home to embrace new goals and such companions as neither suburbia nor the city streets could offer. He brought together in North Beach in San Francisco and in Greenwich Village in New York jaded socialites as well as Thirties survivors now washed clean of their former poverty and radical sincerity but bored by their new financial security and eager to see Beats with their own eyes and perhaps make contact with their primal joys and expression. Yet it remained for writers other than Kerouac to fill out the real story of Beat living.

It was readers, not news media, who made famous another college dropout, deep in drugs, homosexuality, and ecstatic searches. Part of his trauma certainly derived from family anguish. Yet it was curious that he was hailed as a successor of Walt Whitman; indeed, one publisher, trying to sell a book about Whitman, advertised him as a "nineteenth century Allen Ginsberg." Yet Ginsberg's verses were the reverse of Whitman's, being based on the hatred of America common among his friends. Whatever its ultimate literary value, Ginsberg's *Howl* (first issued in 1956 by a Beat literary center, City Lights, in San Francisco) struck a chord which the youth, and many beyond youth, found valid.

> I saw the best minds of my generation destroyed
>   by madness, starving hysterical naked,
>   dragging themselves through the negro streets
>   at dawn looking for an angry fix.

Ginsberg detailed such degradation in all its forms: marijuana, benzedrine, peyote, opium, heroin, turpentine, and kaleidoscope images of sex; and he interlaced them with generalized social references, clearly imputing their catastrophic nature to the "scholars of war," the creators of "the hydrogen jukebox," the bleakness of American society, the cruelty of police and hospital attendants. His friends had "burned cigarette holes in their arms protesting the narcotic tobacco base of Capitalism."[9]

Ginsberg's poem led to a court case on obscenity, but its international fame grew from sympathy with the belief that Ginsberg and his friends were victims of a degraded society, yet superior to it. This conviction added force to other impulses within dissident youth and made of drugs and sexual deviation partial causes in themselves, related to civil rights and arguments over what constituted legitimate living. Such issues complicated the question of what society ought to be willing to accept, just as drug addiction was beginning to spread to nightmare proportions in cities and on campuses.[10]

Music. A strong thread of song accompanied all youth movements and was recognized for its binding power. Jazz and the physical excitement it encouraged were deplored by conservatives in the Twenties, who did not fail to notice the central position Negro players and composers had won in the field. During the Thirties Jazz became more a diversion than a cause, except with intense young people who could somehow divert their attention from troubles of the times. Protest songs were often mechanical and linked with political commitments, but there were folk songs, American and foreign, spirituals, and satirical tunes and words to fill out the musical space between the tragic-popular "Brother, Can You Spare a Dime?" and "Sing Me a Song of Social Significance," the latter a tune in *Pins and Needles*. This musical was originally

9. For a view of *Howl* in the context of Beat writing see Gene Feldman and Max Gartenberg, eds., *The Beat Generation and the Angry Young Men* (New York, 1958), 164–174. An interesting view of Ginsberg sees his work as "pre-poems": material intended to set before the reader Ginsberg's personal vision; see Kingsley Widner, "The Beat Generation in the Rise of the Populist Culture," in W. French, ed., *The Fifties* (Deland, Fla., 1970), 168.
10. A court case of even greater challenge involved William S. Burroughs's *Naked Lunch*, published in America in 1962 and telling of a drug addict's extreme fantasies. Highly literate, it declared its social relevance in satire of unfeeling people, southern bigots, and others, and survived legal action, being widely approved as a work of genius in best-seller figures. Oddly, it also seemed to offer itself as an antiaddiction document, thus involving in the fight against drugs the people it condemned.

produced by the International Ladies' Garment Workers' Union
in 1937. A twenty-fifth anniversary recording in 1962 featured the
then little-known Barbra Streisand.

The genius of the Thirties and beyond was Woody Guthrie,
who created in himself a legend of the wandering minstrel, one of
the people, responsive to their needs, their sorrows, their consola-
tions. He made up songs recounting their feelings; made poetry of
their flat, unadorned phrases; or interpreted them in words which
took on classic sonance. "This Land Is Your Land" became all but
a national anthem, yet one emergent not from the elite, but from
some vast common demoninator of people everywhere. Guthrie
was not deflated by the prosperous years. As late as 1950, before
he had been reduced by disease to a shadow of himself, he was
asking attention for victims of duststorms:

> *I stood a while, I rode a while, I talked a mite with young
> and old weather birds. . . .*
>
> *I heard folks talk and cry about the dust storms all out
> across our 16 middlewest states. I saw that lost gone look
> on their faces when they told me the government didn't
> follow the plan of FDR and so our land is still a dustbowl
> hit by duststorms . . . and the hearts of the people are
> sickly worried. . . .*
>
> *I wrote up these eight songs here to try to show you how
> it is to live under the wild and windy actions of the great
> duststorms that ride in and out and up and down.*[11]

Guthrie was far from alone, in style or interests. Singers drifted
with their guitars into coffee houses, radio stations, publishing
houses, sometimes "making it," like Burl Ives, or receiving honor
from radicals, as in the case of Pete Seeger. And everywhere there
were circles of students who met to sing the tangy songs of love,
murder, radical dissent, blues, spirituals, cowboy ballads, and the
rest.

Guy Carawan was one of them, a Los Angeles college student
with North Carolina highlands roots, who was inspired by folk
song interests to travel over the country and hear and sing its
songs:

---

11. Woody Guthrie, *Talking Dust Bowl* (Folkways Records, 1950; FH 5212).

After I got out of U.C.L.A. in 1952 with an M.A. in Sociology, I took my first trip across the United States in an old car. The next summer two of my fellow folksingers . . . piled into this same car and we headed south. We spent 10 weeks in North Carolina and Tennessee, earning our way as we went singing on street corners, in country stores, gas stations, saloons, at folk festivals and on the radio.[12]

Here was a different odyssey from Kerouac's, and different music. The Kerouacs and their females preferred a dull, flat series of notes, more random and personal than did the spirited folk singers. And yet the two treks met in unwillingness to settle down or accept middle-class premises. Carawan encountered scores of singers, traded songs with them, instrumental styles, and ideas. They held in common regard such folk singers—"authentic and unauthentic"—as Seeger, Guthrie, Leadbelly, and Dyer Bennett. Carawan noted that their followers ranged from earnest students of folklore interested in "correct" interpretation, to hybrid types and new musical gestures, where good and bad, sincere and phony were difficult to distinguish. In 1957 he attended the Sixth World Youth Festival in Moscow: "It was a remarkable experience—to see there in one city 36,000 youth from the far corners of the earth."

Yet all the pomp and power of such a gathering had a less immediate future than domestic jazz. Indeed, the Russians were soon to lose what prestige they still retained among youth, who concluded they were "just another imperialist power," and sought heroes elsewhere. W. C. Handy, composer of "St. Louis Blues," foresaw this during the Depression. He quoted Noble Sissle, a famed exponent of jazz, as holding in 1934 that their music derived from suffering which found relief in jazz. "Then the Depression came, and white people suffered the pinch along with their darker brothers. With us, of course, being broke and low-down is an old story. . . . But it took a woeful depression to teach this trick to white America."[13]

One of Handy's dearest concerns, the preservation of unusual arrangements of spirituals, first experienced a militant revival in

---

12. *Songs with Guy Carawan* (Folkways Records, 1958; FG 3544).
13. W. C. Handy, *Father of the Blues: an Autobiography,"* ed., Arna Bontemps (New York, 1941), 232.

civil rights activities, then ran into rough sailing. The younger
generation of Negroes and whites were both finding the past a
"drag." They were attracted, as were many of their elders with
more or less sophistication, to the sense of the present elaborately
developed by Jean-Paul Sartre. "Existentialism" was as widely
bruited among the young as "Freudianism" had been a quarter
century before. A perceptive critic, Hazel Barnes, however, in her
The Literature of Possibility (1959) noted a difference between
the youth and the Existentialists. The latter believed in involvement, "engagement"; the Beats had practiced disaffiliation.

Meanwhile, they, with other youth, waited for tocsins to
sound and received music covering a complex series of aural options, from aimless and grinding series of drumbeats and trumpet
notes, heard in dark rooms, to the varied and directed songs of the
balladeers. They gave themselves to this mixed fare with an intensity largely indifferent to books or families. About them, and
everywhere, were traditional jazz initiates, many of them made
famous in nightclubs and concert "festivals," such as Louis Armstrong, Benny Goodman, Ethel Waters, Artie Shaw. They had
their own idols, like Bix Beiderbecke, who became a legend of
subtle cornet playing and creativity.[14]

They gave themselves to jam sessions, to intense relations,
and not infrequently to liquor and drugs. Ethel Waters expressed
some of their dedication and curious reverence:

> *I was learning a lot in Harlem about music and the men
> up there who played it best. All the licks you hear, now as
> then, originated with musicians like James P. Johnson. . . .*
>   *Men like him, Willie "the Lion" Smith, and Charlie
> Johnson could make you sing until your tonsils fell out. Be-
> cause you wanted to sing. They stirred you into joy and
> wild ecstasy. They could make you cry. And you'd do
> anything and work until you dropped for such musicians.*[15]

---

14. "As far as I could see, they didn't have any arrangement worked out, or tune
    either for that matter, but when the technician came in and gave them the
    high sign, they took off. Away they went. Away down." Nat Shapiro and Nat
    Hentoff, *Hear Me Talkin' to Ya: The Story of Jazz* (New York, 1955), 176:
    Hoagy Carmichael on Bix, Tommy Dorsey, and others. An important aspect
    of the musical revolution still to be probed is the relationship of "white" jazz
    to "black"; see, for example, Tony Russell, *Blacks Whites and Blues* (New
    York, 1970).
15. Shapiro and Hentoff, *op. cit.*, 176.

All of this was less remote from social impact than might appear at first glance. 1956 was a year for two major sensations. Tennessee Ernie Ford had been raised in hillbilly country, exposed to gospel songs, blues, work songs: the heritage of poor whites. He neither rejected it, nor loved it deeply; an unruffled attitude helped him rise through radio shows to his own TV show. As one commentator put it: "The informal breezy manner of Ford enables him to sing a blues song and switch over to a folksy joke or a bit of local gossip without a perceptible pause." Ford diverted his auditors with "Shotgun Boogie" and "The Ballad of Davy Crockett," as well as spirituals and such songs as "Who Will Shoe Your Pretty Little Foot."

In 1956 he introduced a Thirties song which should have been of no interest to a nation that had forgotten it, or to its children. Instead, "Sixteen Tons of Number 9 Coal," with its bitter message of unremunerated work, was a sensation. It sold two hundred thousand copies in nine weeks, over five million that year, to young and old.[16] It suggested things held in common for Americans but not yet crystallized in that generation, certainly not through renditions by Ford delivered with little pain, and by Lawrence Welk, belted out with none.

Vastly more significant, therefore, was the other phenomenon of that year, also drawn from Tennessee soil. Elvis Presley was a very young truckdriver who had been raised on hillbilly, blues, and fundamentalist tunes, and who may have carried some psychic memory of Holy Roller shouting and gyrations. In 1954 he cut himself a record with which to invite stations to use his services. "My Happiness," "That's When Your Heartaches Begin," and other tunes introduced The Hillbilly Kid to moderately appreciative audiences. He developed his mixture of primitive, revivalist, popular, and highly emotional music along with bodily movements which stirred the young and amused his Border State elders.

In January 1956 he made his first New York appearance on television and caused such a sensation as had not been witnessed since the advent of Sinatra. Yet there were differences. Sinatra, as a frail, almost sickly-looking youth, had attracted hordes of screaming females; unsympathetic critics had commented on the

---

16. *Look Magazine* (June 12, 1956), XX, 73 ff.

girls' taste negatively at a time when burly soldiers were presumably at work manning democratic outposts. Young Presley was
a more hearty specimen, though this made him no more interesting to the critics who viewed the new screaming teen-age armies
with disgust. His soft, full lips, legs spread apart, hips swiveling,
caused unprecedented public controversy. Although the singer
averred, "I never made no dirty body movements," and may have
been sincere at the time, there could be no question what his female admirers made of exhibitions which were condemned as "a
strip-tease with clothes on." They were augmented by the singer's
irregular stress on words and syllables, synchronized with movements and underscoring their purpose. Presley's greatest moment
of triumph came on the nationally viewed Ed Sullivan Show—a
"family" show—which endorsed the tumultuous fealty of the
teen-agers and was evidence that it could not be rechanneled elsewhere.

The intellectuals and hippies did not openly honor Presley,
though some of them may have quietly responded to his work, but
they could see that adult America was either impotent to stop it,
or secretly sanctioned it. Presley went on to earn millions with
empty amorous ditties and motion pictures which received no formal respect, but circulated with great profit among multitudes of
urban and rural youth. He had, however, exploded his firecracker:
revealed deep wells of sexual compulsion which would challenge
social standards for years to come, and form part—perhaps the
most important part—of the mounting youth movement.[17]

Civil Rights. James Wechsler, now editor of the New York

---

17. Did the news media "make" Presley and other juvenile rages of the era? Did
    the commercial houses deliberately puff up inconsequential singers for the
    delectation of the thoughtless masses, possibly in order to save the money
    which would have been necessarily expended on richer talents and more ex-
    pensive orchestras and equipment? So critics of the musical fashions have sug-
    gested. Certainly the record companies planned first of all to make money
    and to save money wherever possible. Certainly the media voted their prefer-
    ences as best they could without being discredited as poor reporters and un-
    satisfying commentators. But it seems unlikely that the media or recording
    companies could foist on their shrieking tribunals "fave-raves" (favorite en-
    thusiasms) they did not fancy and did not demand. Numerous singers shouted,
    gyrated, looked wistful, and otherwise conducted themselves in ways intended
    to draw attention and hold it. Most of them disappeared and left no trace.
    The ultimate choices were the public's.

LONG LIVE THE SPIRIT OF GEORGE JACKSON JESSEL LAWRENCE ATTICA !!

Photo by Scott Wheeler

"a student seeks a sense of proportion at an embattled College . . ."

Max Eastman

Charlotte Perkins Gilman

Dr. Mary Walker

Adah Menken

Emma Goldman

feiffer

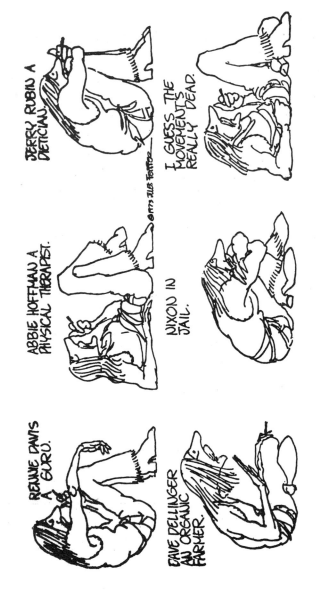

Alan Seeger

(Historical Pictures Service, Chicago)

Maxwell Bodenheim, 1893-1954

"It's simple. We use Vietcong tactics. Sneak into some little jerkwater midwest town. Strike a blow against the Establishment. Then simply fade among the population."

Post, found himself by 1960 frustrated by what seemed to him trivial and irresponsible youth attitudes. His anger was set off by a 1958 Hunter College meeting which featured Kerouac. Wechsler was astounded by the number of students who came to hear him and who vibrated to his every word. He was appalled by Kerouac's rambling discourse which took none of life seriously and treated those aspects Wechsler tried to interpose without comprehension or interest. Wechsler, concerned for United States-Soviet relations, the A-Bomb, McCarthyism, fear of a growing right wing, felt that the Beats and their admirers were missing much of life. As a past leader of youth, he was outraged and alarmed.[18]

One of the issues of serious moment to him was that of augmenting Negro rights. He saw it, however, as an issue dividing congressmen and parties, with neither doing an adequate job:

> *To Lyndon Johnson [then leader of the majority faction] civil rights has become an obsessive preoccupation of certain Eastern and Northern groups. . . . His strength, his survival, his position, his unique place in politics rested on the assumption that civil rights could be deemed number twenty-five on a list of forty-seven major national problems.*[19]

Wechsler paid tribute "to the stoic valor of the young Negroes who stood passively at segregated Southern lunch counters [in the winter of 1960] enduring vile taunts and physical attack and turning the other cheek," and deemed them different from the non-caring Beats. In fact, the civil rights movement was one of many elements, of which the Beats were one. More important than any other elements were the attitudes which crystallized during this period to direct thought and commitment.

Fanatically read by the youth, for example, was J. D. Salinger's *Catcher in the Rye* (1951), the story of a confused sixteen-year-old, with blunt views, mostly uncomplimentary, of his elders, but none of himself. Not unrelated was the phenomenal success of David Riesman's *The Lonely Crowd* (1950), with its key view of Americans as inner-directed or outer-directed, and

---

18. James A. Wechsler, *Reflections of an Angry Middle-Aged Editor* (New York, 1960).
19. *Ibid.,* 120–121.

seeing them as mainly the latter: isolated from each other, and seeking or receiving guidance from others, rather than from their genuine feelings and wants. Also related to emerging youth values was the vindication of Henry Miller, earlier read as a scabrous author, and purchased under counters for his narratives of unadorned sex. In 1959 Karl Shapiro, a well-recognized critic of poetry, called him the greatest living author.[20]

In the late 1950's Paul Goodman, an avant-garde author, would complete his only important book, *Growing Up Absurd* (1960), a work which would keep him visiting college campuses continuously in order to satisfy the hunger of students to see him and "rap" with him. In effect, Goodman deplored irrational social sanctions and false motivations. Students did not fail geometry because they could not learn it; they could not concentrate upon it because it offended their human outlooks. Goodman recalled talking with some "kids" who were fatalistically preparing themselves for unappetizing careers in society:

> *I turned away from the conversation abruptly because of the uncontrollably burning tears in my eyes and constriction in my chest. Not feeling sorry for them, but tears of frank dismay for the waste of our humanity (they were nice kids).*[21]

In effect, Goodman juxtaposed the world in which one had to live with the world which ought to be. So he protested the idea of driving homosexuals out of parks in order to make them livable for others. Where else (he asked a journalist, Pete Hamill) would you have them go? ("Hamill thanked me for my letter and resolved to use his head a little harder in the future.") And Goodman protested the lighting up of streets and dark city corners as a type of intolerable "social surveillance"; "without alleys and basements how will kids, who can't afford hotels, ever have sex?"[22]

Such sentiments were not calculated to alienate restless, disorganized or incompetent youth, and they attracted many who

---

20. Karl Shapiro, *In Defense of Ignorance* (New York, 1960), 313 ff.
21. Paul Goodman, *Growing Up Absurd* (New York, 1960), 35.
22. Goodman, *The Society I Live in Is Mine* (New York, 1962), 75, 129.

were not so and who looked about for better goals than those offered by affluent government, private industry, or the families that
had raised them. The civil rights movement drew impulses and
personnel from such youth. It was even inspired in part by such
a phenomenon as *The Three-Penny Opera,* originally born in the
Germany of the radical dramatist Bertolt Brecht and musician
Kurt Weill, and brilliantly adapted by Marc Blitzstein as an off-
Broadway musical in 1954. By December 1961 it had been shown
2,707 times and gained its sponsors almost three million dollars
on an investment of $8897. All America knew Mack the Knife and
his precious crew of knaves and harlots. Most of the youth, however, were too unsophisticated to realize that he represented a
product of Fascism; many of them took him to be the prototype
of the revolutionary.

Those who did, also revered the career of Lenny Bruce, who
emerged in 1961 as a defender of the right of free speech, in court
cases which first accused him of using obscene language in his
nightclub turns, and later broadened to portray him as a drug addict. In the course of his voyage across the times which extended
to August 3, 1966, when he "fell off a toilet seat with a needle in
his arm and . . . crashed to a tiled floor and died," he stirred national attention in much the same way as did Ginsberg, Kerouac,
James Baldwin, and others whose lives and work declared the need
for change. It was significant that Bruce's autobiography, *How to
Talk Dirty and Influence People* (1965), originally appeared in
serial form in *Playboy Magazine,* which itself attracted outstanding
intellectuals and public figures to argue politics, religion, morals,
and society.

Bruce claimed to challenge the hypocrisies which overlaid not
only bigotry but liberal democratic thought. He blamed not the law
for his harassments, but his nightclub auditors, whom he often
challenged to leave if they found his language, made-up dialogues,
or ruthless comments on unconscious prejudice unpalatable. In
time he became less good-humored, less sought-after by nightclub
proprietors: an aging Beat. He saw himself as a cause, and took
pride in the numerous celebrities who publicly endorsed his creativity and courage. It was no accident that the *San Francisco
Magazine* should have put his book in the class with C. Wright

Mills's *The Power Elite* and George Orwell's *1984*. After his death he was enshrined in a musical, *Lenny,* which played successfully on Broadway and treated him as a martyr and immortal.[23]

Yet Bruce consistently lied over the years to innumerable people, especially doctors who provided him with testimonials covering his need for drugs as a health measure. Bruce was a total, long-term addict, whose battle against social oppression, to be justified, had to be linked with civil rights and hatred of a masochistic government more capable of slaughter and destruction than any addict.

The fact that nightclubs could become centers for social criticism gives some sense of the heavy curtain of concern which lay on the public scene awaiting clarification. Tom Lehrer, the nightclub satirist, ridiculed the Folk Song Army, with its glib and abstract concern for poverty, war, and oppression, and suggested that its slogan should be: "Ready, Aim, *Sing.*" He wrote a marching song for World War III, with the young hero (presumably armed with an atom bomb) promising his mother to be home in an hour and a half. He urged others like himself to fight the battle for smut under the banner: "(Let's hear it for the Supreme Court): *Don't Let Them Take It Away!*" Such satire did not so much contradict the social criticism of a Lenny Bruce as help underscore how immanent were the issues.

The personnel of the original civil rights drive of the post-World War II era were more disciplined than any Bruce or Goodman could work with. The earlier civil libertarians were not indiscriminately young. They grew out of Urban League and NAACP efforts to develop new tactics for fighting race discrimination. CORE, first organized in 1942 (Congress of Racial Equality) sought many ways to dramatize issues of segregation and discrimination. Its white supporters were its flying wedge. Although it won small victories and a few adherents, over the years it made relatively little impact.

In 1947 a small group of whites and blacks, eight of each, undertook a Journey of Reconciliation, intended to implement a

---

23. Paul Jacobs and Saul Landau, *The New Radicals* (New York, 1966), 326, places Bruce in a succession of events which created the New Left.

Supreme Court decision which declared segregation in interstate travel illegal. Their sword and shield was nonviolence, which they studied earnestly, especially the art of avoiding provocation. Nevertheless, they were threatened and in physical danger. Three of them, Bayard Rustin, a Negro, and Igal Roodenko and Joe Felmet, whites, served time on a chain gang. Although the journey did not open transportation facilities without prejudice, it was counted a landmark in the drive to do so.

New strength was provided by the historic decision of 1954 by the Supreme Court in *Brown v. Board of Education of Topeka* which outlawed segregation in education, but turned the spotlight on discrimination in any field. The next year, the Montgomery, Alabama bus boycott by Negroes led by the young Reverend Martin Luther King, Jr. held the attention of the country. King then established the Southern Christian Leadership Conference, and young activists, Negro and white, bestirred themselves to find ways to cooperate.

In February 1960, four youths from North Carolina Agricultural and Technical College at Greensboro sat down at a white lunch counter and demanded service. This first "sit in" attracted not only attention, but concern. Out of this and subsequent efforts (including "jail-ins") grew the Student Nonviolent Coordinating Committee (SNCC). Early members practiced courtesy, fortitude, and spirituality expressed in song. Guy Carawan had introduced at the Newport Folk Festival of 1959 a spiritual, "We Shall Overcome," which had earlier become a tradition among Negroes and unionists and now became the anthem of the antidiscrimination drive.[24]

Howard Zinn, a SNCC activist, argued in *The Southern Mystique* (1964) that the South was far less united against change than common opinion held. His view was curiously affirmed by Strom Thurmond, South Carolina Democrat, who held that there was much more segregation and discrimination in New York City than in his own state. Radicals could explain this paradox by perceiving the same attitude toward Negroes in the North and South.

24. *New York Times*, July 23, 1963. See also *The Nashville Sit-In Story* (Folkways Records Album, 1960).

Thus proper programs to effective civil liberties drives became serious and responsible questions.

From 1959 to 1961 young activists became increasingly remote from the Urban League and NAACP, both of which worked for courtesy, patience, and the growing power of public opinion. In 1961 white and Negro students once again tested southern segregation practices, this time not on a Journey of Reconciliation, but as Freedom Riders. They met beatings, antagonism, and malice, but also found sympathetic Southerners along the way, from Washington to New Orleans, and successfully reached the latter city. Behind them were new, victorious "sit-ins" and "jail-ins," accompanied by intense white-black unity and appeals to spirituality. James Peck, a white veteran of the 1947 march who received fifty-three stitches on face and head, published his *Freedom Ride* (1962) with a foreword by James Baldwin and an introduction by the white Georgian Lillian Smith, whose own pioneer novel, the best-selling *Strange Fruit* (1944), had graced an earlier equalitarian drive. In it Peck noted often the warmth and dedication which kept his fellow workers strong even on the chain gang, swaying and singing "We Shall Overcome" and other songs indomitably. The shield of religion which "activists" carried to deter their opponents from violence against them continued to accrete national sympathy, as millions were made aware by mass media of great student gatherings as in Albany, Georgia where more than a thousand were arrested for demonstrating in September 1962, and in Jackson, Mississippi, where the next month a Negro, James Meredith, defied violence to become the first of his race to be received as a student in the University of Mississippi. Such events highlighted plans and actions everywhere in the nation to rouse attention, bring mass media to the scenes, and win related victories at schools and colleges, department stores and manufacturing plants, and in the entertainment industries. Oddly, there was more white-black cooperation in the South than North, where "Caucasians" (as they were then called) predominated in the campaigns. "The difficulty persisted. Early in 1962 a young white professor, recently fired from the University of Missouri because of his CORE work, was 'very discouraged' because so few Negroes had joined the local chapter. Chicago Southside CORE's black chairman lamented, 'We have not had the support we have hoped for from the community.' . . . As late as the spring of 1963 all except two demonstrators on a Chicago CORE picket line were white."[25]

Still, there was a sense of a civil rights movement on the march. By 1964, it caused the new President Lyndon B. Johnson to announce a war on poverty and to push for and get a Civil Rights Law. It caused mass demonstrations and boycotts by the thousands and brought out of the schools and homes students and their parents by the millions, with more millions viewing the events in newspapers or on television. A new sense of power affected Negro leaders and would-be leaders. And though civil rights leaders appealed to CORE and SNCC to declare a moratorium on demonstrations until after the national elections in November, the appeal was rejected by both James Farmer, speaking for the one organization, and John Lewis speaking for the other.

Nevertheless a species of adjustment seemed in the making. The John F. Kennedy assassination had produced shock that anything like it could occur; there was no expectation that so monstrous a crime could be repeated. Civil rights turbulence continued, but so did passage of meliorative legislation. Government agencies attracted young people eager to aid change. The Peace Corps attracted others who carried the word of American determination to aid positive change at home and abroad. President Johnson identified himself with the movement, quoting the now-familiar "We shall overcome."

What undermined all efforts for natural, substantial integration and social welfare programs was the war in Southeast Asia. Its expansion without a plan for either winning the war or abandoning it lost the government its prestige and encouraged the growth of great antiwar forces which a liberal government was reluctant to put down with traditional military and civil means. This fact, plus the continuing prosperity and an unprecedented civilian relationship to the fighting front through instant television, making it an "armchair war," resulted in an equally unprecedented youthful upheaval.

Bob Dylan. Clark Kerr, then president of the University of

---

25. August Meier and Elliott Rudwick, *CORE* (New York, 1973), 195.

California at Berkeley had opined in 1959 that "employers will love this generation. . . . They are going to be easy to handle." Kerr had in mind mainly the campus youth. But they had been subject to a growth which diminished differences between campus and noncampus. They had met perfunctory teachers interested in little beyond "professional advancement," and they had been "processed" by teaching assistants who were themselves underpaid and underprivileged: a servile class. For many students, their best experiences were off campus, in coffee houses and bars, frequented by drifters and Bohemians.

Moreover they were continuously fed from high schools in which youth moodily undertook to estimate its chances in a world of cold war, deteriorating cities, unsettled family and race relations, and an adult establishment which seemed inadequate for its role. Throughout the 1960's the teen-agers of every grade would feel the impact of peers who would consciously or unconsciously represent hedonistic principles as just and preferable to the dreaming and slow growth previous classes had experienced. Eating, drinking, the tangibles of sex-pleasure and of drugs would be offered them throughout the 1960's and make empty and meaningless such basics as literature and philosophy which had enthralled earlier children in their growth period. Nor did the new youth have to feel uneasy in their new stances. The magazines in their homes featured such advertisements as one by a clothing manufacture: "Take advantage . . . you've got the edge. Youth. Daring. Imagination. Widen the Generation Gap!"[26]

Robert Allen Zimmerman was one such youth who came to Minneapolis in 1959 at age eighteen, presumably to study at the University of Minnesota. Apparently, he had already awarded himself a new name, Bob Dylan, as part of a fantasy life which had gone on for some years and taken shapes having nothing to do with the family in Hibbing, not far from Duluth, Minnesota, which had given him birth and growth. As such, he was ready to join great regiments of others like himself who were engaged in creating a world within the American world, one excluding their parents and all they represented.

---

26. Kenneth L. Fish, *Conflict and Dissent in the High Schools* (New York, 1970), 37.

Dylan's world was composed of lost, resentful fragments of life making up one definition of freedom and personal euphoria. Enshrined in it was James Dean, sullen hero of the motion picture *Rebel without a Cause*, killed in 1955 in a speeding car accident. Some of his worshipers could not believe him dead and lit candles before the photograph of his young face. Like Dean, Dylan—then still Zimmerman—begged from his father the money for a motor-cycle, and on it sported dark leather jacket, greased "ducktail" haircut, big boots and tight pants, and cigarettes. He made early entree into the world of young females, and was wholly absorbed in the tunes which went along with his guitar, tunes like "Your Cheatin' Heart" and "Rock Round the Clock."

Such young persons had curious parallels with their parents, when they were not hard-working and forthright parents like Zim-merman's. Elders and young were both often anxious to be off and going, though nowhere in particular. The father was often ab-sorbed in his "fishtailed" automobile, and, like his son with his motorcycle, passionately washing its wheels and sides and inspect-ing its motor intensely. If the father hunted with rifles, the young played "chicken": a game requiring them to rush at each other at high speed in motorcycles or cars, the palm going to the desperate youngster who closed in deepest with his opponent, causing him to swerve to avert a collision.

A lower level of youthful action created the motorcycle gang, committed to highspeed riding in unison on speedways, and some-times through towns. Some of this activity was fairly harmless, if alarmingly futile. Ultimately it created the Hell's Angels organiza-tion, blown up beyond size perhaps by reporters seeking sensa-tional reports, but touching youthful imaginations. The Angels themselves were sometimes malicious as well as arrogant.[27]

Dylan was not one of these, but he shared their hatred for authority and contempt for structured thought, their Beat language and attitudes; and he doubtless met some of their kind in the off-campus circles he joined in Minneapolis where he began to per-form as folk singer. At this point he was no more than another aspirant to fame and wealth, or even to tolerance or acceptance by

---

27. Hunter S. Thompson, *Hell's Angels* (New York, 1967).

the cafe crowd. The nearby university was the merest shadow to them; as Dylan later ad libbed, after he had attained shining pinnacles, talking between songs while strumming his guitar:

"Met a teacher who said he didn't understand what Blowin' In the Wind means," ... Laughter through the house; the kids knew all about those stupid teachers. "Told him there was nothin' to understand, it was just blowin' in the wind. If he didn't feel it in the wind, he'd never know. And he ain't gonna know, I guess. Teachers."[28]

The youth had secrets and could laugh at the folly of adults who thought they were simply loud and unsubtle in words and tunes. Right wing critics presumed to see the revolutionary message which thoughtless parents ignored: "Rock singers are in constant communication with our teenagers—promoting attitudes and ideas which, if they were aware of the message, would blow the minds of most parents."[29] It was unlikely that anyone among singers or auditors was being gulled any more than in the case of Presley. Bold obscenity and open appeals to lust and a hunger for drugs could not be misunderstood and were increasingly made. Involved was nothing less than a confrontation of generations, with more ground being given by the older than by the younger. As one critic observed:

One of the leading manufacturers, Columbia Records, runs a series of advertisements in the underground press, the theme of which is "The man can't bust our music" and "Know your friends." The implication aligns "us" against "them," and the context of the advertising design and illustration is interracial, hippie, pot-smoking youth.

Is Columbia for legalization of marijuana? No. Columbia is for making money. Thus the investment in music aimed at long-haired youth.[30]

The point was that in wheedling money from hippies, the manufacturers did not lose appreciable funds from the hippie's

---

28. Anthony Scaduto, *Bob Dylan* (New York, 1971), 157.
29. Gary Allen, "More Subversion than Meets the Ear," *American Opinion* 12 (February 1969), in R. Serge Denisoff and Richard A. Peterson, *The Sounds of Social Change* (Chicago, 1972), 151.
30. Ralph J. Gleason, "The Greater Sound," *ibid.*, 137.

parents. Nor were the singers the source of this cultural-financial phenomenon, only its servants. Joan Baez, having come up with the Folksingers 'Round Harvard Square, aged eighteen, sang "Kitty," "So Soon in the Morning," and "Careless Love." Having risen soon after on the tide of musical rage, she continued to sing the more popular of such songs, but often having preceded her rendition with an antiwar avowal.[31] The implication was that "love" was a negation of war—or, as one of the coming slogans had it, "Make Love, Not War." But elemental hunger for feeling and sensation preceded the political idea.

Dylan had begun by dreaming of emulating Presley as a rock singer, but the friends he made contributed to his thought, as did odds and ends of left-wing and avant-garde notions; his name, of course, derived from that of the vibrant Welsh poet, Dylan Thomas, dead of drink at thirty-five in 1955, who had been a legend of intemperance on American college campuses. Bob Dylan had seen a light in Woody Guthrie's saga and music. Thereafter he stepped up his fantasies of being an orphan, a child of poverty, a wanderer born of Okies. He had read or skimmed John Steinbeck's *Cannery Row* and savored its earthy, dissolute circle of outcasts; he was not apparently much interested in the more austere and responsible *Grapes of Wrath*. Somewhere between the Beats and the folk singers of hard times and weary hopes Dylan found a style which he could attach to his odd jargon, composed of deliberate illiteracy and trumped-up camaraderie.

His subsequent success in New York as the "free-wheelin' Bob Dylan" was less illuminating of him than of the millions of enthusiasts who chose to make of his *Blowin' in the Wind* all but the trumpet call of a youth crusade, taking off from where the obsolete pieties of *We Shall Overcome* concluded. Dylan's vogue completely overshadowed those of such tried veterans as Pete Seeger, but for all that, they too profited substantially from the stormy events of 1965–1970. The reason for Dylan's triumph over them appears to have been that it was precisely Dylan's vagueness

---

31. " 'This one is dedicated to President Johnson and his marvelous foreign policy,' she would say, smiling, then sing a rock and roll hit of the Supremes, 'Stop in the Name of Love' " (Jonathan Eisen, *The Age of Rock* [New York, 1969], 6).

and indirection—as compared with Seeger's hard-core social
shibboleths—which could touch and excite youth to whom "social
significance" was unreal. Real to them was personal identity, fear
of the draft, and a yearning for fun and psychedelic truth. For such
ideas they could fight or sympathize. "A Hard Rain's A-Gonna
Fall," "Honey, Just Allow Me One More Chance," and numerous
other Dylan songs, some old, some made up, mixed the bleak
chance of war with the dreams of uncomplicated love. Also important was Dylan's delivery, which mixed a lost-waif's stance with
a pretended humility. ("It's a hard song to sing. I can sing it sometimes, but I ain't that good yet.") For better or worse, the "activist" portion of the youth uprising had their troubadour.[32]

LSD and the "Love Generation."

*We are in a magic theater; a world of pictures not reality.
Tonight at the magic theater for madmen only. The price
of admission your mind.*

—*Hermann Hesse*

It was the contention of emancipated youth—unshackled
from family, duty to society, or to the nation—that their hypo-
critical elders operated by rote and evasion, and that they tolerated
horrors of war and oppression which they, their children, would
not accept. Many of the children, however, engaged in little activity touching on either war or oppression. A heavy concentration
on the permutations of sex and drugs made it difficult for them to
operate consistently in other areas. Nevertheless the more thoughtful of them were persuaded that they lived in and were contributing to widening the options of freedom—options from which
everyone would ultimately gain. They added touches of Zen and
other quasi-religious stances to suggest that their search and commitments were the world's.

Although some "far gone" elements of the new youth disturbed and even angered more politically or action-minded youth,
they were rarely willing to disturb the unity which kept them

---

32. For a critique of Dylan, including an explication of *Blowin' in the Wind,*
    Albert Goldman, "What Sings Doesn't Alway Read," *New York Times Book
    Review,* September 30, 1973, 42–43.

aligned against their elders. And since those who sought pleasure as a primary goal were many times more numerous than their dedicated or austere comrades, they could provide a seedbed from which activists of various types could spring.

Of primary importance to the freedom generation were the Beatles, more so even than Dylan. Dylan's themes suggested social action, however superficially. The Beatles were more like John Osborne's young men, except for his anger and intelligence. Osborne's Jimmy Porter vilified church and family and repudiated traditions of patriotism and reverence for workers. The Beatles were untroubled by any such concepts. Profane, casual, whimsical, they were interested in little else than the people who drifted in and out of the Cavern Club in Liverpool where they performed people looking for fun and a tune. The Beatles cut several records; they became fads in West Germany, then in England, then in the United States and around the world, appealing first of all to the young, then to their elders as well.[33]

The Beatles took all this with genuine aplomb; they had no reverence and rode high on the torrent of young passion they conjured up. They knew it had something to do with their hair, which unbound numerous inhibitions, and soon encouraged—not Beats, not winos—but middle-class children to let their hair go where it willed, and their clothes, and cleanliness, and their concern for the attitudes of shopkeepers and administrators, let alone parents. They evolved. The females shed ensembles and enticements to become their all but naked selves; the young males experimented with headbands, beards, torn jeans, sashes, and other bits and badges, groping generally toward some identification with American Indians, who became a cause as well as their psychological parents: "native Americans" who could be juxtaposed with their cruel and imperial conquerors, as well as a source of the

---

33. "It was fantastic around here then. . . . I always had people at the door hollering they were agents and waving contracts around and asking if we had any more groups like them.

"It was nothing to see Rolls-Royces pull up at the door and fancy people from London trying to squeeze their way in here. You couldn't move in this place." The manager of the Cavern Club, in Raymond Coffey, "Beatles Shrine, Cavern Club, To Be Torn Down," *Cincinnati* (Ohio) *Enquirer*, February 18, 1973, 5-G.

spiritual inspiration induced by drugs. In contrast with their "beat" elders, they displayed themselves as Hippies: hip, aware, and joyous.

The Beatles, ridiculing in their motion pictures the pompous gentlemen who had fought the Battle of Britain and stopped Hitler, were enchanters who were bringing together the bored and purposeless younger generation, and especially the young females, as Sinatra had their mothers. The singers were nevertheless pawns as well as principals. They wrote songs with no purpose, or so they said. "But in a week [said one of them, Paul McCartney] someone else says something about it, . . . and you can't deny it. Things take on millions of meanings."[34]

In fact, they took on only a few powerful, simplistic meanings, as simple and powerful as those of the early Lenin. The message was sex and drugs. Both were lightly bandied about in songs and at concerts attended by awed and abased worshipers. Privately the message was as grimly and purposefully developed as a military campaign, both by the Beatles and their "hep" acolytes. "Groupies," dedicated to sex, music, and drugs, proliferated. Young males and females gyrated toward one another with new, magnetic "vibes" unhampered by older sanctions. Children fifteen, sixteen, and seventeen years old on unimaginable adventures needed heart for their new lives, and heart could only be provided by drugs.

Drugs were not new. Bohemians of the 1930's had experimented with them.[35] But their use had been limited by social circumstances. The middle classes had rigidly proscribed them; narcotics had belonged to the degraded poor and to the artistic or indulgent elements of the elite. A few scientists studied the characteristics of drugs and discussed them with other scientists.[36] William James had pondered aspects of drugs in his *Varieties of Religious Experience* (1902).

Timothy Leary, associated with Harvard's Psychedelic Research Project, began as a sincere student of the human potential

---

34. Eisen, *Age of Rock*, 138.
35. W. Gard, "Youth Gone Loco, Villain Is Marijuana," *Christian Century* 55 (June 29, 1938), 812–813.
36. S. Weir Mitchell, "The Effects of Anhelonium Lewinii (The Mescal Button)," *British Medical Journal* 2 (1896), 1625–1629.

of drugs, and at least one among a number of psychologists was earnest in pointing to the "public health implications of drug-associated rapid personality change."[37] Different fates unfolded for investigators of scientific or adventurous bent, but all of them together made less of a dramatic tale than did the breaking down of social sanctions, despite a forest of laws and local ordinances which would cause the arrest and conviction of thousands of petty and substantial dealers in drugs, and their patronage by millions, especially among the young.

Vital was the role of mediators between demanding youth and the degenerate addicts with a stake in reaching them as customers and allies. Many among those with responsible places in schools and communities took it upon themselves to adopt what they saw as a realistic view. Drugs were a fact of life, they insisted, and the use of drugs among the young was also a fact of life. To proscribe them was merely to drive the youth and their drug habits underground. Marijuana was harmless. A wise program would legalize it and prevent the inhuman jailing of persons with no police record who might be alienated and embittered by such experiences. LSD was a stronger drug, true, but properly used could do no harm and much good. A student community manager at Antioch College lectured the college president, who happened to be a doctor of medicine, informing him that "a warm, supportive atmosphere is the best setting for an LSD session." It was the duty of administrators to advise their drug-taking students of the dangers inherent in drugs and also to admit the drug's positive qualities, if they wished "to establish a more credible position in the students' eyes."

The idea that elders had to win credibility with the young, rather than the other way around, would attract many of the young and many of the elders. For the near future, it was impractical. A youthful vanguard had already democratized drugs, and, as a matter of record, the drive from marijuana toward the bewildering and enslaving drugs had created a rabble and a mob combined, aided by huge numbers of consenting adults. To the sound of Beatles' music, ragged communities took shape from New York to San

---

37. Sanford M. Unger "Mescaline, LSD, Psilocybin and Personality Change," in *LSD The Consciousness-Expanding Drug,* ed., David Solomon (New York, 1964), 222.

Francisco, many of them adjuncts to campuses, while their counterparts among the "squares," wearing "mod" clothing (also
sponsored by the Beatles) became entranced with drugs and "psychedelic" images (lurid whirlpools of color), which were translated on canvasses and in films into a new art form.

Wrote the jazz fancier and would-be radical activist Nat
Hentoff, "Something's Happening and You Don't Know What It
Is, Do You, Mr. Jones?"[38] Actually, Mr. Jones knew. It would
have been difficult to avoid knowing, with children pouring out of
American homes to seek quick rapture in the legendary centers of
hippiedom, and furnishing material for countless columns of news
in periodicals everywhere. Liquescent, yet viscous, they seemed
like a mighty wave of youth able to convene at will wherever they
preferred. They might choose to make Denver their main center,
or London. "The proof of the ease with which they can swoop
down and congregate any place was the New York Peace Demonstration in April 1967, when more than 200,000 young assembled
to march."[39]

Hentoff and many others sincerely imagined that an irresistible revolution was in the making, challenging attitudes and tearing
apart old ways of life. As Jerry Rubin, first a student then a social
radical, was to say:

> *History has chosen us—the inheritors of the best that*
> *money could buy—to vomit up our inheritance. To rip off*
> *the white skin, tear off the American mask, flush those*
> *credit cards down the toilet.*
>
> *People are emotion-freaks. . . . What determines think-*
> *ing is the freaks. . . .*
>
> *Pot is central to the Revolution. It weakens social con-*

---

38. In Eisen, *Age of Rock,* 3 ff. Hentoff took the phrase from a Dylan lyric.
    (From "Ballad of a Thin Man," © 1965 Warner Bros. Inc. All rights re-
    served. Used by permission.) It does not seem to have occurred to the pros-
    pective revolutionaries that the "Squares" had their own music, and that as
    absurd as it might sound to uninterested ears, it moved and activated the
    antirevoluntionaries. For one statement of the breadth and content of "square"
    music, with unspelled-out political implications, see George P. Jackson, *White
    Spirituals in the Southern Uplands* (New York, 1965 ed.).
39. Nicholas von Hoffman, *We Are the People Our Parents Warned Us Against*
    (New York, 1969), 47.

ditioning and helps create a whole new state of mind. The slogans of the Revolution are going to be "POT, FREE-DOM, LICENSE."[40]

In one of the two great bastions of anticipated change, San Francisco, an investigator saw a "thin, hawknosed, witchlike girl in a dirty buckskin jacket, looking like some unbathed Indian squaw" go up to a boy, tap him on the shoulder, and when he turned around, shove a sandwich she held into his mouth. He bit into it. They talked a while, then she went on. The investigator moved over to ask the boy if he knew the girl, to have eaten the food out of her mouth.

> *Again the wise, patient, old man's smile (he must have been nineteen). "Man, you haven't been around here long, have you? This is sharing, this is love, man. She's giving me part of her food because she wants to share part of her-self with me, and it doesn't have to be sex. This is an act of giving. We're all one. This is what it's all about, man. Stay around a while. You'll learn."*[41]

This was the famous Haight-Ashbury "scene," informally be-gun by high school drug connoisseurs who called attention to themselves in what had been a varied group of streets and tenants, some quite staid, near Golden Gate Park. The youngsters had entered an unused house for their festivities, and left it conspicu-ously filthy. The area rapidly attracted every species of youth ini-tiate and acolyte. Cafes, bookstore, and other landmarks sprang up, several of their owners achieving some notability, though none were more important than the dealers in drugs.

A variety of experimenters had broken ground for the Flower Children, as they came briefly to be designated, and they entered into the lore of the district. One was Ken Kesey, author of *One Flew Over the Cuckoo's Nest* (1962), a friend of Kerouac's, a renegade from squaredom who had set up a community south of San Francisco which had featured drug and sexual pranks. The Diggers, as they were known, planned to make of Haight-Ashbury

---

40. "Thoughts of Chairman Jerry [of the Yippies]," *Avant Garde* #7 (March, 1969), 33.
41. Burton H. Wolfe, *The Hippies* (New York, 1968), 103.

a utopia which would welcome all good people, feed them, minister to them, and turn away none. Young enthusiasts concocted rituals to the sun, to inner harmony, to universal love. As in the Fifties, when tourists came to view the Beats, so now new tourists gathered, jamming the streets of Haight-Ashbury, to see the Hippies sitting around, panhandling, meditating, tinkling bells or strumming guitars: youth of every complexion and in every garb, coupled or alone.

An intense throng going nowhere, and yet determined to get there. As one of them said of a girl he was attempting to win over to his way of life, and who was "stoned" on STP: "She's been up about forty hours now. . . . I think she's beginning to come down. I gave it to her. She has to learn about herself, the way I did. She has to change with me or I'm going to have to get rid of her. I don't think she's learning."[42]

The most obtuse tourist could not fail to see and smell the overbearing presence of drugs—drugs of all types, and having every effect, from feverish exaltation to sprawled collapse. Tales were endless about the variety of the people who swept in and out of the area, the numerous drugs they used, the filth which attended their labors. Venereal disease had been all but conquered by the 1950's, thanks to "miracle drugs" such as penicillin. The indiscriminate coupling, concentrated in Hashbury, as some called it, but widespread elsewhere, among the educated as well as the uneducated, gave a new strength to VD and made it a notorious product of Sixties social history.

Much the same happened elsewhere. As North Beach traditions had failed to fill the needs of the new Hippies, so, in New York, Greenwich Village failed to meet the requirements of urgent mixtures of white and Negro youth. East Village arose in the area of Tompkins Square, once a solid and respectable ethnic mixture with children who played in the park. Now, new children moved in in droves, bringing with them needles, syringes, grass, crystals, and all the jargon and paraphernalia of their new life. The course of events was the same in both San Francisco and New York, particularly in the first, which had billed its summer season as a

---

42. Hoffman, *We Are the People Our Parents Warned Us Against,* 58.

"Love-In." Their minds expanded through LSD and other drugs, they were about to lead the world into a new era.

San Francisco and New York became advisory centers for hundreds of working youth enterprises. Many were offshoots of campus plants, but others were set apart in communes proposed as the obverse of the meagre spirit and services available under capitalism. There youngsters joyously united, in spite of neighbors whose chagrin and hatred often added piquancy to emancipated living. Or they set up enclaves in rural places, sought to grow crops (including crops of marijuana) and otherwise make themselves independent of the outside world: a world, as they saw it, of official brutality, TV commercials, and other sterile delights.

The Hippie idyll was short and doom-ridden. The heralded "Summer of Love" in San Francisco in 1967 became a nightmare. The district was shaken by an almost continuous series of murders, muggings, knifings, break-ins, and unspeakable atrocities. The defenders of the Love Generation recognized that the most inhuman commercialism underlay the battles between big dealers in drugs, accounting for much of the carnage. Yet they could not concede that drugs had no future. The problem was with the outlawry of drugs. If drug purchases were made legal, the barbarism would cease.

Yet the Haight-Ashbury regulars were repellent even to those who had been attracted there from the nation at large:

> They slept like litters of stray cats in doorways, halls, abandoned houses, and panel trucks that had a stench sufficient to asphyxiate a full-grown skunk. They hauled filthy, discarded mattresses and rags out of trash receptacles and used them for bedding. They lived for weeks in the same clothes without washing themselves or what they were wearing. A farmer would take better care of his pigs than they took care of themselves.[43]

A similar scene unfolded in East Village, New York, which the brief saga of a Linda Fitzgerald memorialized. The daughter of wealthy parents, she entered the drug world and East Village

---

43. Wolfe, *Hippies*, 190.

was home. Thoroughly alienated, she veered between school, parents, and her real life, at one time supporting herself by panhandling around Washington Square. "She kinda got a kick out of begging," another of the Hippie legion recalled. One of the boys thought it was cool and funny. She also drew: "distorted women's faces, heavy lidded eyes, dragons, devils, all hidden as in a thick jungle of flowers, leaves and vines, interspersed with phrases in ornate script: Forever the Mind, Flyin High, Tomorrow Will Come."[44]

For her it came October 7, 1967 in an East Village boiler room where she had "shot up" a gram and a half. One Thomas Dennis, a twenty-seven-year-old drifter from Philadelphia later pleaded guilty to having killed her young male companion, and Donald Ramsey, a twenty-eight-year-old ex-convict and "black nationalist" dispatched her. "No motive was established."

The campus scene did not differ materially from drug-oriented locales like Linda's, who had abandoned campus jargon and pursuits. Dissidents and drifters helped students create pads and interstate drug contacts. They glanced at or read the torrent of "underground newspapers" for information about such favored places as Detroit, Madison (Wisconsin), and Boston. Some prided themselves on good control of their drug routines. Others of more neurotic bent, uneasy psyches, or a death wish, plunged into depths from which there was no return. Many campuses saw such scenes as the classroom in which a student sat sullen or stupefied, suddenly to pull a needle out of her bag and inject drugs into a vein before other students and a nonplussed instructor.

They were all children of prosperity. John Steinbeck, who had lived in Monterey during the Depression, found loathesome the Hippies "and their tasteless girls." He compared them with his own young companions who had been active and alive on little money, had sung and worked and made love, and created life. But one reporter who observed the new youth in their degradation did not despise them. "The hippie movement may be a flight from reality into a world of drug-induced illusions. Or it may be a revo-

---

44. J. Anthony Lukas, *Don't Shoot—We Are Your Children!* (New York, 1971), 200.

lution against war, violence, racial prejudice, materialism, and puritanism. . . . But it is more than that."[45]

The Hippie, he thought, was a perceptive individual who saw that the American way was wrong. America made catastrophic war on defenseless people. It divided the cities by races and "built upward into dozens of Manhattans." He saw the Hippies as victims rather than as aggressors. The criminals were the American people and their representatives. This was a view of affairs maintained by many youth who were not prostrated by drugs, by their mentors, and by older associates. They worked to further what they called the "counterculture," and along with it, actions intended to overthrow what they deemed a malignant civilization.

---

45. Wolfe, *Hippies,* 193.

7

Youth Eruption

Then there was Bigger No. 5 who rode the Jim Crow street cars without paying and sat wherever he pleased. I remember one morning his getting into a street car (all street cars in Dixie are divided into two sections: one section is for whites and is labeled—FOR WHITES; the other section is for Negroes and is labeled—FOR COLORED) and sitting in the white section. The conductor went to him and said: "Come on, nigger. Move over where you belong. Can't you read?" Bigger answered: "Naw, I can't read." The conductor flared up: "Get out of that seat!" Bigger took out his knife, opened it, held it nonchalantly in his hand and replied: "Make me." The conductor turned red, blinked, clinched his fists, and walked away, stammering: "The Goddam scum of the earth!". . . The Negroes experienced an intense flash of pride and the street car moved on its journey without incident. I don't know what happened to Bigger No. 5. But I can guess.[1]

Black Power. When ex-President Lyndon B. Johnson died, the liberal cartoonist Herblock memorialized him with a monu-

---

1. Richard Wright, "How 'Bigger' Was Born," *Saturday Review,* XXII (June 1, 1940), 4.

ment bearing the inscriptions: "Civil Rights Act of 1964/ Voting Rights Act/ Immigration Act/ Economics Opportunity Legislation/ Education Acts/ Legal Aid to Indigents/ Medicare/ Housing and Urban Development Acts/ Anti-Pollution Programs/ Teacher Corps/ Appalachia Aid."

If such were indeed his achievements, it would have been difficult to recognize them in the stormy years he suffered during the presidency he won at the polls in 1964. His major roadblack to popularity with the belligerent white youth was the expanded Vietnam War. Yet he received no greater regard from the Negro youth who, for the most part, played a minor role in antiwar activities. There were numerous Negroes, young and old, who had direct reason to be grateful to Johnson for jobs, for legal or financial aid, for desegregation actions. But they could not mollify a surging Negro youth tide that swept away all regard for Johnson, holding his achievements as too little, too late, mere products of "white guilt" or of fear, cunning efforts to avert the mighty wave of revenge and revolution about to fall on all white civilization.

The tocsin was sounded by a young college graduate and SNCC activist, Stokely Carmichael, a native of Trinidad, on the heels of an attempt to murder James Meredith in July 1966. Meredith had been engaged in a protest march in Mississippi. The tocsin followed other indignities and aggressive responses to civil rights laws which indicated that they would not immediately be honored.[2] Students had been arrested in great numbers at numerous southern colleges. In 1963 six Negro children had died in Birmingham, four as a result of dynamite exploded in a Baptist church. In March of 1964, Malcolm X, a Black Muslim, had broken away from his organization to raise the banner of black nationalism and repudiate nonviolence; his assassination the following February created for the stirred-up Negro youth a martyr, vaguely identified with white racist oppression—a martyr of militancy.

By 1966, when Carmichael led the battle for "Black Power" (a slogan he had found in Richard Wright's 1954 book entitled

---

2. Compare, however, the circumstances of 1966 with those described in John Bartlow Martin, *The Deep South Says "Never"* (New York, 1957).

Black Power, but referring to the ferment of African politics), a relatively small but verbal and determined group was prepared to give a new program to the Negro community and its numerous white sympathizers. It was on the surface a "go it alone" program. But it was expected to create a higher level of equalitarian action throughout the nation. Carmichael was thoroughly disillusioned with civil rights. On many campuses, in lecture halls and at conferences, he held their white and black attendants breathless with his sweeping repudiation of all that had created his imperious program. In view of later scorn expressed by Negroes as well as whites that Carmichael had been a mere opportunist who had struck it rich in Negro discontent, left the country, and settled in easy affluence abroad, it seems fair to observe that he had almost from the beginning adopted a revolutionary and Pan-African stance intended to link black dissidents for world upheaval.

His hatred of the United States was no doubt aided by his foreign birth, yet it raised equal exultation in many native-born black and white American youth. Nor did Carmichael think it paradoxical that he, chairman of the Student Nonviolent Coordinating Committee, should advocate violence. He was, he declared, for full, universal peace. But it would have to be attained by destroying American society: "This country is a nation of thieves," he told a thrilled student and faculty audience at a Berkeley, University of California mass meeting. "It stands on the brink of becoming a nation of murderers."[3]

A voting registration drive had been one of the great objectives of the civil rights movement. But the vote in this country, Carmichael now insisted, would always be "irrelevant"; it was no more than a "honky trick." Many of the "bourgeoisie" advised him that they did not like Brother Rap Brown to say, "I'm gonna burn the country down." Carmichael noticed, however, that each time Brown made such declarations, another poverty program was born.

Carmichael was not really interested in such half-measures as poverty programs. Nothing more nor less than full restitution from fascist America would do. He quoted with approval the posi-

---

3. Ethel N. Minor, ed., *Stokely Speaks* (New York, 1971), 59–60.

tion of the Cuban revolutionary, Che Guevara, calling for hatred "as an element of the struggle, relentless hatred of the enemy that impels us over and beyond the natural limitations of man, and transforms us into effective, violent, selected and cold, killing machines."

Many observers of television, which faithfully reported these and similar sentiments, felt that the "news media" were derelict in their duty by giving national and international coverage to such firebrands and such messages: that the media had taken insignificant characters with no achievements or novel ideas, raised to eminence one, and spread the others like seed everywhere. It seems more likely that the newspapermen who followed Carmichael about and permitted him to voice his incendiary rhetoric were no more than giving the public what it desired to turn over in its collective mind.

Carmichael admitted that the great civil rights drive of pre-1964 had been a "necessary stage" on the march to bigger things. But he, and even more his excited white and black sympathizers on campuses and in cities, had been impatient with, when not contemptuous of, Martin Luther King, Jr.'s effort to maintain black and white unity, and they had probably planned to leave him behind as they had Roy Wilkins and the NAACP, which they tarred with the general "Uncle Tom" brush.[4] King's assassination in the spring of 1968 gave them further ammunition with which to condemn American civilization.

Major explosions of discontent had taken place in 1964 in Harlem and the next year in Watts. In 1967 occurred the horrors of arson and pillage in Detroit: a major uprising doing at least forty-four million dollars' worth of damage. This accelerated the movement, chiefly of whites, out of the city and into the suburbs. Some reporters were baffled by the destruction; it seemed to them the equivalent of individuals shooting themselves in the foot. All noted that it was primarily a youth uprising, aimed, theoretically, at white proprietors, but seriously affecting Negro housing and enterprise even more. Efforts were made by activating Negro ministers, civic leaders, and heads of organizations to curb the

---

4. For the revolutionaries' "get rid of King" perspective, see Robert Scheer, ed., *Eldridge Cleaver: Post-Prison Writings and Speeches* (New York, 1969), 50.

looting and assaults. All admitted they could not control the youth.

And yet these leaders included some of the most notable people of the general community. John Dancy was the son of a distinguished Negro of the previous generation. The elder Dancy had been a brave, educated, and intelligent man, formerly United States Collector of Customs at Wilmington, North Carolina, later Recorder of Deeds for the District of Columbia: a friend of Booker T. Washington and others of various races. The younger Dancy was himself educated, highly informed, and for twenty-five years had served the Detroit community with distinction, creating baby clinics, libraries, and other facilities, and, above all, giving personal help in times of trouble without which hundreds and thousands of Negro Detroiters would have suffered everything from prison to extremities of disease.[5]

Black Panthers. Many careers like Dancy's were now ended as young blacks marched toward confrontation. A few, Carmichael included, put themselves forward as leaders of a new quasi-military movement called Black Panthers, and assigned themselves the names appropriate to rival governments: Minister of Defense, Supreme Commander, Minister of Information, Chief of Staff, and others: titles which were regularly reproduced in such publications as the *New York Times* and received as official pronouncements by the National Liberation Government of Vietnam and the government of mainland China. So well received were the handful of Black Panthers that they were able to make household words of such relatively fledgling personalities as "Huey," "Stokely," and even "Bobby," the latter being recognized as Bobby Seale, in such graffiti as "Free Bobby." Even Carmichael's frank antisemitism and his declared belief that Hitler had dealt appropriately with the Jews of Germany failed to dampen the campus enthusiasm which he inspired.

The Black Panther drive was a guerrilla-type operation which depended on such sympathy as it could muster among Negroes and the general population. For their own people, the young partisans proposed a species of welfare program which in Oakland, Cali-

---

5. *Sand against the Wind, the Memoirs of John C. Dancy* (Detroit, 1966).

fornia, and Harlem included free food, clothing, and promises of greater things coming. Although this program was little more than a propaganda gesture, it secured more coverage in the press than did great sums expended by civic bodies and foundations for community aid and enterprises.[6] For those outside the Negro community, combinations of threats, demands, and emotional appeals served well. The latter included vivid expressions of feeling and attitude, selling their personalities as dedicated and ardent, and bringing home to the readers of their publications their sense of oppression.[7] They also spawned new organizations, all of which were treated solemnly in the press as viable projects. Thus Newton, as Minister of Defense of the Black Panthers, sent official greetings to "the Republic of New Africa and [its] President Robert Williams." The latter planned to establish a separate black nation to be located in several southern American states. As they groped for language appropriate to their plans, the young revolutionaries veered between "street people's" talk, strongly infused with obscenity of a somewhat limited range, and Marxist jargon. On occasion, they reverted to the forthright English they had learned from parents and teachers. Working between separatist ideas and international perspectives, they suffered more criticism from revolutionaries than from the "chic radicals," mostly white, who patronized them as legitimate in their anger.[8]

One who profited outstandingly from Black Panther popularity

6. See, for example, photographs in *To Die for the People: the Writings of Huey P. Newton* (New York, 1972), which includes a curious photograph of the young author, sitting in state on a woven-straw lawn chair, holding a spear as sceptre.
7. As in the "biography" by James Forman, *Sammy Younge: the First Black College Student to Die in the Black Liberation Movement* (New York, 1968): a confiding, agitated account of Alabama happenings in the Tuskegee area. It did not hesitate to condemn the moderation of the Negro community in that University town. See also Phil Husch, ed., *Listen, White Man, I'm Bleeding* (New York, 1969), representative of many collections of "terrifying true accounts of black men and women faced with the inhuman cruelty...of a white world they never made."
8. For example, William L. Patterson, a veteran Communist, complained of the Black Panthers' "weaknesses...on the ideological and programmatic fronts," and thought that "if not systematically and persistently combatted they can lead to deterioration," *ibid.*, 169. A famous essay caught the phenomenon of hollow empathy with what affluent New York liberals imagined Negro "revolutionaries" to be; see Tom Wolfe, *Radical Chic & Mau-Mauing the Flak Catchers* (New York, 1970).

was Eldridge Cleaver, like many of his associates a veteran of prisons: a fact which was taken to impugn the prison system, rather than the prisoners. Their major tenet was that they harbored legitimate grievances against a system that impaled them, and that they were revenging not only their own outrages, but what they generalized as four hundred years of oppression. Cleaver, convicted of narcotics activities and rape, saw his latter exploits as "probably a combination of business and pleasure"[9]—a view which was approved not only by the editors of *Ramparts,* a "muckraking" publication which employed him, but by reviewers who estimated his *Soul on Ice* (1968) as a work of genius, and, in 1968, by some 200,000 voters, most of them assessed as white, who endorsed Cleaver for the presidency of the United States on the Peace and Freedom Party ticket.

Murray Kempton, who served as an ironic and embittered columnist for the *New York Post* before becoming a sports commentator for *Esquire,* concluded that the Black Panthers had basically furnished entertainment for newspaper and television watchers: thrills and amazement at their bold talk and promises of excitement. Nevertheless the attention accorded their views cost a number of the embattled dissidents their lives and put out of working society such others as Cleaver, who was forced to become an exile. One young militant, George Jackson, like some others possessed of an impassioned style and sense of wrong, acquired a gun with which he attempted in August 1971 to shoot his way out of San Quentin, a maximum security prison. In the action three prison guards died of slashed throats and two white prisoners as well. Jackson was the second of his family to die in such an attempt. His bereaved father told reporters that if the Negroes were not to lose all their most talented young men they would have to curb their anger.[10]

---

9. Scheer, ed., *Cleaver,* 204.
10. For Jackson's book, *Soledad Brother* (New York, 1970), with an introduction by Jean Genet, see *New York Times Review,* November 22, 1970, 10. A curiosity of his effort to break out of San Quentin was that there was apparently no way in which he could have hoped to escape. An educated "con" anonymously surveying the situation in the *New York Times* concluded that Jackson was not going anywhere, but, with no future, sought death as a proper ending to an unexpectedly brilliant year.

Yet the Black Panthers had accomplished at least two things. Such slogans as "Freedom is obtained through the barrel of a gun" had succeeded in alienating large numbers of generous donors, despite Roy Wilkins's expressed hope that the white American majority would not be "piqued" by the words and actions of black revolutionaries. The donors had subsidized the expensive plane trips, purchases, and hotel expenses which had become standard among the top-ranking black youthful revolutionaries. As Cleaver's editor put it: "Cleaver took easily to freedom and women and food and Scotch and Berkeley and Bobby Dylan and the soul food near the Panther office."[11] The drying up of "honky" funds also affected the work of Negroes more modestly involved in the improvement of schools, clinics, housing operations, and other communal facilities. Negro leaders were thus required to reassess their resources. For a while, Black Panthers popularized the concept of "Pigs" as descriptive of policemen, but working Negro politicians were required to reconsider its validity as they themselves took civic office, and sometimes the highest office, in cities, and were directly resonsible for the well-being and self-esteem of the police force.

The most significant achievement of the revolutionary young was their revival of the concept of black. A major reform battle of the 1920's and 1930's had been to cease identifying Negroes by color, on grounds that this raised invidious social and legal distinctions, especially unfair or malicious, since many Negroes were far from black. The Black Panthers had made a political point, forcing Negroes to choose between unity under the flag of blackness and themselves, or to be condemned by militants as "Uncle Toms" and "Aunt Tinas." Most Negroes appear to have accepted the distinction as just, at least in public, and were joined by the great mass of whites in so doing, some doubtless for racist or political reasons of their own.[12]

---

11. Scheer, ed., *Cleaver,* xxvi-xxvii.
12. However, a major academic project of the time went under way as a "Dictionary of American Negro Biography," such a designation being deemed more suitable to the long-term views of this people and the majority of its subjects, and gave evidence that the subject was far from resolved.

Hatred of America as a Unifying Force. The Negro separatist tendency was paradoxically aided by strong, activist integrationist forces from Hippie communes to campuses, at one in wholehearted anti-Americanism. Joan Baez, among many others, expressed contempt for the nation, declaring "The Star-Spangled Banner is just so much trash."[13] Gary Snyder, an associate of Allen Ginsberg, wrote a highly esteemed poem entitled "A Curse on the Men in Washington," which spoke of his disgust with his own past as a crew-cut Seattle boy. The "Christian" in himself was long dead; he would now kill the false American in himself, returning the spirit to the true one, seen personified in the American brave, Chief Joseph, and in Buddha.[14]

Such commitments, passionately expressed and with no qualification, permitted strange fruit, such as the 1967 meeting in Chicago of the National Conference on New Politics which attracted white liberals, old-line radicals, and new ones. "Angry blacks" in attendance caucused privately, and then boldly demanded full control of the conference on grounds that the Negro people had suffered unspeakably, and that they themselves were in the shadow of death because of their battle for justice. Many of the blacks there as elsewhere were amazed when these violent assertions were applauded and their wishes wholly granted. At the Chicago meeting, once they had the power they did not know what to do with it, so black and white, in argumentative discord, spent the better part of a week confusing the national news media which had come believing they were covering important news.[15]

Weak as were such alliances, and differently oriented, they added relevance to each other's programs. The Black Power drive gained greatly from such convictions as Gary Snyder's and others with status and place in larger establishments.

Norman Mailer's essay on "The White Negro" in 1959 and Jerry Farber's "The Student as Nigger" in 1967 give a sense of the

---

13. *Fact,* II (January-February), 1965, 8. The entire symposium on the merits and demerits of the National Anthem is worth perusal, involving as it does a wide range of public personalities.
14. Hoffman, *We Are the People Our Parents Warned Us Against,* 127.
15. *Ibid.,* 131.

distance the subject had traveled.[16] Mailer viewed the Negro as his
timeless rival in sexual achievement. Farber was a young instructor
in a California college who saw the students' plight as comparable
to that suffered by Negroes as a race. Both were demeaned, frustrated by sterile, perverted administrators. Farber's dream of a free
and radical education was published in the *Los Angeles Free Press,*
a small, independent paper. The strong response it generated indicated that readers believed the campus to be a key factor in their
search for a new America.

Campus and off-campus elements joined for the campaign.
A transitional figure was Herbert Aptheker, long a scholar in
Negro revolt and member of the Communist Party. He had often
been brought to campuses to present his viewpoint and was about
to enjoy a wave of campus popularity which would take him from
coast to coast. His daughter's name, Bettina, would briefly join
those of others who could be identified without recourse to sur-
names. Aptheker's *Laureates of Imperialism* (1954) attempted
to prove that esteemed historians were no more than servile frauds.

Such partisans found their cause pinpointed in the troubles
of a young historian of admitted competence who had been denied
advancement in the history department of the University of California, it was surmised, because of his ardor for social issues.
Richard Drinnon, who was to publish an excellent biography of
Emma Goldman, professed himself a friend of democracy. He despised "the liberal technique of failure," however, and confessed
himself radical in believing that where the courts refused to function
for civil rights, direct action was justified.[17] He and others created
Studies on the Left in 1967, with such talents as James Weinstein,
Warren Susman, Staughton Lynd, and Tom Hayden, to probe
ways and means for radicalizing the campuses. By 1965 they had

---

16. Mailer's essay is contained in *Advertisements for Myself* (New York, 1959);
    Farber was himself surprised by the success of his locally reproduced piece,
    and reprinted it with several other pieces in *The Student as Nigger* (North
    Hollywood, Calif., 1969), 114 ff. This success, like a number of others, was
    clearly the product of youth interest and demand, and had nothing to do with
    news media influence or other agencies of propaganda or prestige.
17. Peter Loewenberg, "An Interview with Richard Drinnon," *Studies on the
    Left,* II (#1, 1961), 76–81.

repudiated "irrelevance" in scholarship. It was a short step to the declaration of one of their editors that "a turn towards radical politics remains the sole alternative to a new and disastrous capitulation to the forces of liberal accommodation."[18]

Many young historians emerged to discover a backlog of American experience which warranted hatred rather than respect. Thomas Jefferson, once an inspiration to radicals as well as reformers, now appeared as a slaveholder first, anything else second. Lincoln the Emancipator lost his potential for stirring creative ideas in the present. Abolitionists, Populists, and Progressives had long received variants of lip service or contempt from historians plying liberal or conservative theses. Now a solidified "New Left" group, using their *Studies on the Left* as a fulcrum, set out to portray in detail a United States which was a giant without a head, a materialist without a heart. Gabriel Kolko, William Appleman Williams, Staughton Lynd, Jesse Lemisch, and others, working different historical threads or eras, labored to expose venom and frightening stupidity in the classic and current power structures.[19]

The Negro counterpart of New Left history put western history in the pillory, but without footnotes, and at the mercy of emotional attitudes. "History books tell us that nothing happens until a white man comes along," Carmichael declared. The cliche circulated among enthusiasts that, after all, Columbus had not "discovered" America; it had been in the good hands of Indians before that doubtful event occurred. Rap Brown wrote off William Shakespeare as a racist and "faggot." Nat Turner, the Virginia Negro insurrectionist of 1831 was blown up into mythic proportions, though little was then known of his actual life and circumstances. The legend was multiplied by a best-selling novel which gave

---

18. Robert Wolfe, in *ibid.*, VII, January-February, 1967, 21.
19. A vast literature accumulated, the purpose of which can be perceived in such titles as James Weinstein and David W. Eakins, eds., *For a New America* (New York, 1970) and Barton J. Bernstein, ed., *Toward a New Past: Dissenting Essays in American History* (New York, 1968). See also Arthur Lothstein, *"All We Are Saying . . .": The Philosophy of the New Left* (New York, 1970), and Irwin Unger, ed., *Beyond Liberalism: The New Left Views American History* (Waltham, Mass., 1971). For a sensational review of these authors' methods and materials see Robert James Maddox, *The New Left and the Origins of the Cold War* (Princeton, N.J., 1973).

partisans occasion for heated statement at the expense of reality.[20]

One who profited most from such discontent with recorded history was Dick Gregory, a "stand up" comedian in nightclubs and on television of deserved reputation for wit and ethnic insight: a man of feeling, as his autobiographical *Nigger* (1964) indicated. At first involved in desegregation challenges, he moved on to such successful presentations on campuses as to change his style and approach. His protests against injustice became indictments of American civilization, and, more elaborately, historical critiques. Ultimately, he published two books which appeared serious in presuming to interpret American history and politics past and present.[21]

Since Gregory delivered his lecture to several hundred thousand students, professors, and others, at a reported fifteen hundred dollars per lecture, usually paid from college funds allotted for student activities, his crusade was symptomatic of college circumstances. Gregory's humor and debatable historical assertions constituted a kind of public relations for the civil rights drive, and an extremely effective one. Gregory declared he was not violent, but would not press his views on militants. "I didn't heat them up, and I am not going to cool them off." Carmichael and Rap Brown, he thought, had dared to become as bitter as Patrick Henry. He mocked the "discovery" of America, and the Pilgrim who, "on his way to find his freedom . . . stole *us*." He marveled that the Senate and House in Washington had debated for months on a Clean Meat Bill, and asked whether such a question should be debated.[22]

All such assertions and declarations appear to have impressed his student-faculty audiences as irrefutable. They helped indicate the deep chasm between the established humanities and their stu-

20. Minor, ed., *Stokely Speaks,* 80; H. Rap Brown, *Die Nigger Die* (New York, 1969), 21; William Styron, *The Confessions of Nat Turner* (New York, 1967); this last heatedly answered by a number of Negro writers in John H. Clarke, ed., *William Styron's Nat Turner* (Boston, 1968). The subject was more calmly and competently handled by a scholar, Henry I. Tragle, in *The Southampton Slave Revolt of 1831: A Compilation of Source Material* (Amherst, Mass., 1971).
21. Richard Claxton Gregory, *No More Lies: The Myth and the Reality of American History* (New York, 1971); and *Dick Gregory's Political Primer* (New York, 1972), both volumes edited by James R. McGraw.
22. Dick Gregory, "Breaking Out: a Black Manifesto," *Avant Garde* #6 (January 1969), 24–27.

dent attendants, and between the campuses and the larger communities. The shouts of laughter and applause which Gregory was able to evoke in crowded halls—at the height of his popularity at two or even three campuses on a single day—were calculated to fill the auditors with a sense of power and unity and a belief that they could and must change the world.

Berkeley. The fulcrum of the first civil rights agitation had been the South, seen as monolithic in its efforts to maintain a caste system. The movement had drawn young white crusaders and religion-shielded blacks who, by a series of symbolic gestures and tactics, had made their appeal to the nation—an appeal which had forced democratization of social deportment and status. Although these changes in the South had caused some impatience among dissatisfied Negro elements, they seem to have been treated as progressive by a variety of leaders in the Negro community.[23]

The situation in the North was more complex, and required different tactics of the youth. Civil rights drives were rendered more political than moral, thanks to the network of civil rights laws already in operation in the North and the high percentage of black populations in the great cities. The civil rights drive, therefore, important though it was, and employing many black and white youth in vanguard postures, could be clearly distinguished from the student eruption which activated the burgeoning "war babies" generation, and which was largely general-staffed by whites.

There were avant garde colleges which made a point of soliciting student participation as part of their educational program. Students were, in one measure or another, brought into "decision making" situations. They were permitted to aid in selecting teachers from among candidates for positions, asked about the validity

23. See, for example, Roy Wilkins, "One Man's Struggle," *Dayton Journal Herald*, October 15, 1973, honoring a successful young Negro businessman of New Orleans who had moved through a succession of jobs to become an outstanding automobile salesman. Wrote Wilkins: "There is, of course, racial discrimination.... One has to live with race prejudice and not let it get one down.... That takes time, fortuitous office holders (which means intelligent voting), and self-control: not bowing, agreeing or acquiescing, but not tearing up the pea patch, either.... The vociferous and disillusioned blacks are in the minority."

of courses, teaching effectiveness, and the like. Civil liberties and male-female relations were never far from the minds of either administrators or students and could cause debates which grew heated in and out of campus conferences and student publications. Former "activists" of youth movements, who were now teachers or administrators, were sometimes conservatives, or still "radical" in thought, however conservative they might be in practice. But in any case, they were constrained to deal with popular student attitudes which tended toward sympathy with student peers who professed radical goals, promising greater freedom of movement or choice to all.

It was, however, at the highly populated universities, public and private, that discontent arose. There, student identity was at a minimum. Courses were routine and largely taught by assistants whose tenure lacked dignity or hope. Fraternities, "homecomings," sports, and spring frenzy satisfied a large percentage of the registered student personnel. But such events were wearisome or worse to a substantial minority which now inherited the experiments and convictions of previous student generations.

That their unrest should have become first conspicuous at Berkeley, California, in 1960 was an accident of time and place. The seizure of power in Cuba by the revolutionary Fidel Castro the year before, and exacerbated United States-Cuban relations thereafter, encouraged young radicals. Cynicism caused by detailed evidence of fixed television shows which were supposed to demonstrate superior knowledge did not increase youthful respect for age. Continuing tensions, mainly in Europe, raised possibilities of war and therefore of the draft; this inspired some male youth to continue on in school, even past graduation, in order to take advantage of deferment regulations. It also encouraged them to seek moral justifications for their marginal places in life. Differences between liberals and conservatives widened as President Eisenhower's term of office ended; in California, the Nixon candidacy for president particularly underscored those differences, as also did, in San Francisco, investigations of subversive activities in the area by the House Subcommittee on Un-American Activities.

In the Fall of 1959 Fred Moore went on a hunger strike on the Berkeley campus against compulsory ROTC. That year students demonstrated in Berkeley, at San Quentin, and elsewhere against the execution of Caryl Chessman, convicted of and given the death sentence for kidnaping and rape. Chessman was a talented criminal who had won national attention with self-taught legal maneuvers which had fended off execution for a record eleven years. He had written eloquent and keen-minded denials of the crime which had kept him on death row and raised doubt and admiration in many minds. Chessman's courageous death in the gas chamber was closely attended by the Bay Area students, many of whom kept a final vigil and reported all harrowing details to the campuses. The event increased disrespect for law and administration.

Of equal relevance were claims of repression of faculty, some of whom, like Richard Drinnon, were concerned for the Chessman case. Another case involved an assistant professor of biology who, in a letter (actually published on another campus) advised students limited to awkward "necking" sessions, of the ready availability of contraceptive devices. His subsequent dismissal reverberated among students. As promising of future turbulence, however, was the attitude of publishers who made these events and others memorable. Their publications included accounts of riotous demonstrations against HUAC sessions in San Francisco's City Hall which resulted in fire hosing, police action, and arrests. The protests brought thousands to the scene, some to gloat and to taunt students with their lack of interest in Hungary's agony under the Soviets, but more to choke with indignation at police repression and to join or support other protest actions. Wrote one publisher's man, introducing an account of Berkeley happenings:

> *National attention has been given Berkeley student efforts to influence the major issues of our time.*
> *More than 18,000,000 Americans have seen a distorted film about them.*
> *Students . . . no longer accept outworn and empty slogans. Their re-examination of these meaningless ideas has led them to decide on action on the major issues.*[24]

These and similar declarations reflected media conviction that

---

24. David Horowitz, *Student* (New York, 1962), [i]. The author identified himself as a teaching assistant in English at Berkeley.

the general public was interested in student phenomena and would encourage it by giving it the attention it needed to flouish. One result of such seethings and maneuvers was a demand for expanded definitions of free speech, which focused on HUAC as a major enemy but looked to broader views of freedom on several fronts. Interesting was radical Berkeley's repudiation of both HUAC *and* official Communism, and the calling for a New Politics hostile to both Soviet repression (as in Hungary) *and* American antagonism to Cuba. "If the students are radical in their critique of the market system, they are radical as well, in their critique of Marxist solutions."[25] Embattled Berkeley looked forward to a free speech fight, which was soon to materialize in over twenty campus organizations.

As important to the momentum of events were actions on other campuses concerning civil rights or free speech. Thus, at one relatively small midwest college, Antioch, in Yellow Springs, Ohio, some 250 students capped long efforts to desegregate a local barber shop by locking arms and sitting down in the street in mass protest against the stubborn barber's policies. Great numbers of police were brought in from neighboring cities to disperse the demonstrators. The police employed tear gas and fire hoses and eventually read the Riot Act. They then arrested over a hundred of the students and their associates, dragging them without resistance to police wagons for jailing and court processes. Such incidents, carried as news to other campuses and in an increasingly "underground press," marked steps in the growing student revolt.[26]

Berkeley continued to be the center of personalities and ideas intended to advance autonomy of students on and off campus. It was not accidental that the university's president was a famed liberal, Clark Kerr, though events later made it evident that liberal or nonliberal administrations made no difference to the revolutionaries. Indeed, they soon made it a tenet of faith that their worst and most dangerous foes *were* the liberals because the meliorative policies of the latter impeded the quick march of radical change.

---

25. *Ibid.*, 157.
26. The demonstration is memorialized in Philip Roth, *Portnoy's Complaint* (New York, 1969); see also Laurence Leamer, *The Paper Revolutionaries: the Rise of the Underground Press* (New York, 1972).

Although in their first wave of action the campus radicals made gestures indicating an appeal to sympathy and public support, they dispensed with such tactics when there was sufficient student strength for more basic challenges to authority.

Counterculture. Much of the student revolt in the next several years seemed unbelievable to the great mass of television viewers and newspaper readers, who did not understand what the students' goals might be. They were therefore stigmatized as irresponsible, pawns of subversive groups, or, more gently, as utopian. "Utopian" some of them may have been in a technical sense, but in practice most of the participants gave little thought to the future. Enthralled by the present, they were able to generate a passion and determination of high intensity. As a Mark Rudd later declared, during a major effort at Columbia University: "If we win, we will take control of your world, your corporations, your University, and attempt to mold a world in which we and other people can live as human beings."[27] Such sentiments thrilled equally present-minded supporters into fancying that they were heading toward a genuine revolution.

Grass-roots support pervaded campuses from coast to coast. In dormitories, at rallies, in thousands of cafes and private sessions they could hear and experience evidence of what an empathetic instructor called a *counterculture.* It was spelled out by the "dialectics of liberation," as explained by Herbert Marcuse and Norman Brown, among others. The "counterculture" advocate deplored the misuse of drugs, but he could not fault a basically "healthy" youth in protest against the authoritarianism of technology. He himself joined the students in rejecting "objective consciousness" in favor of a warmer, more spontaneous and fulfilling personal reality.[28]

The future appeared to move swiftly, as Stanford female students made public declarations that their bodies were their own, to dispose of as they chose. They thus endorsed a condition which had operated informally on campuses: the "shacking up" of as-

27. *Columbia College Today,* Spring, 1968.
28. Theodore Roszak, *The Making of a Counter Culture* (New York, 1969).

sociated males and females. This had previously been attended with some inconvenience and expense in as much as a student was compelled to pay dormitory fees while also being charged rent at other addresses. Deans of Women rapidly disappeared from official catalogs, the women involved being given other duties, sometimes academic. Adjustment of family relations and understandings were more slowly achieved, if at all; but, in sum, the militants, themselves already liberated from society, could see many allies gathered for their cause.

Thus a former Swarthmore editor and student community leader recalled his contribution to the "generational line" of his associates. His paper had asked a random sample of fifty Swarthmore student males whether they would mind if the female they thought to marry was not a virgin. He recalled his sense of shock when all but two answered yes. "We decided not to publish the results."[29]

The rationale for such suppression of evidence was that what would be called "male chauvinism" ought not to be encouraged, and, by implication, that female freedom of choice ought to be positively motivated, if not forced, since some females were unduly influenced by family ties and tradition. So, once more, a spirit of war between elders and offspring was implemented which students could find stimulating and adventurous. It was soon further implemented by a "woman's liberation" movement which was not strictly a youth movement, nor especially interested in youth causes. Betty Friedan's *The Feminine Mystique* (1963) sparked a wide variety of female protests in demand of more and better jobs, equal pay, day care centers, equality in familial roles, and other issues, which, though separated from the youth movement proper, gave indication of a soft social underbelly at which it could strike.[30]

In some ways a more novel development in the new morality

29. Lewis S. Feuer, *The Conflict of Generations* (New York, 1969), 422.
30. Friedan herself made much of family-type dilemmas which touched the younger females hardly at all; see her "We Don't Have to Be That Independent," *McCall's*, January 1973, 18, in which she declared: "It is a relief now to realize that we can admit our need for love and home, be soft as well as hard with our children and our husbands, admit our dependence on them without giving up our identity."

was the dignifying of "rip-offs" as legitimate means of attaining social restitution. The process was clearly seen in the philosophy of Bobby Seale, whose view of the nation flowered when he was still a youngster:

> *In school, when a little white liberal walked by, I used to come up with my knife and say, "Give me your lunch money or I'll cut your guts out." And he'd give me his lunch money. Pretty soon, I'd say, "Tomorrow you bring me two dollars." And the next day he'd bring me two dollars. Because that two dollars was mine. Mine because of four hundred years of racism and oppression. When I take two dollars from you, pig, don't you say nothing.*[31]

As detailed by Seale, it was a philosophy which appeared attractive to white audiences. It was also espoused by his colleague, Rap Brown, who proudly recounted his visit to the White House in 1965 as part of a delegation to protest police action in Selma, Alabama. Brown was dissatisfied with the President's attitude, "[a]nd to show the ———— what I thought about the whole meeting, I stole some stuff out of the White House. I liberated everything I could! Sure did."[32]

This approach to morality, shortsighted in that it failed to take into account long experience with the dynamics of theft, nevertheless seemed exciting and persuasive to "activists" of various types. In January 1963, the left-wing student leader at Berkeley was apprehended in book-stealing from a local bookstore. He sought to justify his act by arguments that "probably" ninety percent of the population in the country could be jailed for criminal conduct. "Our laws are outdated, our penal system prejudicial to the wealthy and white, and our police force brutal and grossly unfair."[33]

Such views helped give a sense of status to numerous persons who might otherwise have had to demonstrate character and fitness, and who in many cases had an obvious stake in raising

---

31. Scheer, ed., *Cleaver*, 189.
32. Brown, *Die, Nigger, Die*, 53.
33. Feuer, *Conflict of Generations*, 419.

hatred and contempt against others who did their work and kept
the world turning.[34]

The year 1964 was the wonder year of Berkeley, swirling
with movement and debate. It evolved as a free speech issue the
right to obscenity—another prodigy which was to add credence to
the belief that the times were really changing. Despite the ups and
downs of court cases which forced a brilliant publisher, Ralph
Ginzburg, to spend some time in prison, obscenity and sex-laden
matter proliferated for the literate and illiterate, providing proof
that the world of repression and evasion was disappearing. Key
"evidence" included the dizzying success of *Playboy Magazine*
which mixed common female forms with philosophic essays by famous academics and public personalities. The youth who declared
for open sex openly arrived at seemed to be endorsed by the highest authorities.

Mario Savio, a philosophy student, emerged as leader of the
free speech fight at Berkeley. Of all his actions and words, drawing
in deans, flouting official orders, inspiring sit-ins and mass meetings, little could be recalled after the revolt on campuses across the
country was unleashed. He did, however, popularize a phrase,
"blowing the mind," which was curiously interpreted as referring
to a fresh intellectual wind. Savio himself, using language common
to his crowd, seems rather to have meant that it was their business
to bewilder and disarm the public, the better to compel them to accept student demands. That, in any event, was what the radicals,
supported by a loose federation of sympathizers with experimentation and euphoria, sought to achieve.

---

34. The standard work in the field is Abbie Hoffman, *Steal This Book* (New
York, 1971) which explained numerous ways of outwitting the system and
fattening at its expense; gave much information on acquiring the best of
drugs and other commodities; resentfully noticed that "racist penny-pinchers
of Mississippi dole out only $8.00 a month," but that New York "dishes out
the most with monthly payments up to $120.00." The author knew "cats"
who by various means "parlayed welfare payments up to six hundred dollars
a month." The author's general principle was that "pigs" [law enforcement
officers] have small brains and move slowly," and so continuing success could
be predicted. Hoffman was also witty: "Remember, January is Alien Registration Month, so don't forget to fill out an application at the Post Office,
listing yourself as a citizen of Free Nation. Then when they ask you to 'Love
it or leave it,' tell them you already left!" (p. 213.)

Vietnam.

> Hey, hey, LBJ
> How many kids have you killed today?

What gave them focus for their discontents was the war in Vietnam, and yet not so much the war as the unprecedented coverage which it was accorded by the news media. It had been the intention of the government and the military since the Kennedy era to involve the general public more intimately in the program of pacification in the Far East, so that it could better appreciate the difficulties in the way. Newsmen cooperated, showing army efforts to strengthen border communities so that they could better resist Communist infiltrators, showing the military distributing Christmas gifts, showing them rebuilding war-damaged abodes with modern American housing materials, and otherwise carrying out acts of mercy as well as of security.

The newsmen and photographers had learned their craft well. Unleashed from traditional military censorship that had been in effect as late as the Korean War, they broadcast reports from the very front lines, making it evident that the actions were costly, continuous, and with no end in sight. It was difficult to explain that despite overwhelming power, American troops had to maintain a purely defensive posture if they were not to raise dangers of direct Soviet confrontations and the specter of World War III. Moreover their cameras and reports highlighted the weakness and corruption of the Saigon government and the shoddy lives of American servicemen in Saigon bars and other entertainment centers. Astounded television watchers saw cargo ships filled with army materials and supplies literally being stripped before their eyes by black marketeers as the ships proceeded up inland waters.

Although numerous Americans were unwilling to give up faith in their government or its decisions in the untidy waging of war, its escalation—on television, and through drafted soldiers—added fuel to student unrest and gave them their most popular and fruitful cause. Students for a Democratic Society had been founded in 1960, and for some time had shared the program and perspectives of the civil rights movement. SDS esteemed itself the New

Left: less tired and dogmatic than the Old, more aware of the "human" factor, the "psychological" variables which could start and direct change. It separated itself from the dying Progressive Labor group which clung to Old Left dogma.[35] So, though SDS still talked socialism, adored Mao, and talked world liberation, it also welcomed the philosophy of simple disruption, of guerrilla warfare, of Hippie euphoria—a stance which gave it entree to youth sessions fighting segregation or enjoying drugs. As Carl Oglesby, an SDS leader put it, their program was "to make love more possible. We work to remove from society what threatens and prevents it."[36]

Protests against the war took irregular forms in 1965, but all methods employed supported the rest. A "revolutionary" mood made heroes of the Viet Cong, and villains of the Americans. The youthful antiwar conviction gained from new "lifestyles" which transformed campus living and also donated many male and female bodies to demonstrations. In the spring of 1965 occurred the first "teach-ins" on Vietnam at the University of Michigan: an event largely sponsored by the SDS and involving faculty as well as students. "Teach-ins" spread swiftly to hundreds of college campuses. The hordes of students attending these sessions overwhelmingly favored peace, though it would then have meant the fall of the Saigon government. The effort of the American government to use the domestic "teach-ins" by sending speakers to defend United States policy only added fire to the SDS program, which called for closing down ROTC operations on all campuses, forcing college administrators to renounce all government "war-related" contracts, and even driving off Peace Corps representatives from campus on grounds that they were a branch of American imperialism.

The youth cried peace, and that spring of 1965 staged the first of the great marches to Washington to protest the war in Vietnam, bringing to the capital some 25,000 demonstrators. Nevertheless, like their civil rights comrades, they were not averse to

---

35. Richard E. Peterson, "The Student Left in American Higher Education," in Seymour Martin Lipsit and Philip G. Altbach, *Students in Revolt* (Boston, 1969). 206.
36. Marjorie Hope, *Youth against the World* (Boston, 1970), 269.

violence when done in a righteous cause. Their major inspiration in this respect was Che Guevara, their enthusiasm for him being strangely augmented by evidence of his ineptitude as a revolutionary leader and administrator. His "Marxism" was as dull and dogmatic as any the Old Left had ever lucubrated, and probably meant little to most of the youth who taped life-sized pictures of him on their walls. A sympathetic commentator, who anticipated that "the older generation" would write Guevara down as a hopeless romantic perhaps driven by a suicidal impulse, put the matter clearly:

> *The youth see him better. To them he appears as an admirable example of that complete commitment, that absolute dedication to the advancement of mankind which they instinctively feel represents the highest and noblest attainment an individual can achieve. The vanguard youth are therefore taking Che as their own.*[37]

Guevara was as poor a symbol of revolution as the times produced, leaving a trail of failures in Cuba, in Africa, and in several South American nations. Yet within weeks of his death posters reminiscent of those which followed James Dean's death proclaimed that "Che Lives." The key to this dedication was, at least in part, the hopelessness of his cause. As a guerrilla warrior, Che thrilled American adventurers who saw themselves as opposing the might of "fascist" America. But whereas such revolutionaries as Mao had seen guerrilla warfare as an adjunct to the more serious business of rooting their affairs in the life of the people, Che had made of guerrilla tactics a thing in itself, which would somehow roll up a revolutionary wave and bring the final victory.[38] Such tactics appealed to an urgent youth, like him outsiders in a land they had repudiated, like him eager for action and reluctant to believe it could only be made valid by careful planning, by clear, disciplined minds, and attention to such interminable and unglamourous matters as crops, diplomacy, statistics, traditions, and the nuances of culture.

---

37. Joseph Hansen in *Che Guevara Speaks,* ed., George Lavan (New York, 1967), [7].
38. Jay Mallin, ed., *"Che" Guevara on Revolution: a Documentary Overview* (Coral Gables, 1969), 30.

Demonstrations and Festivals. A bitter critic of the youth uprising later saw them as patent scum: "a mélange of narcotics,
sexual perversion, collegiate Castroism and campus Maoism." He
was controverted by a psychological study of 240 activists which
found them to be above average intelligence, many the recipients
of esteemed fellowships and scholarships.[39] It is evident that the
antagonists were not talking about the same thing. One concentrated on the youthful decay which expressed itself in aimless
euphoria, drugs, and revolutionary jargon as shabby justification.
The other fixed on such personalities as Thomas Hayden, Herbert
Aptheker, and Staughton Lynd as leaders of a youth uprising
against debilitated campuses, football-drunk television audiences,
and a government which waged doubtful war abroad. Between
these two extremes lay great masses of sympathizers and followers
who were the real basin of sustenance for the utterly lost, on one
side, and the Robespierre-incorruptibles, on the other. Both were
dependent for justification on their belief that the great American
public was beyond redemption. As Lynd and Hayden, students of
academic history, put it: "Our country has been significantly imperialist, ethnocentric, indifferent to the cultural riches and human
worth of dark-skinned people, from its beginnings."[40]

Throughout this era there were innumerable manifestations
of student unrest abroad. Protest ranged from Canada, where university reforms were asked, to India, where there were riots over
the English-Hindi language issue. The French outbreaks were outstanding in Nanterre and at the Sorbonne.[41] They inspired sympathetic strikes replete with local issues in Italy and elsewhere.
Brazil, Japan, Yugoslavia—these and other nations—saw masses
of students pour out into great city centers, or stage sit-ins within
university buildings, because of academic regulations, because of
the quality of the food served, or because they wished to bring
down the government. Local issues in Mexico City were noticed
world-wide when they escalated into student-police confrontations

---

39. Jack Newfield, *A Prophetic Minority* (New York, 1967), 136. Newfield himself noted an "appalling anti-intellectualism among the newer SDS members"
(p. 87), but felt called upon to justify their overall validity.
40. Staughton Lynd and Thomas Hayden, *The Other Side* (New York, 1967 ed.),
202.
41. Alain Touraine, *The May Movement* (New York, 1971).

which on October 2, 1968, resulted in forty-nine dead, many of them women and children.[42]

But though these great swellings of student unrest necessarily included numerous fools and inept camp followers, none quite produced prototypical leaders of the nature in the United States of Abbie Hoffman and Jerry Rubin. Among the Germans Rudi Dutschke was a literate left-winger. Daniel Cohn-Bendit ("Danny the Red") of the French uprising was sufficiently qualified to pass the Sorbonne examination in sociology the season following his May morning of leadership of the "uncontrollable spontaneity" movement which he had imagined would result in a new self-generating organization.

Hoffman and Rubin made no plans, imagined no future. Yet David Dellinger, a veteran "peace" advocate, asked Rubin to become project director for the National Mobilization's antiwar demonstration in Washington. " 'People in Berkeley [where Rubin made his start] think we ought to try to shut down the Pentagon this fall with massive civil disobedience,' I told Dave. He grinned, a twinkle in his eye. He's in his early 50's, but he's a kid at heart, a born troublemaker. If there were a million Dave Dellingers, there'd be no generation gap."[43]

Although Rubin's and Hoffman's actions and words were calculated to outrage "square" sensibilities, in line with the classic Bohemian concept of shocking the bourgeoisie, they had a plan of sorts which would be repeated in variations by hundreds of their admirers and accepted by thousands more. Spelling out their methods was part of their program, so that, being emulated by others, it would persuade the enemy that they were faced by an invincible tide. In effect, and for a while, the "Yippie" leaders, heading a paper Youth International Party, did bring young masses to their feet, did create damage and disorder and a species of martyr who served time in jail for arson, stealing, endangering life, and other crimes, and did draw media sympathy for their civil rights and good intentions.

---

42. For an unforgettable account, Elena Poniatowska, *Massacre in Mexico* (New York, 1971).
43. Jerry Rubin, *Do It: Scenarios of the Revolution* (New York, 1970), 67.

As Hoffman, "master at the art of media manipulation," explained:

> Get them to promote an event before it happens. Like the thing about Washington, Chicago, the Pentagon demonstration, uh, to get them to write about an event. In other words to do an ad, you know, to make an advertisement for the event. . . . You gotta study the techniques that they use in advertising, and the one thing they don't do is have very straight press conferences.[44]

In time, Hoffman would lose his "mastery," and doubtless have to reconsider what had given it to him in the first place. Rubin, again, dedicating his book to "Nancy, Dope, Color TV, and Violent Revolution," and urging readers to be "stoned" while reading, might also in time have to reconsider his life premises. But his concept of "guerrilla theatre" as life combined entertainment with serious issues which affected the era.[45]

Their major premise—and the premise which gave them and their supporters and adult defenders a sense of firmness in the right—was their faith that nothing could be more obscene than the war in Vietnam, that nothing could be more devastating and destructive than the "Amerikan"[46] policy toward Negroes (this category was broadened to include Mexican-Americans and Indians) and that the nation was a prison of infamy which had to be razed.

They were not to be satisfied by partial victories. Rubin, having spent a bit of time in prison, expressed the thought that all prisons everywhere, that is, in the United States, ought to be emptied. Hoffman, burning dollar bills on the floor of the Chicago Stock Exchange, obviously imagined that everyone should have anything he desired. Any repression in drugs and sex seemed to them intolerable. There were, to be sure, several extreme manifestations of their definition of freedom: a young male and female

---

44. Leamer, *Paper Revolutionaries*, 71.
45. See *The Wedding within the War*, by one of Rubin's acolytes, Michael Rossman (New York, 1971), which quoted Mario Savio's arresting thought on the firing from the Berkeley presidency ("good riddance to bad rubbish"), offered "Reflections on the American Theater," and detailed other Rubinesque exploits in wreckage and charades.
46. Spelled so in order to equate American ways with Fascism.

who coupled in a Haight-Ashbury street, a New York lesbian who did the same with a partner at a Woman's Lib conference, presumably to encourage others like themselves to "get out of the closet." But these were seen as vagaries in an essentially correct uprising of the crushed and the abashed.

Had there been no My Lai (a coarse episode of murder by American military personnel), had there been no other well-reported tragedies of warfare on the American side, had there been no regularly analyzed record of American loss of blood and treasure supported by harrowing film, many more citizens would have been revolted and activated by the public flouting the New Left and their "Yippie" associates dealt out. But the tiring and continuous war made it difficult for adults, with a sense of their own inadequate use of the prosperity they had enjoyed, to stand up firmly against their tormentors or even to give encouragement to a brilliant core of conservative youth which solicited support for American foreign policy and the older morality.[47]

Mass demonstrations continued on campuses and in the major cities and in Washington. They employed every tactic of emotionalism, from reading the names of the American dead in Vietnam to the doubtful piety of candlelight vigils, presumably for the repose of their souls. The demonstrations drew contrivers and buffoons, but mainly they depended on the steadfastness of the mass young who, for different reasons, had come to believe they stood for something better than what the nation offered. Such a youth was "Dave Goldring," son of Old Left parents, raised in a quiet college town, who was "turned on," first by rock and Presley, then "activated" by a "Fair Play for Cuba" march on the state capital, and roiled by television news featuring civil liberties confrontations. Visiting in Paris, he made connections between the Algerian war and the "war" in Mississippi. Visiting Israel, he reluctantly concluded it was an American imperialist outpost.

---

47. Best known was William Buckley, who began his public career at twenty-two with a bitter book about his mentors, *God and Man at Yale* (New York, 1951), and who went on to establish a vehicle for sophisticated conservatives, the *National Review*. Many others in his general field emerged to conduct polemics, appear on television, write syndicated columns, and otherwise feed their philosophy to the nation. See Edward Cain, *They'd Rather Be Right: Youth and Conservatism* (New York, 1963) for an overview of their condition in the Sixties, including a discussion of Young Americans for Freedom.

Harvard University, which he attended, he came to see as an "institution of the ruling class." He mixed trucking work and communal living with intensive reading in imperialism; and as an SDSer helped make Defense Secretary Robert McNamara's Harvard visit memorable with shouts of "Murderer!" He helped frame a "We Won't Go" avowal of antiwar students in the area, had himself thrown off an army base while trying to get antidraft information to pre-induction draftees, and was arrested for sitting-in at the Massachusetts State House with welfare mothers seeking larger clothing allowances for children. Although he was energetic in the April 1969 Harvard takeover of University Hall in protest against ROTC, he avoided arrest during a subsequent police "bust" which netted 197 arrests and 45 injuries, since, having graduated, "he no longer enjoyed the immunities of a Harvard student."[48]

Such persons, conscious of being part of the New Left, and with a dream rendered more vivid by their temporal enjoyments of pot, rock, sex, and other tangibles distinguishing the drab old world from the coming one, stocked the campuses from coast to coast.

The 1969–1970 school year brought nearly 1,800 demonstrations, with numerous cases of arson. Campuses were closed down. One college president died of a heart attack induced by importunate confrontations, and others were threatened with similar mishaps. Many administrators resigned due to loss of morale or credibility, and new ones were brought in to stem the tide with new energy and resources. Veterans of campus imbroglios traveled the country as visiting functionaries, helping to administer local efforts, or encourage them with speeches. Yet it is likely that as much was accomplished through the mounting wave of festivals throughout the era, as by the demonstrations proper.

The use of festivals was better understood by libertarian than by democratic theoreticians of youth. From 1947 on they were held regularly in Prague, East Berlin, North Korea, Warsaw, and Moscow. They drew thousands of youth from everywhere, thrilled by their own variety, by the dances and music which galvanized hundreds of performers, by pointed political and dramatic shows,

---

48. Lukas, *Don't Shoot—We Are Your Children!*, 10.

and by their sense of being attuned to great historic forces which were remaking the world. Meetings, discussions, and speeches linked the participants to current events.

They were excited by a spirit of internationalism not to be infused by mere pamphlets, or even by domestic demonstrations against "imperialism."[49] However, disillusionment with Stalin and his regime and a turn to euphoria and campus issues as a new frontier dulled the edge of the old internationalism. The need for festivals where mass emotion could be generated increased. The new festivals convened a more indiscriminate assortment of young, but their increasingly formidable numbers provided the dynamo for Hippie and student action.

The first Newport Festival of 1954 had featured such jazz players and singers as Dizzy Gillespie and Ella Fitzgerald. Its success, and that of others, multiplied festivals all over the nation. In 1959 nine of them had played to 311,000 people and grossed $975,000; the avant-garde musician Miles Davis scorned them as "jazz supermarkets,"[50] curious evidence that they were not so much "far out" from society as simply the other side of the same cloth. Monterey, California, in 1958 inaugurated a festival which ultimately created a landmark in the youth movement.

As the youth movement reached its height, little separated the spirit behind festivals from that of demonstrations, except the rhetoric and placards necessary to the latter, and the inevitable "squares"—Dr. Benjamin Spock, Reverend William S. Coffin— who lent tone to demonstrations, but not to rock festivals. Rubin was doubtless correct from his point of view to say that he would not trust anyone who was not potted. The heavy pall of incense could be smelled and seen at festivals and demonstrations, and it embraced both during the memorable Chicago demonstration of 1968. As one grim student of affairs reported:

A survey of a sample of the disrupters showed that almost four-fifths of the respondents—432 in number—were imbibing marijuana at least once a week, 40 per cent were

49. Richard Connell, *Youth and Communism* (New York, 1965), 137 ff.
50. John S. Wilson, *Jazz: The Transition Years: 1940–1960* (New York, 1966), 147.

taking hashish weekly, 29 per cent were consumers of LSD,
11 per cent of methadrine, 10 per cent of mescaline, and
4 per cent of heroin.[51]

The Monterey Festival of 1967 was quickly made more famous than any by the inordinate number of youth it attracted, by
the exhibitions made of themselves by Jimi Hendrix and Janis
Joplin, and by the success of such groups as the Jefferson Air-
plane: all recorded on film and rapidly circulated throughout the
country. Hendrix, in effect, was unsheathed Presley; Joplin a
species of American Piaf: decadent, narcissistic, and wretchedly
insecure in her emotionalism—a mixture which could be received
with sympathy.

If *Monterey Pop,* the film celebrating the event, showed a
youth joyous in its freedom, the most famous of the festivals, at
Woodstock, New York in 1969, seemed to show the youth as established. Hoffman with good reason entitled one of his books,
written in three days, *Woodstock Nation* (1969): a collage of
thoughts, threats, attitudes set down as from a secure base. Tour-
ing campuses, controverting air stewardesses, men of affairs, and
others as he roamed to meetings and rendezvous, he could view
faces like his own, warm with greeting and regard. Woodstock,
more than the 1968 Chicago riot, was the fulfillment of his dreams
and those of his following. As one of their celebrants said, in a
volume of photographs which sought to capture the bliss of Woodstock:

> *I think about my friends among these young people and*
> *their houses . . . and it seems to me now that there is often*
> *a lovely feel to them: a softness, a delight which come*
> *more and more often, an ease and surety, a sense of being*
> *at home. . . .*
>
> *It is that world—in women or solitude or comrades—*
> *that now holds us and cradles us; it rocks us within it, and*
> *it is all a form of worship, the slow pouring of life into life,*
> *a letting out and entering, a slow ease and delight in the*
> *body of the beloved World.*[52]

---

51. Feuer, "Student Unrest in the United States," *Annals of the American Academy,* 404 (November, 1972), 175.
52. *The Free People* (New York, 1969), intro., Peter Marin [8, 13–14].

But where, someone asked him, are the "free people" without rich parents? The question troubled him. Yet he could not deny the quest of the "tender-limbed" seekers of beauty. It seemed to him good. Hoffman boldly declared it was the only quest. He quoted a line from a rock group's song: "We want the world and we want it NOW." That, he said, was good enough politics for him.

McCarthy, and RFK–68. Nevertheless, a strong faction of youth thrust itself forward in an effort to put more direct pressure on the larger body politic. The youth movement was being polarized. The "free people" had no energy or biceps for coping with society. The bid for the presidency took a breed of youth who could talk to citizens. It now emerged in 1967 to meddle with American politics.

To do so, however, it had to accept a traditional youthful role. Although the battle of new Democratic candidates for the bulk of advocates was composed of older people, members of women's organizations, veterans of antiwar bodies, teachers, social workers, and not a few isolationists, outraged by the heavy governmental expenditures outside the country: an Adult Crusade, rather than a Children's Crusade.[53]

Johnson's overwhelming victory of 1964 had created a sense of national euphoria which had been as narcotic as that which was disarming the young. The President had promised, October 21, 1964, that "[w]e are not about to send American boys nine to ten thousand miles away from home to do what Asian boys ought to be doing for themselves." He had said no more than Woodrow Wilson and Franklin D. Roosevelt had said in their time, before entering into war. But he could not now muzzle a discontent which involved everything from economic depression in the midst of war —a novel condition—to the war itself, which escalated with no clear end in view. Frustrated housewives as well as their jobless elite husbands looked to an end and a beginning, neither of which the president could set before them. Among the troubled Americans came former CORE and SNNC leaders, members of the Unitarian Universalist Association, of Americans for Democratic Ac-

---

53. Richard T. Stout, *People* (New York, 1970), 170.

tion, and of scores of other social action groups. And they raised such an exaltation among the malcontents as the youth themselves could not match. As one Tiffin, Ohio woman said of her work for McCarthy: "Personally, I would not have worked harder for Jesus."[54]

The "kids" worked hard, too, shaving beards, donning neckties, or dresses not calculated to anger or perplex New Hampshire Democrats. Their leader McCarthy had no clear program for Vietnam. What he offered was mainly a change, and his "loose-jointed and almost anarchic campaign structure . . . was uniquely suited to the temper of the young people who rallied to his cause."[55] That effort was complicated following the New Hampshire "triumph" (though Johnson polled more votes than McCarthy) by Robert F. Kennedy's entry into the Democratic race. A "new politics" seemed in the making, though both McCarthy and Kennedy had been administration supporters and had indicated no counterprogram promising victory against Republicans.

Riot. The first of several ultimate confrontations between youth and their adult peers now materialized. The Democratic Party Convention in August of 1968 in Chicago was firmly in the hands of party regulars. Their actions were not unrelated to the events which took place on the city streets; four years later Senator George McGovern would repeat endlessly that those who had been out in the street had been brought into the hall. His subsequent campaign, therefore, became a judgment upon this achievement, and upon the youth movement to which it pointed.

The organization of a youth demonstration against the Democratic Party Convention proceeded as naturally as a festival, bringing together "Yippies" planning a Festival of Life, National Mobilization leaders and others from the Committee to End the War in Vietnam, Detroit-based People against Racism, and many others. A delegation of "Headhunters" came from Posen, Illinois, representing their motorcycle gang of some seventy-five to a hundred members. Plans were gone over for coping with the police. A Medical Committee for Human Rights was set up to treat their wounded.

---

54. *Ibid.*, 123.
55. Sidney Hyman, *Youth in Politics* (New York, 1972), 376–377.

All such matters were observed by news media and by the police while negotiations, which came to nothing, proceeded for a permit to conduct an "open convention." Practice sessions in karate were conducted under blue skies. An air of cheerfulness prevailed.

The city's plans were more complex, including security measures, the staking out of parks and the Loop, fire control, and the agreement on strategy which previous demonstrations had taught. This last was resented by the demonstrators. Dellinger explained:

> *What the present system will not tolerate is the continued functioning and growth of a protest movement which relies not on speeches and articles, not on candidates and legislation, but on direct confrontations either between the oppressed and their oppressors or between an aroused and disillusioned people and the government.*[56]

A university administrator was soon to suggest with outstanding restraint that he did not think universities "ought to permit themselves to be destroyed."[57] In effect, that was what they were being asked to do, and the cities as well. As Tom Hayden, one of the Chicago organizers, put it, in his *Rebellion in Newark* (1968): "[T]actics of disorder will be defined by the authorites as criminal anarchy, but it may be that disruption will create possibilities of meaningful change." From Rubin to the more political SDSers, the goal was not to tease or taunt, but to pile "disruption on disruption."

Booing and oinking, continuous provocative insults and even actions could be covered by civil liberties concepts. However, they shielded other, guerrilla-like quarrels and duels with the police, all intended as prelude. One poster in Lincoln Park referred to work already accomplished: a Molotov cocktail thrown into an induction center; revolutionary words and obscenities sprayed on buildings; plans for letting animals loose in convention delegates' hotels. The poster went on to advise: "If we get into enough things, they don't have to be that big, we can close down and uptight the whole town, as far as the people who run the System are concerned."[58]

---

56. Abbie Hoffman, Bobby Seale, *et al.*, *The Conspiracy* (New York, 1969), 101.
57. Chancellor Alexander Heard of Vanderbilt University, at *Inter-American Dialogue on Student Activism and Higher Education* (New York, 1970), 65.
58. Daniel Walker, director, Chicago Study Team, National Commission on the Causes and Prevention of Violence, *Rights in Conflict* (New York, 1968), 142.

When finally violence became the rule, continuing for days, a species of war between demonstrators and police broke out, punctuated by marches, speeches, gatherings in several parks, and a bewildering succession of individual incidents and arrests. Impressive was the cohesiveness of the ever-growing number of demonstrators, and the hatred and malevolence toward the police which they were able to engender among bystanders and sympathizers.

The dissidents never ceased raising new cries, new projects which kept the police in pursuit of them. Each project spontaneously brought together young men and women to strike, shout, march, and overturn. Before the week's events had been concluded, almost two hundred policemen had been hit, burned, bitten, and otherwise wounded. Of the recorded hospitalized demonstrators—almost certainly many more had not been counted—101 were counted. Six hundred sixty-eight men and women were arrested, of whom 276 were Chicagoans.[59]

An approving witness saw "the kids" as right and triumphant, manipulating the police at will:

> With a brilliant use of distance and provocation, rocks, bottles and firecrackers, with the march in the street and other demonstrators acting as agitators on the sidewalk, [the kids] backed up north on Michigan, gaining the exultant support of traffic stopped on the street and people crammed on the sidewalks. The agitators on the sidewalks shouted slogans, as if they were part of the crowd. "Peace now," "Streets belong to the people," "Dump the Hump," etcetera. They did not attempt to disguise themselves as utterly innocent bystanders, and sometimes the ones on the sidewalk would openly talk with the marchers in the street about whether one or the other wanted to change places for a while. It was an effective gimmick, and the sympathy of the crowd on the sidewalk was stimulated. The agitators moved north on the sidewalk parallel to the march, leisurely, with an easiness about them that was good to feel, an elite cadre air. One tossed the elbow of

---

59. *Ibid.*, 352–353, 357.

another and said, "It's happening, man, its happening."
And the other answered, "Beautiful, beautiful."[60]

The author had seen, he thought, a revelation of the human spirit which was "immensely trustworthy, imaginative, quick, cooperative and individual," and he could only marvel that indictments had not been returned "against those who decided to block all aspirations of the dissenters in the streets." However such indictments could have been worded, it was clear that the revolution was moving determinedly wherever it could, and with a sense of victory in the offing. It had destroyed the Johnson presidency, it believed, and would change society as well.

The Weathermen and "Charlie" Manson. The projected revolution had certainly contributed to Johnson's discomfiture, though the election of 1968 scarcely showed the revolution on the move. Nevertheless, there were dynamics which continued to demonstrate youthful muscle. The "conspiracy" trial of a number of leaders of the Chicago riot caused one of them, Tom Hayden, to conclude that "[n]o one, including the press, understood what was going on. From the judge to the most liberal journalist there was a consensus that we were engaged in a put-on, a further 'mockery of the court.' "[61] What was really going on was the continuing creation of a "new consciousness" which would align revolutionaries to world forces leading to the overthrow of effete "Amerika." During the trial itself efforts were made to arraign the presiding judge as neolithic in his comprehension of issues; and this was an effort which not only won the defendants acquittal, but was largely agreed upon by liberal observers. The revolutionaries continued to magnetize adult sympathy in most other directions. Thus a columnist happily observed that "[o]ne spinoff of the Vietnam Moratorium was the discovery that it is safe to walk the streets of Washington at night." All that was necessary was 35,000 people carrying candles during such a peace vigil as she witnessed. She contrasted the ordinary terror of Washington life with the vision she had enjoyed of the streets "filled with light and song. The glow of

---

60. John Schultz, *No One Was Killed* (Chicago, 1969), 198.
61. Tom Hayden, *Trial* (New York, 1970), 35.

thousands of candles shone on happy faces, and gusts of peace-
songs swept along the line that ambled by the White House."[62]

During the following month of November 1969, the greatest
rally in Washington history, involving some quarter-million people,
mostly youth, convened to protest the war. It was reported as
mostly peaceful, though "[s]everal thousand unsuspecting marchers were led into [a] melee by the radicals," estimated at about a
thousand, who had smashed windows and thrown a smoke bomb
against the Justice Department building. As a result, tear gas
had been used extensively. Present at the rally were such digni-
taries as Eugene McCarthy and Mrs. Martin Luther King, Jr., plus
student leaders in great number, parade marshals, and other paraphernalia of protest. The sea of posters included such slogans as
"Ho Chi Minh was a Jeffersonian Democrat," and "The World
Will Long Remember What We Do Here Today." An American
flag, passed through the line of parade, was furiously torn to pieces
by the marchers; another was carried upside down. Dominick V.
Amgerame, 20, of Buffalo, was arrested for allegedly painting a
purple peace symbol on the Washington Monument. The curi-
ously-named Daniel Webster Billings, Jr. walked the entire route
dragging a three-hundred-pound wooden cross over his shoulder.
He believed Christ, if there, would have impeached the President
and Lyndon Johnson.[63]

We Are Everywhere (1971), Rubin declared; and so it must
have seemed to many of his followers. Yet though they continued
to assert their power and prestige on campuses, in demonstrations,
and in the courts, forces and incidents appeared which diminished
their strength and numbers. The massive impediment to further
growth of the youth movement was undoubtedly the winding down
of the war in Vietnam which had given the youth their strongest
argument. The antidraft-conscientious objector-student deferment
motifs had contributed much and many to the youth movement,
including ways for fooling and increasing disrespect for the government.[64] But soon there would be little left of all the symbolic ges-

62. Mary McGrory in *New York Post,* October 20, 1969.
63. *Washington Post,* November 16, 1969.
64. For example, Peter Romay Clark, "How to Beat the Draft without Claiming
    to Be a C.O., a Fag, a Psyche, or a Moron, and without Going to Jail,"
    Fact, IV (January-February, 1966,) 14–17.

tures and confrontations but the appeal for amnesty for deserters: a cause which could not use celebrants of the free life.[65] From all the confrontations, too, the government had learned sophisticated techniques for dealing with problems which had kept it off balance in the 1960's. The old ideal of a citizens' army was being discarded; a volunteer army was in the making. Its potential was widely discussed, but in no ways involving the youth as an outside force.

The possible onset of a major economic depression was also chastening to good spirits and hope. Private foundations, once happy to grant funds for experimental purposes which might reveal new ways to encourage creativity or rehabilitate neighborhoods, grew shy of making lavish gifts for uncertain use. Government disbursements under Johnson had been earnestly intended to satisfy all elements of society, and had kept administrators busy preparing budgets, scales of need and desire, grants and financial encouragement for all articulate persons. Carefully prepared volumes had circulated detailing ways in which funds could be requested without, inadvertently, transgressing guidelines which would prevent further requests for other funds. The new administration showed distinctly less willingness to provide comparable funds for education, welfare, and social purposes generally. Money which had once been given even to street gangs in hopes of creating "pride," leadership aspirations, and the like dried up and was not renewed. Threats of new uprisings in the ghettoes or among the youth suggested ideas for new techniques for social control, rather than for new sources of funds.

Parents, too, were increasingly less able to give youth money if only to rid the house of them. Yet many of the youth continued unwilling to "shape up," and exhausted ingenuity in trying to create livable conditions in communes, in the wilderness, in abandoned old houses. Many of them had been originally "refugees from affluence"[66]; increasingly they became refugees from poverty and rootlessness. Later assessments indicated that communes which were not rooted in such middle-class economics and aspirations as savings, routine, cooperation, regularity, concern for

---

65. Roger Neville Williams, *The New Exiles* (New York, 1971).
66. "The Youth Communes," *Life,* 65 (July 18, 1969), 16B ff.

others' privacy, and a willingness to defer present pleasures for future gain tended to fall apart.[67]

None of this aided youth to whom the "Third World" of colonialism and imperialism was a reality into which they had poured their young years at the expense of a dream period of adolescence and an appreciation of family and cultural heritage. The apparent momentum of revolutionary forces abroad, disaffection at home, an interpretation of events which saw American fascism stopped by indomitable National Liberation-Hanoi troops in the Far East—all this multiplied the anger of young revolutionists, and made them impatient to see their victories consolidated.

Fred Hampton, a young Black Panther shot and killed by Chicago police December 4, 1969—it became an article of radical faith that he had been sleeping when fired upon—had declared that "[w]hen one of us falls, 1,000 will take his place." Some of the avant-garde radicals now held that youth power was being restrained by more cautious associates. The trial of the "Chicago Eight" for conspiracy in October 1969 seemed to them a good time in which to express not merely their solidarity with the defendants, but their open hatred and determination to destroy and hurt in retaliation for the legal web which insulted their plans. Tom Hayden, one of the defendants, was startled by their grim readiness for battle: "helmeted, with heavy jackets, clubs, NLF [National Liberation Front] flags." Hayden hesitated to address them, remembering that this could be an invitation to another indictment, and he expressed nervousness over the presence of photographers. He said "a few words praising the spirit of their new militancy," and got away as soon as possible. He was candid enough to notice that the once New Left was now beginning to look like another Old Left, "with too many radicals falling into the rut of teaching and monogamy, leaving Che and Malcolm and Huey only as posters on their walls."[68]

Hayden was convinced that what the Weathermen did in the next four "Days of Rage" in which their handful of some two or three hundred militants tore at and warred with the police was

67. Richard Fairfield, *Communes USA* (Baltimore, Md., 1972).
68. Hayden, *Trial*, 92–93. Hayden himself married Jane Fonda, the movie queen activist.

"deeply wrong." His colleague Hoffman thought the difference between the Weathermen actions and the subsequent violence during
the Washington Moratorium gathering was the difference between
structured, artificial violence (Weathermen) and natural, spontaneous violence (Yippie). What Hayden failed to understand was
that the Weathermen had hoped to raise thousands who would join
their hundreds in wrecking the American social machine. He himself gratefully remembered combinations of organization and spontaneity which had brought memorable days: "Tens of thousands
participated. The youth ghetto in Santa Barbara exploded and the
Bank of America was burned down. Stores were trashed everywhere. Bombs were placed in buildings from California to New
York." Thus, the ends were the same; the problem was only with
tactics. What many of his friends were reluctant to believe, and
what the Weathermen found unbearable, was the possibility that
the "revolutionary situation" was drying up, and that mild or
murderous tactics might make little material difference.

A number of events created dividing lines for great hordes of
youths who were eager to have all the fun and thrills available, but
who were unwilling to die or even to have their options for getting
and spending limited. A moment of pause was created by the bizarre unfolding of the Charles Manson saga. Rubin, for one, did
not hesitate. He "fell in love" with the man when first viewing his
"cherub face and sparkling eyes" on television. He hastened to see
him in prison and would have embraced him had they not been
separated. They spoke a common language, having a rap, assessing
the pigs, and defending Manson's lifestyle. Hayden was a bit cooler
with respect to Manson's place in their affairs; Manson represented
the *id* of their generation, he thought, rather than its conscience.

Less consequential revolutionaries thought it best not to tread
the waters of Manson's accomplishments too boldly, and it became
a species of bad taste to discuss them. Yet they contained elements
enlightening of events. For example, film-director Roman Polanski, bereaved husband of the best-known of the Manson-murdered,
Sharon Tate, on first knowledge of the killings believed they had
been done by one of their own set—one which the *New York
Times* characterized as mod, wealthy, talented, self-indulgent, but
not harmful.

And in fact Manson was not far removed from people of their kind. The long-time thief, cheat, pimp, professional liar, and possibly worse was also an entertainer who played original rock songs on a steel guitar and made several recordings. He had planned business enterprises with Hollywood personnel. Manson was involved in pornographic film productions and planned a script on Jesus as a black man. He was also in touch with persons whose contacts in production mixed with and touched upon those by Polanski. Manson was well known in Hollywood, and he, in turn, knew enough about Polanski's set to plan the murder-theft atrocity which put them all in the news.[69]

They had dope in common. Abigail Folger, of the coffee family, a Radcliffe College graduate, was reading and smoking the drug MDA when interrupted by the Manson visitors. Her Polish lover, a survivor of Nazi concentration camps, was in the next room, about to endure a Calvary of substantial proportions. He had helped her overcome "that damned Protestant Ethic" which she had already learned to derogate in college. Her new, though brief, acquaintances were also averse to the ethic's implications.

Manson was also a legitimate element of Haight-Ashbury. He had learned "Scientology" in prison. He had mastered Dr. Eric Berne's concept of transactional analysis—involving group therapy, but not unrelated to groupies or communes, or, in Manson's case, to organizing a bevy of prostitutes. In Haight-Ashbury, in its flower-children phase, he had set up a kind of hostelry which received or found a variety of females and useful males who passed through, or stayed if they had assimilated enough of Manson's "charisma" to become his willing slaves. Robert Henlein's science-fictional *Stranger in a Strange Land* (1961) helped, along with occult ideas, and a mod vocabulary of "share water," "come to Now," and "Grok." Drugs and a good command of Biblical passages were important parts of the Manson program. An imperial force in his thinking were the Beatles, whose *Magical Mystery Tour* became a Bible in itself, full of implications which Manson abstracted in his creation of a "new" religion.

---

69. For a pre-Sharon Tate murder of a Manson associate a $25,000 reward for information was offered by Peter Sellers, Warren Beatty, Yul Brynner and others (Ed Sanders, *The Family* [New York, 1972 ed.], 249).

No one was more of the "love" generation than Manson. His exploits in the field put him far ahead of any brothel, and were rendered "profound" by his tenets of complete giving, dying and being born, symbolic foot-kissing, LSD as a sacrament, and the like.

Nor was Manson isolated from the radicals. Indeed, following his last jail term, he came to Berkeley as a wandering minstrel with his steel guitar, immediately making a conquest of a female University of Wisconsin graduate who was working at the University of California library. Other females who became his camp followers included the daughter of a stockbroker, the thirteen-year-old daughter of a reverend who himself became enslaved to drugs and Manson, and others who were not waifs or of submarginal intelligence. His commune idea, though "sexist," as Rubin disapprovingly noted, was part of a new world being born; and Manson's vision of a black uprising, after which he would come to power, was not unrelated to revolutionary dynamics. As Manson said: "Now it's the pigs turn to go up on the cross."

Manson fancied himself a second Christ, had himself symbolically hung on a cross, granted immortality, and followed contemporary thinking in believing that a sensual Christ had been deposed by envious and life-hating Christians; a concept which later reappeared in the film success, *Jesus Christ, Superstar*.[70] His development as a satanist, emphasizing ritual, absolute obedience, magic, witchcraft, and the values of killing, blood, and desecration (even when mixed with such common goals as stealing, which Manson's "family" industriously pursued), was a full and legitimate flowering of all their potential. Part of the stimulus for one of them was the Beatle song "Piggies," inspiring to one who had fully assimilated the meaning of "pig."[71]

Manson's "family" strove for artistry in its work. Said one, of a murder which followed the offing of the Sharon Tate set:

---

70. A showing of this in Burlington, Vermont was almost wholly attended by youths who listened in deep silence and what could only be construed as reverence. A sample of its verse indicates its quality. In the Last Supper episode, the "apostles" look forward to retirement, when they will write the Gospels ("Always hoped that I'd be an apostle"). As a result, people, they imagine, will "Talk about us" when they've died.

71. Sanders, *The Family*, 314.

> [S]he picked up the fork and went over and left the fork
> in the man's stomach. . . .
> She sat and watched it wobble, and she said she was
> fascinated by it.
> Tex, she said, carved "War" on the man's chest. When
> Katie told me that, I flashed and said: "Wow. Pretty far
> out."
> I thought it was pretty far out.

Bernardine Dohrn, of the Weathermen, had a comparable reaction. Although she offered numerous remarks appropriate to
Third World thinking, it is probable that those she found to express her admiration for Manson and his forces would perpetuate
her name:

> Dig it. . . . First they killed those pigs: then they ate dinner
> in the same room with them; then they even shoved a fork
> into a victim's stomach! Wild![72]

Also not helpful to sustaining the enthusiasm of admirers of
revolution was the September 1970 holdup of the Brighton branch
office of the State Street Bank and Trust Company in Massachusetts which netted the bandits $26,000.

As they left the bank, they sprayed it with gunfire, killing
Boston Patrolman Walter A. Schroeder. A bank camera having
caught one of the participants, he identified his comrades as two
paroled longtime criminals, both of them Brandeis University students under a federally financed Student Tutor Education Program, plus two females, one recently graduated from Brandeis
magna cum laude in English and American literature, the other
from Denver, a sociology major and an SDS activist. Her room
was found to contain an arsenal, including materials stolen from
the National Guard building in Newburyport, Massachusetts: evi-

---

72. Anthony Esler, Bombs, Beards, and Barricades (New York, 1971), 287; Alan
Adelson, SDS (New York, 1972), 247. Nor were these humans unique in
their regard for Manson. A graduate student in Columbia University's film
program opined that if Manson were released from prison, "he could make a
handsome income for himself on the college lecture circuit. He wouldn't even
have to write a book." T. E. D. Klein, "Manson's Fan Club," Xenia (Ohio)
Daily Gazette, April 6, 1972.

dence that there was political motivation in their capers and some expectation of acquiring funds for radical causes.

Brandeis authorities were shocked, and immediately set up full scholarships for the nine children of the dead policeman. Others covered all his family debts for a year and created trust funds for the orphans. Brandeis administrators pointed out that there were numerous such programs as STEP, and that it had resulted in a high percentage of rehabilitated cases. Revelations respecting their daughters confounded their progenitors, who had had no inkling of such plans and outlooks. Such was evidence, not confined to desperadoes, that hypocrisy was not wholly an adult characteristic.

What made the crime memorable was its aftermath. The male criminals were presumably hardened in the ways of assault and escape, yet both were quickly captured. One of them evaded a dragnet, was recalled by a bartender in New Hampshire as deeply drunk and mumbling about killing "all the pigs," and soon seized. The females, however, disappeared. They thus gave support for Rubin's view that their kind was everywhere. They implemented the Dohrn woman's view that, as fugitives, they could, like her, be everywhere, meeting many people with their "new identities," watching TV news of their bombings with neighbors and "friends" who did not know they were Weathermen: "What we once thought would have to be some zombie-type discipline has turned out to be a yoga of alertness, a heightened awareness of activities and vibrations around us."[73]

One of Dohrn's more interesting views was that dope was one of their weapons. "The laws against marijuana mean that millions of us are outlaws long before we actually split [disassociate ourselves from the nation]. Guns and grass are united in the youth underground."[74]

Although the program of winning adherents to the "revolution" by welcoming them "stoned" seemed peculiar, more like the expectations of degenerates than Socialists, it underscored a problem in perspectives which other youth would have to meet.

---

73. Dohrn in Bruce Franklin, ed., *From the Movement toward Revolution* (New York, 1971), 154.
74. Thomas Powers, *Diana: the Making of a Terrorist* (Boston, 1971), 213.

An explosion, also in 1970, that wholly destroyed a wealth-laden townhouse in Greenwich Village also spelled out choices which were being given to youths and to their elders. The explosion killed two Weathermen and a Weatherwoman who had been engaged in making bombs. The latter was identified by the fingerprint on a severed finger. Her brief annals as the child of wealthy parents, her radical influences, her transformation from student and teacher to hardened terrorist—her young mentor had told her that her teaching was only delaying the revolution—all this was spread over the newspapers of the land and assimilated in various ways by absorbed readers.

More enigmatic was another explosion in August 1970; this one on the Madison, Wisconsin university campus which destroyed the Army Mathematics Research Center and killed a young researcher, a husband and father. Students expressed regret for this accident but stoutly held that protest against the Vietnam War which was still continuing could not be faulted or impeded; that one death, regrettable though it might be, was a trifle compared to the thousands of deaths which had been perpetrated in Vietnam and were still imminent.

This was an argument which appeared to impress many readers who were neither patriots nor Weathermen. How it would affect official judgments of the participants became an open question when one of them was apprehended and brought to trial. To his defense the young man brought some pacifist "stars" as witnesses, including antiwar partisan Phillip Berrigan, the unofficial discloser of the "Pentagon Papers" Daniel Ellsberg, and former United States Senator Ernest Gruening of Alaska. All testified that the defendant's act, though wrong, "pales in comparison with the calculated deaths of thousands in the Vietnam war."[75]

Most likely to achieve general reprobation as unwarranted was the May 4, 1970 shooting by National Guardsmen of some thirteen students during confrontations at Kent State University in Ohio. Four of the students died. All the background for the event was lost in a sense of the immediate denouement. The long

---

75. *Dayton* (Ohio) *Daily News*, October 26, 1973.

harassment and revolutionary intent behind Kent developments;[76] the burning of its ROTC building; the small but dangerous "rock-and-canister" throwers—all were forgotten. As the most thoughtful of analysts concluded, following exhaustive investigations:

> *We have dissected all adverse evidence, explored each ugly*
> *rumor, but we cannot convince ourselves that murder was*
> *committed by the Guard. It was an accident, deplorable*
> *and tragic. If evidence should surface to prove there was*
> *collusion or that certain Guardsmen boasted on Sunday*
> *night that "tomorrow I'm gonna shoot me some students,"*
> *this conclusion will look ridiculous, but such evidence was*
> *not available to us, even though we searched for it most*
> *diligently. There was death, but not murder.*[77]

Nevertheless there would be many who preferred the uncomplex tale told by I. F. Stone in his *The Killings at Kent State* (1971) which saw the prime cause of the trouble President Nixon's decision to invade Cambodia. Where such a view prevailed, the right and wrong of the tragedy would be seen through partisan interests, the dead being but pawns.

Related to the tragedy, and partially explanatory of it, was its most famous relic: a photograph which showed a girl with classic features, her face distorted with grief, her arms half prayerfully lifted above the body of a dead student. It seemed to angry friends of youth symbolic of the brute force which had swept among earnest and defenseless students, to their grief.

It was only later that equally concerned citizens could call attention to the fact that the girl was not a student, and was one of many who had involved themselves in Kent's troubles with no responsibility for their solution. The girl, Mary Vecchio, had thrown rocks with the rock-throwers, and denounced guardsmen as SDSers had, though she had no idea what SDS stood for. Although she was five feet ten and amply built, she was no more than fourteen years old: a Florida runaway who had drifted among Hippies in Atlanta, Georgia, accompanied some boys north to Youngs-

---

76. Terry Robbins, one of the Townhouse dead, had "led the first rebellion at Kent State less than two years ago," according to Dohrn; Powers, *Diana*, 213.
77. James A. Michener, *Kent State: What Happened and Why* (New York, 1971), 410.

town, Ohio—they had come south to attend a rock affair; and she had joined others who went over to Kent, where the action was.

Back home, her parents tried to make money from the photograph, but had problems with Californians who were selling it on posters and T-Shirts: under it the words: *Now Will You Listen.* Mary, who had run away many times, had no immediate plans to run away again. "Why should I? I have friends now. I'm a celebrity."[78]

More touching, perhaps, was the account of the events following the shooting by a reporter from nearby Elyria who saw a guardsman huddled in a jeep. The soldier pushed down his helmet to hide his tears. "My God," he said, "they were just kids." Yeah, thought the reporter, and you, you too, you're just a kid.[79]

---

78. *Ibid.,* 545 ff.
79. Joe Eszterhas and Michael D. Roberts, *Thirteen Seconds: Confrontation at Kent State* (New York, 1970), 176.

8

Retrospect and Outlook

But meanwhile things were not going over harmoniously at Maryino, and poor Nikolai Petrovitch was having a bad time of it. Difficulties on the farm sprang up every day— hired labourers had become insupportable. Some asked for their wages to be settled, or for an increase of wages, while others made off with the wages they had received in advance: the horses fell sick; the harness fell to pieces as though it were burnt; the work was carelessly done; a threshing machine that had been ordered from Moscow turned out to be useless from its great weight, another was ruined the first time it was used. . . . To crown all, the peasants began quarrelling among themselves; brothers asked for a division of property, their wives could not get on together in one house; all of a sudden the squabble, as though at a given signal, came to a head, and at once the whole village came running to the counting-house steps, crawling to the master, often drunken and with battered face, demanding justice and judgment. . . . Then one had to examine the contending parties, and shout oneself hoarse, knowing all the while that one could never anyway arrive at a just decision.

Turgenev, Fathers and Sons

Youth movements were a function of American society almost from its beginnings. Having taken forms deriving from traditions not inherent in other societies, they gained momentum from the encouragement given them by others who were not preternaturally young, or of radical bent. Poe, who was anything but a Bohemian, had become the patron saint of early Bohemians, and the ascetic Thoreau was hailed as a forerunner by patently sensual and even licentious types. Walt Whitman, patriot and mystic, was claimed by uprooted materialists.

But, more important, a strong current of American tolerance —obscured by violence which afflicted Irish, Negroes, Chinese, Italians, and almost all others—permitted cults to flourish and religions to grow all over the land. New Harmony in Indiana, Modern Times on Long Island, the "free love" Oneida Community in western New York, and Mormonism in several locales were only a few of thousands of experiments which took root in American soil, some permanently.

The twentieth century produced youth who became active in unprecedented numbers and in novel ways. Factors which contributed to these phenomena included land space (though in diminished quantity), periodic affluence, multiethnic relations, and religious unrest. Not to be minimized was simple American curiosity about the youth potential, which often entertained an over-busy people who periodically awoke to ask questions about what they might be missing. The activities and attitudes of youth sometimes produced extreme discomfort and frustration in their communities before a harassed element of society decided how to adjust the situation created.

Youth flourished between the tolerance of the city, based on indifference and a hands-off attitude, and of the more rural areas, where individuals could be counted and assessed. The frontier had constituted an extreme of free-wheeling America. There, in a society based largely on the gun, the quickest eye and the fastest draw had rated with wisdom and integrity and had produced so odd a hero as Billy the Kid: William H. Bonney of Brooklyn, New York, a twenty-one-year-old delinquent. Billy, in his brief moment as a symbol of unfenced youth had been a partisan in range wars of Lincoln County, New Mexico, and was notorious mainly because of his prowess with firearms.

City conditions were more complex, if not necessarily deeper; and such youth movements as emerged from urban terrain made intellectual as well as primal appeals for regard. Randolph Bourne asked for "trans-national America," in effect demanding that the ethics, the feelings, the preferences of new American immigrant groups be consulted in a new formula for Americanism. John Reed, turned political, envisioned a new, revolutionary internationalism. Mixed with their social ideas, however, were youthful desires for more individualistic, more picturesque living than American traditions seemed to allow. Some of their aspirations were actually achieved in modern designs, more leisure, streamlined cars, more efficient bathrooms, and less formal family relations. Whether such "progressive" developments retrospectively impugned conditions which had produced a Thomas Jefferson and an Abraham Lincoln, an Abigail Adams and a Charlotte Perkins Gilman, was open to question.

Similarly, youth movements in the 1920's influenced the career of jazz, progressive education, freer sexual attitudes, sports, antiwar sentiments, and always with the cooperation or tolerance of large segments of the older generation which were persuaded that to keep young, to appear youthful, was a prime necessity of life. The severe depression of the 1930's forced more sober goals and appeals, and though youth leaders in that era became adjuncts of highly centralized radical movements, they attained some autonomy. They became the best propagandists against war, arguing that youth had the most to lose by it. They demanded jobs and educational opportunities. And they added beauty and artistic talents to rallies, song festivals, dramatic presentations, and the like.

During World War II youth movements were swallowed up in nationalistic labors. Afterwards, they could make no propaganda of the war crisis, as had the youthful debunkers of the 1920's. Apathy became the weapon of malcontents in the face of an apparently indomitable military-industrial complex. Beats became Hippies, but they could have gained neither numbers nor consequence, except for factors they did not create. The awesome deterioration of the cities which had been a hundred to three hundred years in building, the decline of the family, and the massive, pachyderm-like educational establishment processing millions of young with hundreds of thousands of mentors and administrators posed social control dilemmas.

Although there were some efforts, especially by conservative national leaders, to return to "traditional" values, many segments of society seemed to accept the new youth-projected programs as inevitable. The *New York Times* had, in 1941, treated John O'Hara's *Pal Joey* as merely contemptible, though the author had made no particular claims for his shabby protagonist. In the 1960's, the *Times* treated as distinguished such authors as Paul Goodman, Norman Mailer, William Burroughs, Henry Miller, and Gloria Steinem, and published articles written with uncontrolled hatred of the United States and adulation of such a figure as Jimi Hendrix, who had presumably exposed its failings.

Many social publicists argued that drug use could not be stopped. The problem was to curb the use of "hard" drugs and provide better facilities for drug victims. The family as it had existed could not be recaptured. Needed were such institutions as day care centers to serve atomized families. Sexual experiments could not be controlled and could only be kept civilized by clinics, contraceptives, counseling services, and material aid. Above all, the battle against bigotry, defined as white bigotry, in living conditions and education had to be pressed without stint, and at whatever cost.

As has been seen, millions of youth had poured their energies and commitments into these issues as well as into the tenets of anti-Americanism, as it was evoked by their jaundiced view of the American past, their hatred of American guns and diplomacy, and their admiration of America's foes. Like previous generations, they had to judge how their crusade had fared.

Youth at Crossroads. By the Fall of 1973, it was evident that their movement as they had known it had crumbled and disintegrated. Its last symbol was neither drugs, nor sex, nor demonstrations, but music. The youth who gathered, July 28, 1973 at Watkins Glen, New York, to the number of 600,000, and who listened to the Grateful Dead, the Band, and the Allman Brothers were obviously seeking to recapture the spirit of Woodstock, with all that it connotated. But, said careful observers—some as eager as "the kids" to see once more the old dream—it was not to be found. Heat and rain there was in plenty, drugs and sex were readily obtained. But to one over-thirty commentator who had, herself, once "squealed and writhed on the floor whenever Elvis Presley did his mid-1950's number on the Ed Sullivan Show," it seemed that the moment had passed. "The party wasn't all that great and getting there wasn't half the fun." And the drugs, at three dollars "a hit," were "downers," "because since Nixon took over, everything has been a downer."[1]

Here and there, a student intransigent refused to admit that any change in the weather had taken place.[2] Names still spotted the news, but as in gossip columns: Bob Dylan, playing in cowboy pictures for money; Rennie Davis, one of the "Chicago Eight," who now worshiped a fifteen-year-old guru; Bernardine Dohrn, who had become a nonperson, earnestly sought by the FBI, but by no one else. There were doubtless enclaves of Beat and Hippie types, Marxist revolutionaries and pan-African enthusiasts, commune habitués and sex experimenters, but their views and exploits adorned small newspapers or sensationalist sheets, and were not of general interest.[3] Abbie Hoffman's *Steal This Book* (1971) was an actual guide to "ripping off" the Establishment, providing detailed advice for theft of every kind. Yet in one institution from which ten percent of the library books had been stolen, his book sat on the library shelf unmolested.

Government scandals now monopolized the press and elicited a type of virtuous statement which veterans of the youth campaign could only have characterized as "bourgeois." Although some youths of the older persuasion attempted to become part of the

---

1. Judy Klemesrud, "Bigger than Woodstock, but Was It Better?" *New York Times,* II (August 5, 1973), 1, 13.
2. See, for example, letter by Anton Alterman, of Northwestern University's Student Mobilization Committee, "The Youth Movement Lives," *ibid.,* December 19, 1972.
3. For the tragedy of Marshall Bloom, an Amherst College "activist" and typical of some aspects of 1960's youth, see David Eisenhower, "Campus Activism Fading," *Xenia* (Ohio) *Daily Gazette,* May 9, 1973.

changing scene by joining, or even initiating "impeachment" demonstrations against an unpopular president, it was evident that
their relationship to such events could only be marginal. As one
citizen sardonically asked, in a letter to the press, apropos of a
vocal impeachment rally: Whom would the youth prefer as head
of the government? Castro?

There were numerous residues of the late youth uprising.
Here a former youth leader was apprehended and brought to trial.
There a "Satan cult" was uncovered, reminiscent of "Charlie"
Manson's late enterprises. Communes sought to avoid the stress
of life, attempting to convene like-minded persons. Sometimes they
tried to define their goals, such as: "low techno (hand, animal,
solar, earth-powered) self-sufficiency with sharing of basic tools
. . . sexual liberation from stereotyped roles, a big orchard, friendship, room to grow in spirit, and the Whole Works!"[4]

Yet all such ventures moved inward: they excluded, rather
than worked for influence beyond their confines. It was also sometimes difficult to distinguish between mature attitudes and immature on the part of such aspirants. The Whole Works sounded
glorious and vaguely practical, but was it? Did the brave words
hide someone fearful of life and in no better position than the
crushed young man, longing for a lost innocence, who asked a
kindergarten teacher if he could *play with the children*? She denied
him the privilege, saying it would be unnatural.

One youth who had hoped to become an interpreter of youth
as early as March 1971 noted a "pervasive gloom" which tainted
everything which had been hoped from "the culture of ecstasy."
He quoted an underground editor to the effect that "gonorrhea is
everywhere and everybody is flat broke." A year later, "overwhelmed by hopelessness," the young man closed his newspaper
column. He had been a product, he thought, of "youth tokenism,"
but had hoped the country sincerely intended to "behave rationally
and justly." But, no, it had no such plan.[5]

Interesting was a second column, printed beside the young
man's farewell, indited by one of the paper's editors. It deplored

4. *Communitas*, no. 2 (February, 1973), 43.
5. Steven Levine, in *Dayton* (Ohio) *Daily News*, March 7, 1971, April 2, 1972.

his despair. As a Democrat, the editor agreed that the incumbent national administration was undesirable, but we were "basically a pretty decent people," had survived Harding, Coolidge, and Hoover, and we would learn. Meanwhile: "[L]isten to your head. Amazing! You can still hear Louis Armstrong there, and the Brandenburg concertos, the Carter Family and Sgt. Pepper. I think that means there is beauty in us."

There was other evidence that youth causes were far from played out. Women's Lib seemed active, attracting some female young, though not all. Family lifestyles continued unsettled. Students experimented, sometimes beyond their psychic and material means, and appealed with some success for support from elders. Although one Wellesley sophisticate complained that many of the students she knew were really as settled in their routines and commitments as though they were married, the social pattern remained soft and unpredictable. Students suffered insecurity as a result, as did elders. Not unique was a young woman with a compulsion toward order and neatness, who felt compelled to play the emancipated female, though she was neither happy herself nor gave happiness to her emancipated partner.

A journalist made a well-supported study of sexual intimacy as a means for getting to know people. "The use of sex as a means for getting close is contributing to a profound shift in our sexual customs," he thought. It was also convenient that "such intimacy is handily disposable, as durable as an emptied beer can."[6] Although such analyses were convincing in connection with beer cans, they were less definitive on whether America had discovered a new principle of social living, or merely a rationale for aimless wanderings in certain intellectual industries and in a number of specialized communities. They did indicate that the older generation, as well as its offspring, had unfinished business to review.

Assessments. The future of youth depended in part on estimates made of its past, and youth partisans were not slow to make claims for their own. They had, they believed, loosened a social fabric which had become tight and unyielding. They had made

---

6. Ralph Keyes, "Getting to know Anyone," *New York Times*, August 4, 1973.

education more open and relevant. Civil liberties workers pointed with pride to hosts of Negro legislators elected in the South who would have been socially nowhere in the 1950's. Such claims and others relating to politics, the "greening of America," and other fields were made doubtful by the fact that many youth had not, in their days of glory, made any particular claims to social philanthropy, but had merely signed up to do their thing. Others had frankly stated that their goal was not to refurbish American society, but to destroy it. Reform was "rotten liberalism" and to be despised as the first barrier to a better world.

Below such levels of achievement or nonachievement lay more basic questions of life. The young dissidents of the 1960's had accused their elders of maintaining double standards. Parents charged that their children debased themselves with marijuana and unsanctioned sex, that they misused education, lied, cheated, stole. But they themselves used the more deadly hard liquor. They engaged furtively in extramarital sex. They honored dishonorable politicians, pretended to piety in hollow churches, and patronized television shows and commercials which were beneath contempt. They preened themselves on education which was sordid and materialistic in purpose and which lied about the realities of American life. Above all, they were racists who in their living and endorsements hypocritically prevented the freedom guaranteed by the laws.

Much of what the young militants claimed of their elders was true of some of them, though not all. What made the young uncomfortable was to have the state of the nation contrasted with that of other nations. It was sadly obvious that most of their tactics and stratagems, if employed anywhere but in the United States, would have resulted in fierce retaliation. Even the laws of America differed in kind from those elsewhere, where torture, decapitation, hanging, death by firing squad, and other means were normally employed as a control on plotting, riot, and treason such as many of the young imagined to be their birthright under an inadequate Constitution. Government efforts to warn young people going abroad of the harsh drugs laws there enforced often went unheeded, with shocking results; yet the government's friendly effort accrued no additional respect among the militants.

In any event, the argument by comparison did nothing for closing the generation gap. And yet the young were not quite so far removed from their elders as they thought. They were, after all, their parents' children, and had absorbed some of their attitudes, though in reverse. Thus, elements of what might have been called a New Victorianism could be noted under the facade of emancipation. True, the young did not hide sexuality under such rubrics as limbs, busts, and unmentionables. But they had built up a series of sanctions of their own. They had made it, for instance, *bad taste* to expose the shoddiness and disease attending much of their sexual congress. Although they used obscene words, over and over again, respecting what were, after all, private parts, they were less forthright respecting the quality of many of their associates' public minds and bodies.

In addition, a Puritanic morality, worthy of Cromwell, though in reverse, made heroes of outlaws and culprits of civic employees. A landmark of public opinion in this respect was attained by the *New York Times* when, following the riot at Attica Prison in New York in 1971, its editor, striving to be "with it," criticized Governor Nelson A. Rockefeller for having expressed sympathy for the families of guards held as hostages and killed during the riot, but not the families of the prisoners who had died during the action.[7]

Such tragedies, arising from Jerry Rubin types of social expectation, were closer to the permutations of sex and social attitudes than might have seemed possible at first glance. Because definitions of rights and privileges could be as effectively determined by a seventeen-year-old female of no intelligence as by the most experienced sociologist and prison authority. Thus, the young female who, except for an attractive hair ornament and neckchain, stripped naked during a sex education series at Grinnell College in 1969 in order to expose the exploitation of the female form by *Playboy Magazine* may or may not have been making a valid point. But whether she would have done so had she not been "well stacked"—had she been poorly endowed by conventional American standards of the time—might best have been decided by a quorum of representative females.

---

7. Tom Wicker in *New York Times*, September 16, 1971.

Other females who abjured "bras" in protest of exploitation by capitalist and prurient interests were certainly aware that their resulting exhibitions were exciting to immature psyches—and Attica inmates. Students, like "jocks," emphasized biceps, private parts, backsides, and other animal insignia. Clearly, the females were themselves guilty of sexual exploitation, by what plain people called "teasing." They were an excellent argument for prostitution —and *Playboy*—which would free male victims of trifling compulsions and help them look more independently and without illusions for character and intelligence in the woman they courted.

The same was true in other areas involving patent hypocrisy.[8] Those who eagerly sought evidence of American military atrocities in Vietnam, but also conducted candlelight vigils for the American dead—many of whom had presumably participated in "atrocities" —were not aware, apparently, that they were part of a "peace offensive" against the nation. Certainly, their discrimination of news from North and South Vietnam could only be called propaganda and contribute to victory for the strongest, rather than the most pure in heart.

The most serious question raised about the validity of the youth drive related to its standards of humanity. There were numerous individuals who were properly "turned off" by crass parents, dull schools, mean policemen, and all other elements to which all societies were liable. But parents were inevitable. Schools there would be. And police would flourish however defined. The question was what standards of deportment would be tolerated or substituted for those in use. Seen so, the records of the youth as revealing sensibility, compassion, and simple loyalty left much to be explained.

Drug "trips," though said to be revelatory, were often taken at the expense of others: parents, "lovers," children who were exploited and forgotten. A young militant had malevolently declared, during the trial of the "Chicago Eight," "We will bury you, Julie," in somewhat disrespectful reference to the trial judge. But he lived on, and while he did, thousands of youths, feeding on drugs, died catastrophically, or were reduced to zombie-like helplessness. Dy-

---

8. See Mitchell Goodman, ed., *The Movement toward a New America* (Philadelphia, 1970) for these and related matters.

ing drug victims were often flung out of cars on hospital steps, leaving "straight" doctors to try to save these abandoned creatures.

The Berkeley drug pusher who declared that he could not care less about his customers who went "up" and who did not come down (that is, died) was in good standing with the Flower Children, and could doubtless defend his point of view on existentialist grounds. But those who saw enter into the lurid and gray worlds of drugs sixteen- and fifteen-year-old boys and girls, not ready to die, yet condemned to death or worse, showed little sensitivity to their pathetic commitment. The young female veteran of sixty "fixes" who was said to have gone on to new enterprises untouched, was untouched, too, by the tragedies about her, which only the despised Establishment would note in its mortality records.

These tragedies engulfed not only doomed experimenters, but the next rapidly forming generation. Some babies whom the young had not been quick to abort were rendered mongoloid because of their "mothers'" drug use. They would have been less than joyous symbols at festivals and other celebrations; and they were not invited, being left, once more, to the compassionate "straights" for service and companionship.

Nevertheless, the young activists found friends and defenders who, first of all, pointed to splendid, warmhearted young men and women who dressed in Hippie fashion but worked with children, labored against pollution, and lived with grace in mixed marriages or alliances. And where such good companions were not available for the defense, the youth defenders pointed to two mitigating factors. One, the social importance of the youth experience. Youth had dared, and we now understood our American dream better. For example, a Dotson Rader had been against war and oppression. He had also been in favor of violence as "the individual declaring his existence and worth to a system that had reduced him to a commodity." Violence also helped curb alienation; and homosexuality, to heterosexual youth, became "a process of voluntary brutalization and conversion, an instrument for the creating of subversives." Rader's sexuality, he emphasized, was close to his activism; "he had long been turned on by very young girls ('it was the sense of corrupting them which was exciting')." All this, to an older and influential critic made for an "important document of the times," and one worth full review.[9]

Secondly, the young in their disorder were products of a world of war and materialism which the elders had created. In effect, this defense saw the youth as victims, rather than principals: an argument which struck at the roots of their cause and deprived them of hope of dignity and independence. Was youth no more than a defeated fantasy? Could it only be saved by some radical changes in its elders?

Although some of the youth claimed victories, even these were subject to interpretations which could transform them into defeats. For example, they had fought ROTC and resisted the military draft. It was possible that, as a result, their crusade might inadvertently have created an army of volunteers whom they could not claim as brothers and sisters and whom they might meet only as an instrument of the state.

They had resisted the liberal arts as irrelevant to life: it remained to be seen how ready for intellectual discipline their revolt had left them. Economic depression, a tightening society, antiwelfare measures all vaguely resembled a time of crisis calling for a New Deal. But was society willing to grant one? The old New Deal has posited a deserving youth, willing and able to work, honoring health and responsibility, family and traditions. Any drive toward a new program would have to persuade legislators and the public whose votes they needed that such a program was worth pursuing, and would work.

Programs. The generation gap would have to be closed, if any program at all vigorously employing youth was to be in the making. When Randolph Bourne had declared youth was always right, age always wrong, he had expected a display of wisdom which would win the muddled elders to his side. But the new elders were not only unwon; they were increasing in numbers. Estimates were that within a generation, more than fifty percent of the population would be over the age of fifty. Their political clout would therefore be tremendous. What could youth fanciers do to win their regard?

---

9. Eliot Fremont-Smith, "Twilight Cowboy," *New York* (November 12, 1973), 76–77.

Moreover, youth was not secure even within its own citadels. There were gaps within its own generation. Some friends of the youth drive had praised it for refreshing the American scene with their NOW outcries. But others saw not only parched earth, but a hurt youth elite which had resigned the natural leadership which their status had given them. While they had disported themselves with drugs and sex, less picturesque but steadier youth had been acquiring college credits, industrial know-how, an inner position in competition for the best jobs and authority. Mainly from the working classes, this new democratic elite would have to be conciliated if they were to make friends with the dreamers and idealists.[10]

They would need new leaders. Jerry Rubin had been a kind of Victoria Woodhull: not a program, but a symptom of social decay. A healthy society would have laughed his absurdities on to a stage, rather than permitted them into the schools in the name of dialogue. Those who shouted at campus administrators: "You knew we were street people when you invited us here," could have been answered: "We didn't anticipate that you would want to turn this campus into a street." A new youth would want to deal with campus problems in ways appropriate to campus objectives.

The street itself needed attention, but not apart from the country lane, seen too shallowly in mere ecological terms. The countryside was civilization, just as much as the city, though the latter received more attention thanks to its nerve-shaking decay. Although youth activists could not be blamed for this tragedy, and were to some extent victims of it, they had not studied it as a whole but had thrown all their energies and hopes into a one-dimensional, prejudged campaign for "equality" as they defined it, giving no quarter and receiving none. Unfortunately, it was others who were required to suffer for their presumption.[11]

Some views of what could be done for the cities could only

---

10. Peter L. Berger and Brigette Berger, "The Blueing of America," *New Republic*, 164 (April 3, 1971), 20–23. Compare with Charles A. Reich, *The Greening of America: How the Youth Revolution is Trying to Make America Livable* (New York, 1970).
11. See, for example, in the area of schooling, Robert Reinhold, "More Segregated than Ever," *New York Times Magazine*, September 30, 1973, 34 ff., a study of Boston schools.

be called desperate and beyond reason, as in the *New York Post*'s columnist Pete Hamill's denunciation of the government and the entire nation outside of New York City as mean-minded, and his apparently seriously intended program for separating his city from the Federal Union. A more calm assessment of the situation raised questions of what a reconstructed youth movement might be able to contribute.

The antiwar issue was dead; for the moment, the United States had adopted isolation and diplomacy as a way of life. A la mode historians were not only looking more benignly on Herbert Hoover's assessment of world affairs, but showing sympathy toward the so-called revisionists who had been less than trusting of Franklin D. Roosevelt's character and competence. The free speech issue was deflated; student newspapers made no principle of expletives and sought clear English within their capacities. Drugs were defended on technical grounds—legal, realistic—rather than as Bernardine Dohrn had seen them. Sex was reverting to its old public/private equations.

The crucial fact was that the country had run out of money for new experiments, or, at least, was unwilling to find it. Concerned youth would have to study accounting as well as slogans. If they were to have any public impact, it would have to be on an increasingly nonsilent majority of nonyouth. In assessing prototypes for a new youth movement, they could profitably ponder the minds of a Thomas Jefferson as well as of a Lincoln Steffens.

Most important, they would have to reconsider *communication* from its very basics. Emotionalism had reduced communication to chaos even among eye-to-eye radicals.[12] Illiteracy had all but become a status symbol. The youth drive, in emphasizing action over ideas, had tossed away the nation's past, and with it, all the eloquence and penetration of its artists and interpreters. They had tested old ideas with their wisdom. They represented prestige for any new proposals, if they could be understood and used.

A new youth needed not only to ponder with humility the radical writings of Emerson, Thoreau, Veblen, James Weldon

---

12. For an astonishing example of such chaos, see Robert Brustein, *Revolution as Theatre: Notes on the New Radical Style* (New York, 1971), "A Night at the Symposium," 29–48.

Johnson, Charlotte Perkins Gilman, and a hundred others—and the poems and tales which gave them added life—but *criticism*, which could teach them (in Van Wyck Brooks's phrase) the difference between a weed and a rose. Thoreau had, on principled grounds, denied there *was* a difference between flowers and weeds. Still, there was a difference between weeds and trash; and trash had unfortunately proliferated during the 1960's. Richard Hofstadter had termed it "an age of rubbish."

So much for the worst of the movement. But even the finest among the youth—those with good nature, uncorrupted intelligence, cleanliness, an outgoing love of people, with honest records in day care centers, or Veterans Administration facilities where the amputees and the shell shocked lived lone and empty lives, or in schools—even such youth could not expect to advance in influence at the old pace. Prejudice and self-interest were built into any system. Those qualities had been augmented by bitter generational battles and the cold competition of economic depression. The "go it alone" program of Black Power advocates was not calculated to soothe hurt feelings. A give and take philosophy, square as it might sound, was more promising than impotent threats, terror, or rejection.

John Steinbeck had once written warmly of a youth who had respected and loved certain old people more than his father had: Gitano, a Mexican-American whom his father thought too old to hire for work, and the boy's own grandfather, who still talked of the days when he had been the leader of a wagon-train across the Plains to California. The boy's father found the old man irritating and a bore.[13] Since Steinbeck's day, the American family had grown even less close, the young ones demanding day care centers for their babies, the older generation subsidizing nursing homes to free themselves of their own elders. A nation which was unwilling to create communes as Socialist or quasi-Socialist nations did would have to reconsider its free-enterprise program for the old.

Many factors had worked to degrade the old into the mock-respectful status of "senior citizens," and they themselves had not been guiltless in the process. The sum of the results, however, were

---

13. John Steinbeck, *The Long Valley* (New York, 1970 ed.), 244 *et seq.*

appalling: 29,000 nursing, convalescent, and rest homes, less than
half of which were decent by any measure.[14] These institutions
hid deep tragedies of hunger, fire, loss of human companionship
and dignity, all covered over with a heavy odor of hypocrisy in
many ways worse than the pine oil and other deodorizers lavishly
employed to cover up careless attention to dirt, urine, and other
marks of indifference and lack of standards. Yet beyond these lay
the question: Was it good for society to segregate its aged? Senility
was sad enough, though even here kindness could leaven the giver
as well as the recipient. But the drive to get aging people off the
job to make room for the young, and out of the home to save space
for bridge games or paying tenants who were strangers—such a
program could only further dehumanize the home and the nation.

James Reston, writing on "The Nobility of Old Age," reported his ninety-four-year-old mother as clear in mind and critical of much that passed for trouble in the world. Reston was most
persuasive in depicting her integrity, her program for life and
death, and her unwillingness to waste sentiment on whiners and
docile sloganeers.[15] But a young person studying her life might
be perplexed about its usefulness to him or herself. Was Calvinism
necessary to the good life? Ought poverty to be accepted without
protest? How could an admittedly splendid old woman's views aid
in sorting out the puzzles implicit in woman's role, the homosexual's, or ethnicity, industry, and other matters which the late youth
movement had attempted to strike down at one blow?

The answer was, of course, not in a polemical reconsideration
of pros and cons, but in that factor which the youth had first exploited: the idea of love. The "Love Generation" had not loved
very wisely, or well. Cascades of books describing forms of sexual
activity had not brought the mystery of sex closer to solution. Similarly, it was unlikely that "new techniques" of caring for the old—
or the young—would in themselves raise society even one cubit.
The discomfitures both categories suffered, and without regard to

---

14. Richard M. Garvin and Robert E. Burger, *Where They Go to Die* (New
    York, 1968), 10. See also J. J. Schifferes, *The Older People in Your Life*
    (New York, 1962), which treats the aged as a human problem, rather than
    merely in the muckraking manner of guilty people looking for scapegoats.
15. *New York Times,* September 23, 1970.

sex, race, or other condition, resulted not so much from finances or laws as from status. Unless a society materialized which defined legitimate contributions from young and old, both would struggle with the animal attributes of cunning and escape, to their mutual harm.

Youth movements were not necessarily defined by action. The Children's Crusade had, indeed, sought to destroy "infidels" and recapture prized terrain. But the Romantic poets, also revolutionaries, had wanted little more than to sing and create inner joy. Wordsworth had praised the young and the old. New youth of the 1970's did not necessarily need to take up where the 1960's had ended. There were manifest areas of life crying for reconstruction, rather than razing, and which only lacked young ardor and older heads.

Appendix:
Perspectives on Youth

Not enough work—almost none—has been done on the influences, and sheer history of youth as a period of human time having social impact, and a different impact in different eras. The following constitute notes on youth as a phenomenon running through civilizations.

Young men and women there have always been, of course, but their status in society was generally determined by others who dominated institutions and dictated rituals. The young could advance socially by reason of family, individual assets, or by strategic individual qualities, but not by appeal to youth. So gifted a young man as Alexander the Great began at age twenty-two (334 B.C.) the military campaign which by his death ten years later made him master of much of the world between Greece and India. His philosophy, however, derived from his teacher Aristotle, rather than the other way around.

There were numerous brilliant young athletes, army and navy tacticians, and poets who adorned the ancient and later worlds. Their views and ambitions served the state, rather than youth. Scipio Africanus Major, conqueror of Hannibal (202 B.C.), was a young man, but wholly dominated by the patrician family which sired him. Caesar Octavius had superb military gifts and political cunning. Later, as Emperor Augustus, he imposed his *Pax Romana* (Roman peace) on the civilized world. But he was given his entree into important affairs by his grand-uncle Julius Caesar, and all Octavius's triumphs resulted from his manipulation of Roman traditions and power elements. Shakespeare, centuries after, remarked the difference between authority and mere talent. In his confrontation scene between Brutus and Cassius, whom Octavius helped to defeat, Shakespeare bitterly introduced a Poet as a motley and futile element—a "jigging fool"—between the warring generals.[1]

Women as Youth. Young girls similarly made their imprint on history by force of family, personal charisma, artistic, political, and even military arts, as well as because of the vagaries of male minds. Esther, Cleopatra, Messalina, Joan of Arc, Margaret of Navarre (patron of Rabelais, and herself author of the *Heptameron,* a classic of French literature)—here was a scattering of names which might be extended indefinitely, of women who under the twists of time influenced manners or events.

For the most part, as with their male counterparts, they were too subject to social pressures and expectations to stand as leaders of youth. Almost unique among them is Sappho (c. 600 B.C.) in expressing a spirit identifiable with youth as such, rather than with loyalty to family or nation, or with an individualism possible in persons of any age. Her Greek passion and despair faded in human recollection after the fall of Rome, but burst out afresh in later, romantic eras:

> My life is bitter with thy love; thine eyes
> Blind me, thy tresses burn me, they sharp sighs
> Divide my flesh and spirit with soft sound. . . .

> Me hath love made more bitter toward thee
> Than death toward man; but were I made as he
> Who hath made all things to break them one by one,
> If my feet trod upon the stars and sun
> And souls of men as his have always trod,
> God knows I might be crueller than God. . . .

1. *Julius Caesar,* Act IV, Scene III.

> Alas, that neither moon nor snow nor dew
> Nor all cold things can purge me wholly through,
> Assuage me nor allay me nor appease,
> Till supreme sleep shall bring me bloodless ease;
> Till time wax faint in all his periods,
> Till fate undo the bondage of the gods,
> And lay to slake and satiate me all through,
> Lotus and Lethe on my lips like dew,
> And shed around and over and under me
> Thick darkness and the insuperable sea.[2]

The Middle Ages. European society from the late fifth century onward offered less leeway to the young and adventurous, despite troubadours and minnesingers. Symbolic of circumstances for the callow and untried was the pathetic Children's Crusade of the year 1212, preached by a young French dreamer, Stephen of Cloyes. He attracted thousands of children who boarded ship to help free the Holy Land from the Saracens. They fell into the rough hands of slave traders. A German contingent of youthful Crusaders tried to reach Jerusalem by land but died of hunger and disease.

Almost startling in his difference from all such youth, and closer to the outcast and the bandit than the troubadour, was François Villon (1431–1463?), a ne'er-do-well graduate and Master of Arts of the Sorbonne who consorted with cutthroats and prostitutes, and himself barely escaped hanging, if he did. His great *ballades* mixed pious fears of death and infernal punishment with despair over the inexorable march of time, destructive of youth. Unlike Sappho, Villon was poor. For a while, at least, he probably lived from the earnings of a prostitute. Villon describes their routine with sordid detail and somber irony, his refrain employing the royal "we": "Here in the brothel where we ply our trade." His "Ballad of the Ladies of Former Times" recites their names and recalls their loveliness. Its cadences conclude with the agonized lines:

> Where are they, where, O Virgin Queen?
> But where are the snows of yore?

---

2. Algernon Charles Swinburne rendition; see his "Anactoria," in *Laus Veneris, and Other Poems and Ballads* (New York, 1866), 64 ff.

Robert Louis Stevenson did not like Villon. He admitted his genius, but set him down as a self-pitying scamp, without dignity or purpose. Yet Villon's youth, his incapacity to accept the easy clichés of church and state, his tormented sense of human decay, and his human need ("And pray God will absolve us all") recommended him to romantic sympathies and made him a forerunner of future devotees of love and impulse.

Thomas Chatterton. "The world . . . moves under the impulses of youth to realize the ideals of youth." So, much later, wrote the American Transcendentalist E. P. Whipple.[3] He distinguished between youth and young men, "between the genial action of youthful qualities and the imperfections and perversions of youthful character." Certainly, young dissidents had difficulty establishing the valid nature of their cause. Thomas Chatterton (1752–1770)—"the marvelous Boy," William Wordsworth called him in his poem "Resolution and Independence," "the sleepless Soul that perished in his pride"—Chatterton was a martyr and pioneer of youth. A child of poor people in Bristol, England, he haunted the nearby St. Mary Redcliffe Church, of which Queen Elizabeth had spoken so glowingly. Chatterton seems, as early as the age of twelve, to have begun to dream of poems written by a fifteenth-century monk of his imagination, whom he named Thomas Rowley. Chatterton also wrote poems expressing his own visions and thoughts, the life and people about him, and his inordinate personal hunger for fame and appreciation. Apprenticed to a local attorney, he pored over ancient church documents and histories of early England and Bristol, and spent time learning to create[4] old manuscripts, which might be sold and so release him from his servitude and hopeless prospects.

The momentous fact which separated the boy from a large range of forgers and confidence men of his and other centuries was the quality of the poems and plays which he indited in the ancient

3. "Young Men in History," *Atlantic Monthly,* XVI (July, 1865), 1 ff.
4. "Create" seems more appropriate than "forge," since Chatterton invented the poet-priest Rowley and others. "Misrepresent" would be more accurate, though it does not take into full account Chatterton's needs and predicament, among other facts.

manner. With the help of glossaries and an unfettered imagination
he broke with the classical tradition which dominated his time. His
poems opened roads for the coming Romantics. His lyrics and
dramatic scenes expressed oneness with nature, ideal love, and an
uncontrollable pride and lust for freedom. In his amazing play
Alla, Chatterton mixed songs and ballads with his story of love
and battle. In a dramatic fragment, *Goddwyn,* his verse mounted
to an exultant vision:

> Whan Freedom, dreste yn blodde-steyned veste,
>> To everie knyghte her warre-songe sunge,
> Uponne her hedde wylde wedes were spredde;
>> A gorie anlace bye her honge.
>>> Shc daunced onne the heathe;
>>> She hearde the voice of deathe.
>
> Pale-eyned affryghte, hys harte of sylver hue,
> In vayne assayled her bosomme to acale [freeze];
> She hearde onflemed the shriekynge voice of woe,
> And sadnesse ynne the owlette shake the dale.
>> She shooke the burled speere,
>> On hie she jeste her sheelde,
>> Her foemen all appere,
>> And flizze alonge the feelde.
> Power, wythe his heafod straught ynto the skyes,
> Hys speere a sonne-beame, and hys sheelde a starre,
> Alyche twaie brendeynge gronfyres rolls hys eyes,
> Chaftes with hys yronne feete and soundes to war.
>> She syttes upon a rocke,
>> She bendes before hys speere,
>> She ryses from the shocke,
>> Wieldynge her owne yn ayre.[5]

Chatterton's poems in his own eighteenth-century voice
ranged from satire to lyrics, and sharply explored the society about
him and its relationship to himself. He sought to interest in his
manuscripts the antiquarian Sir Horace Walpole, son of the Prime
Minister and best remembered for his concept of "serendipity,"

---

5. *The Poetical Works of Thomas Chatterton, with Notices of His Life, a History of the Rowley Controversy, a Selection of His Letters, Notes Critical and Explanatory, and a Glossary* (Boston, 1863), II, 138–139.

that is, dilettante enthusiasm. Chatterton himself took off for London to join in the democratic movement headed by the demagogue John Wilkes, and to make his mark with plays and poems. Wilkes was imprisoned, and Chatterton publicly denounced as a forger. Proud and defiant, he wrote cheerful letters home and sent gifts, but his last verses were tragic in their loneliness.[6] He committed suicide and was buried in a nameless grave.

He was, however, the author of two notable volumes of poetry, his own and Rowley's, and of an undying legend. The Romantics adopted and followed him. John Keats dedicated *Endymion* to him. Percy Bysshe Shelley honored his "solemn agony." And across the English Channel Alfred de Vigny celebrated him in his play *Chatterton*: one of numerous continuing tributes to the poet, abroad and in America, embodying the conviction that genius ought not to be confined by ordinary law.

The Romantic Movement. The Romantics were not only words; they were deeds. They were also consequences. Robert Burns, first hailed as a rugged work of nature, found that fame did not pay him in material terms. Society may indeed have found amusement in his simple earthiness and lusty stance toward women and drink. ("I have———[Jean Armour] till she rejoiced with joy unspeakable and full of glory," he wrote rather pridefully to a male friend. "O, what a peacemaker is a guid weel-willy p—le!") Nevertheless, his labors as a farmer and exciseman availed him little. Despite his hearty, well-regarded lyrics, including "A Poet's Welcome to His Love-Begotten [illegitimate] Daughter," Burns was constrained, at age thirty-six, and within days of his death, to write his canny publisher: "After all my boasted independence, curst necessity compels me to implore you for five pounds.—A cruel scoundrel of a Haberdasher to whom I owe an account . . . has commenced a process, & will infallibly put me in jail."[7]

---

6.   Farewell, Bristolia's dingy piles of brick. . . .
        Ye spurned the boy who gave you antique lays,
        And paid for learning with your empty praise. . . .
        Farewell, my Mother!—cease, my anguished soul. . . .
        Have mercy, Heaven! when here I cease to live,
        And this last act of wretchedness forgive! (*Ibid.*, I, cxxvi.)
7. J. De Lancey Ferguson, *The Letters of Robert Burns* (Oxford, 1931), I, 200, II, 328.

Byron and Shelley, who succeeded Burns in time, were protected from such desperation by their social status and funds. But as social and sexual experimenters, they expressed democratic ideals which did not sit well with their British peers. They found much of life more easeful and inspiring abroad than at home. Shelley's death by drowning, off the shores of Italy at age thirty, was not unconnected with his ecstatic view of life. Byron's death by fever, while serving with the Greeks in their war for independence against Turkey, further underscored the mixture of egotism and social generosity which marked many of the romantics, and recommended them to the sympathies of later legions of youth.

Paris and Bohemia. Wrote Wordsworth:

> Bliss was it in that dawn to be alive,
> But to be young was very heaven.

The center of such inspiration was Paris, even before the French and subsequent revolutions. Symbolic of the spirit which slumbered under the stiff formalities of Bourbon France was Beaumarchais, no young man when his *The Marriage of Figaro* (1784) became the rage. He filled with mockery and protest his "firecracker which set off the Revolution." As Baron Grimm, friend of the Encyclopedists and an analyst of France in ferment, put it: "[Beaumarchais] depicts, with an audacity to which we have so far no parallel, the way of life, the ignorance, and the baseness of the great; he dares to make fun of the Ministers, the Bastille, the liberty of the Press, the police, and even the censors." The King himself had first stopped the performance, then hoped for its failure on the stage. The passionate appreciation with which the play was received suggests the ennui which the nobility itself felt. It is instructive to compare the role played in its time by *The Marriage of Figaro* with that accorded John Osborne's play, *Look Back in Anger* (1956) a century and three-quarters after. In both cases social feeling encouraged social action. Danton, a leader among the French revolutionaries, hardly exaggerated in saying that "Figaro killed the nobility."[8]

---

8. Compare, page 111.

If he did, another nobility rose in its ruins. The guillotine disposed of the aristocrats, then of the revolutionary children. Napoleon crowned himself emperor. Clever politicians, of whom Talleyrand became the prototype, learned to mix the thrilling lilt of *La Marseillaise* and references to equality with the arts of bribery and advancement. Newly-rich speculators and businessmen and their wives studied gentility and conspicuous consumption. Students, artists, and their girls created a "Bohemia" such as no other country could boast, in reaction to the bourgeois materialism and pomposity of the new French elite.

Henri Murger, a young Parisian, immortalized the rebels in his gay and poignant *Scenes of Life in Bohemia* (1845–1849), later the basis for Giacomo Puccini's opera *La Boheme*. With swift, sure strokes, Murger in his sketches depicted the lover, the poetaster, the artist, the musician struggling with poverty, in need of money, but unwilling to stoop to the values of a society which they were, at least temporarily, repudiating. They esteemed laughter and irresponsibility, and were aware that both had much to do with their young years. As Marcel says to Rodolphe: "[T]his wasting of our days with as much prodigality as if we had Eternity at our disposal—all this must have an ending." That ending not infrequently spelled death for Bohemians and their delightful girls. "Oh, my youth," cries Jacques, the lover of one of them, at her graveside, "it is you that is being interred!"

It was sometimes a short walk for a Bohemian from a garret to the academy, dignified ceremonies, and a potbelly. But not for all. Many of the young Parisians—not Murger's—dreamed of liberty. They mixed with the workers and Socialists. Some of their girls were workers: flower makers, seamstresses. A youth from Périgord, one Lachambeaudie, composed verses intended for workers to sing: *Ne criez pas à bas les communistes* (Don't shout down with the communists). The art of such Bohemians, though meagre, enabled them to perceive some of the insincerities of the French regime and to scorn festivals and parades which were intended to stimulate patriotism and flatter "the People." In the painful days of the Revolution of 1848, which brought the National Guard out against mobs, not a few of the Bohemians mounted barricades along with militants in the working class districts, and bared their breasts to the guns of the soldiers and volunteers.

Victor Hugo, Alphonse de Lamartine, and Alfred de Musset, among others, mixed idealism with individual ardor and appeared to augur social change even when they were not committed to it. George Sand's adventures in love, and her emotional, vaguely socialistic novels, expressed the woman's stake in free thought and a more permissive society. The reform movements of Great Britain, in the same era, lacked a comparable flair and variety-suggestive of youth. The great Chartist movement of the first part of the nineteenth century was humane and democratic. But its artistic and individualistic component was weak, when it existed at all.

Britishers visited Paris as much for its gaiety as for its revolutionary spirit, perhaps more. William Makepeace Thackeray, who became the very model of a conventional Englishman, though a somewhat sad and disillusioned one, spoke for many like himself in his verses on youthful flings—in Paris, not in London:

> With pensive eyes the little room I view
> Where, in my youth, I weathered it so long;
> With a wild mistress, a staunch friend or two,
> And a light heart still breaking into song:
> Making a mock of life, and all its cares,
> Rich in the glory of my rising sun,
> Lightly I vaulted up four pairs of stairs,
> In the brave days when I was twenty-one. . . .
>
> And see my little Jessey, first of all;
> She comes with pouting lips and sparking eyes:
> Behold, how roguishly she pins her shawl
> Across the narrow casement, curtain-wise;
> Now by the bed her petticoat glides down,
> And when did woman look the worse in none?
> I have heard since who paid for many a gown,
> In the brave days when I was twenty-one.[9]

Youth and Society. By the middle of the nineteenth century, youth had become established as a force in human affairs, to be idealized or reprobated, but in either case to be taken seriously.

9. William Makepeace Thackeray, *Ballads and Verses* (London, 1904 ed.), 136.

"Young Italy," "Young Ireland," "Young Germany," and similar
phrases were calls to idealism and revolution. They were also calls
to nationalism, from France, across Europe, and as far as Russia.
The youth were inspired in many ways. In France there was the
pamphlet by Pierre J. Proudhon; *What Is Property?* (1840), with
his classic phrase defining it as theft. Louis Blanc, a journalist and
socialist, that same year issued his *Organization du Travail,* in
which appeared the equally famous view: "From each according
to his abilities, to each according to his needs": a principle Blanc
sought unsuccessfully to translate into his vision of "workshops."

Socialist action and ideals influenced elements of the young,
and diverted some from the self-expression and individualism they
favored. But youth *movements* were more galvanized by the odes
to freedom by such poets as Friedrich von Schiller and Heinrich
Heine than by the pamphlets of the ideologues of class struggle.
Alexander Pushkin was by every description a liberal force in Russia, being of aristocracy, but also of mixed blood and passionate
disposition. Pushkin's inspiration was Byron. His poems gave form
to Russian literature. He died in a duel in 1837, aged thirty-six—
Byron's age—as did also, and like Pushkin also for romantic
reasons, Ferdinand Lassalle (1824–1864), one of the influential
German Socialists of his time.

So youth became conspicuous as a force and also as an enigma. The latter was crystallized in Ivan Turgenev's *Fathers and
Sons* (1862), which gave the world the concept of *nihilism.* The
young doctor Bazarov declares himself a nihilist, one who accepts
nothing that is not plain fact, who scorns authority, civilization,
love. All institutions are to be treated with contempt, and to be
undermined. There will be a time to rebuild later, he says. There
are elements in Bazarov of languor and alienation somewhat reminiscent of the later "Beats,"[10] and perhaps understandable in a
Russia of censorship and secret police; Turgenev himself, though
of the aristocracy, was placed under police surveillance for having
written an admiring article on the satirist Nikolai Gogol.

But neither revolutionists nor the numerous conventional

---

10. Compare, page 110.

readers across all of Europe who pored over *Fathers and Sons* knew what to make of Bazarov's view that people were like trees in a forest; no botanist would think of studying each individual birch tree. "[I]n a proper organization of society," the young man asserted, "it will be absolutely the same whether a man is stupid or clever, wicked or good." Such an opinion distressed idealists, but made it clear that society's values were being questioned.

Challenges to Youth. The symbol of resistance to change was Clemens von Metternich (1773–1859), so effective in his labors for the *status quo* that the very age was identified with his name. Curiously, though attached to royal houses and to law and order more than to the mitigation of human suffering, he was a proponent of peace rather than of war. The famous Congress of Vienna (1814–1815), which he dominated, worked to achieve a balance of power and reached across national boundaries to do so. Metternich's supranational plans premised tolerance of differences between peoples, for instance the Slavs and Italians embraced under Hapsburg rule. Some ardent nationalists, on the other hand, though they praised freedom, nurtured antisemitism and hatred of adjacent nations that promised war more than it did liberty.[11]

However well-intentioned the reign of Metternich, it took the form of censorship, imprisonment of dissidents, spy systems, and the crushing by armed forces of all liberal-nationalistic movements. Giuseppe Garibaldi was exiled from Italy in 1834, and wandered to far places, including the United States, before returning to lead his young "Red Shirts" to victories which built a throne for Victor Emmanuel. The Hungarians were less fortunate in their republican efforts, though their exiled Lajos Kossuth was applauded by Americans, whom he visited in 1851. German revolutionaries, too, failed to establish a republic, and were forced to flee Europe. Carl Schurz was only nineteen years old when he came to the United States to become one of its soldiers, statesmen, and editors.

Henrik Ibsen was skeptical of the militants and their motives.

---

11. The case for Metternich, and skepticism of the potential for good of the young revolutionaries, is spelled out in Peter Viereck, *Metapolitics: the Roots of the Nazi Mind* (New York, 1961 ed.).

His *League of Youth* (1869) portrayed a demagogue, eager for wealth and advancement, to whom Dr. Fieldbo, a man of integrity, observes:

> *Come, my dear Stensgard, pause and reflect. You will be the Voice* [*of the people*], *you say. Good! But where will you be the Voice? Here in the parish? Or at most here in the country! And who will echo you and raise the storm? Why, people like Monsen and Aslaksen and that fatheaded genius, Mr. Bastian. And instead of the flying emperors and kings we shall see old Lundestad rushing about after his lost seat in Parliament. Then what will it all amount to? Just townsfolk in a wind.*

> STEN.   *In the beginning, yes. But who knows how far the storm may sweep?*

> FIEL.   *Fiddlesticks with you and your storm! And the first thing you go and do is to turn your weapons precisely against all that is worthy and capable among us. . . .*

And later:

> STEN.   *I made a false start when I settled here. I fell into the clutches of a clique. . . . But . . . I won't go and wear my life out as a tool in their hands.*

> FIEL.   *But what will you do with your league?*

> STEN.   *The league will remain as it is. Its purpose is to counteract noxious influences, and I am just beginning to realize what side the noxious influences come from.*

> FIEL.   *But do you think the "Youth" will see it in the same light?*

> STEN.   *They shall! Fellows like that should bow before my superior insight.*

> FIEL.   *But if they won't?*

> STEN.   *Then they can go their own way. You don't suppose I am going to let my life slip away into a wrong groove and never reach the goal for the sake of mere blind consistency?*

FIEL.   *What do you call the goal?*

STEN.   *A career that gives scope to my talents and ful-fills my aspirations. . . . In the course of time to get into Parliament, perhaps into the Ministry, and to marry hap-pily into a family of means and position.*

Nevertheless, despite such disillusioning leadership, often less gross than in Ibsen's satire, but no less suggestive of the limits of human nature, young aspirants continued to appear in response to crises of poverty, war, and civil suppression, and to demand their place in the sun. Some assumed Byronesque poses, others identified with episodes in Murger's epic of Bohemia. Some sought to group together for nationalist or socialist purposes. Inevitably, their slogans and associations changed to accommodate new conditions.

Bibliographical Essay

The traumas of the 1960's and their proliferation of memoirs, essays, and ephemera dimmed recollection that they represented only another wave of youth movement, and that previous experiences had to be seen dimensionally, if the latest outthrust was to be comprehended. The odd must be distinguished from the real. The history of youth is as deep and broad as human experience. The present study has concentrated on youth as a separate factor in society, and so must be distinguished from others emphasizing art, or sex, or radicalism, or war, or social protest. A few general references indicate the field which can be probed further for historical roots and topics. Related items are in the text proper.

Arthur Rickett, *The Vagabond in Literature* (Freeport, New York, 1968), first published in 1906, discusses the Bohemian temperament, with arguable views on Whitman and Thoreau, among others. Rowland Berthoff, *An Unsettled People* (New York, 1971) deals with the American setting, in which youth flourished. Albert Parry, *Garrets and Pretenders* (New York, 1933) concentrates on Bohemians and outlandish personalities. The 1960 edition added a chapter on "Greenwich Village Revisited," and another by Harry T. Moore, "Enter Beatniks: the Bohème of 1960."

G. Stanley Hall, *Youth, Its Education, Regimen and Hygiene*

(New York, 1904) is desperately out of date, but informative for that reason, and its chapter VIII, "Biographies of Youth," reviews a variety of historical figures. J. Salwyn Shapiro's concise *Movements of Social Dissent in Modern Europe* (New York, 1962) traces dissenters from Saint-Simon, early social philosopher, to twentieth-century Socialists, some young and expressing youthful idealism. Ivan Turgenev's *Fathers and Sons* (1862) is a major general reference, as fresh today as when it first excited readers. Robert H. W. Woodward and James J. Clark, eds., *The Social Rebel in American Literature* (New York, 1968) strains credibility in placing in one continuum Mark Twain and LeRoi Jones, but is helpful in dealing with the relationship of writers to off-beat movements. Anthony Esler, *The Youth Revolution* (Lexington, Mass., 1974) is a selection of articles, mainly sociological, on European and American youth phenomena.

Literature was so urgent a factor in youth movements as to require understanding of changes affecting its outlook. Thus *romanticism* was a constant in youthful thinking, and is directly challenged in Irving Babbitt's *Rousseau and Romanticism* (Boston, 1919).

F. Musgrave, *Youth and the Social Order* (Bloomington, Indiana, 1965) uses mainly British historical and modern experience—but also some American data—to inquire into youth's place in society. See also John R. Gillis, *Youth and History* (New York, 1974) for a somewhat comparable approach. Richard L. Rapson, ed., *The Cult of Youth in Middle-Class America* (Lexington, Mass., 1971) uses a few essays from Tocqueville to the present. It sees youth as products of democracy, abundance, and other factors, rather than as principals. E. Wight Bakke and Mary S. Bakke, *Campus Challenge* (Hamden, Conn., 1971) looks for universal features in student activism at home and abroad.

From Poe to the Mauve Decade. Henry Murger's classic *The Latin Quarter,* in various editions, continues to give perspective to the American scene. Herbert Asbury's *The Barbary Coast: An Informal History of the San Francisco Underworld* (Garden City, New York, 1933) and *The French Quarter* (Garden City, New York, 1938) perform similar services, the latter dealing with New

Orleans. Even the author's *The Gangs of New York* (New York, 1928) describes scenes which drew and nurtured nonconformists. Also helpful is Constance Rourke's *Troupes of the Gold Coast, or the Rise of Lotta Crabtree* (New York, 1928) and Edmond M. Gagey, *The San Francisco Stage* (Westport, Conn., 1950). See also Joanna Richardson, *The Bohemians: La Vie de Bohème in Paris 1830–1914* (Cranbury, N.J., 1971).

Poe's work requires interpretation to be seen as meaningful to Bohemia. Marie Bonaparte's Freudian *The Life and Works of Edgar Allan Poe* (London, 1949) risks error but is suggestive and frequently enlightening. Walt Whitman continues to confuse youth who think he should be useful to them. The key work is Esther Shephard's *Walt Whitman's Pose* (New York, 1938). Allan Lesser's *Enchanting Rebel: The Secret of Adah Isaacs Menken* (New York, 1947) and E. B. d'Auvergne, *Lola Montez, an Adventuress of the Forties* (London, n.d.) are best used together. Carl F. Lang, ed., *The Swinburne Letters* (New Haven, 1959–1962) put Swinburne's life and art significantly in focus.

Although romanticism remained a constant factor in youthful attitudes until the 1930's, it was modified in post-Civil War decades by materialistic challenges. The European background is well covered in George J. Becker, *Documents of Modern Literary Realism* (Princeton, N.J., 1963). Charles C. Walcutt, *American Literary Naturalism, a Divided Stream* (Minneapolis, 1956) discusses Zola as "fountainhead of naturalistic theory" and works various personalities into its context.

M. M. Marberry, *Splendid Poseur* (New York, 1953), a study of flamboyant Joaquin Miller, is a social history as well as biography, as is James G. Huneker's *Steeplejack* (New York, 1915), the autobiography of the impressionist critic who influenced H. L. Mencken and encouraged "spontaneous" opinions among youth. Too discrete to be fully informative, it gains from Arnold T. Schwab, *James Gibbons Huneker, Critic of the Seven Arts* (Stanford, 1963). See also Thomas Beer, *The Mauve Decade* (New York, 1926), on Nineties writers, and Lloyd Lewis's *Oscar Wilde Discovers America* (New York, 1936).

Victoria C. Woodhull was neither strikingly young, radical, nor Bohemian, yet her brazen exploitation of all three makes her

worth understanding for what she did and did not contribute to
social change; see M. M. Marberry, *Vicky* (New York, 1967),
and Johanna Johnston, *Mrs. Satan* (New York, 1967). There is
dramatic contrast in *The Living of Charlotte Perkins Gilman*
(New York, 1935).

The Classic Era. The first youth movement emerged dra-
matically, but out of social materials already in motion. For a
general view, LeRoy Ashby and Bruce M. Stave, eds., *The Discontented Society: Interpretations of Twentieth Century America*
(Chicago, 1972). Henry F. May's *The End of Innocence* (New
York, 1959) is intellectual history, with a questionable title.
Whether American "innocence" differed significantly as a consequence of World War I, or any war, is a matter of interpretation.
Lincoln Steffens's *Autobiography* (New York, 1931) bids fair not
only to be a classic, but a bridge to John Reed, Hutchins Hapgood,
and others in youth and radical complexes. See also Steffens's *Letters* (New York, 1938). Hutchins Hapgood's *A Victorian in the
Modern World* (New York, 1939) is egotistical, but, perhaps for
that reason, helps explain the Greenwich Village he adorned. Em-
ily Hahn, *Romantic Rebels* (New York, 1967) runs more lightly
over ground covered by Albert Parry, but carries his tale further.
Even lighter, and seeking harder to entertain, is Allen Churchill,
The Improper Bohemians (New York, 1959).

Bernard Duffey, *The Chicago Renaissance in American Letters* (East Lansing, 1954) is academic and throws some light on
sources of unrest and experiment. Richer and more varied is Dale
Kramer, *Chicago Renaissance* (New York, 1966). See also Alson
J. Smith's *Chicago's Left Bank* (Chicago, 1953). Harry Hansen's
Midwest Portraits (New York, 1925) gives contemporary accounts of Sandburg, Sherwood Anderson, Harriet Monroe, Ben
Hecht, and others. Hecht's own *Gaily, Gaily* (New York, 1963)
tells of his newspaper days in Chicago; much better is *Child of the
Century* (New York, 1954) which recounts a memorable career
in journalism, Bohemianism, and the arts.

King Hendricks and Irving Shepard, eds., *Letters from Jack
London* (New York, 1965) describe better than any biography
his several lives as Bohemian and Socialist; see also Joan London,

Jack London and His Times (New York, 1939). Joseph Noel, *Footloose in Arcadia* (New York, 1940) includes London, Ambrose Bierce, and George Sterling in its West Coast story.

This first youth generation made itself felt mainly in terms of its "lifestyle" and impact on the arts. Will Durant's *Transition* (New York, 1927) is almost unique in reflecting youthful turmoil without adhering to youthful solutions of the time and after. Several overall works showing youth active in the arts are Horace Gregory and Marya Zaturenska, *A History of American Poetry 1900–1940* (New York, 1946); Bernard Rosenberg and Norris Fliegel, *The Vanguard Artist* (Chicago, 1965); Frederick J. Hoffman et al., *The Little Magazine* (Princeton, N. J., 1947); Helen Deutsch and Stella Hanau, *The Provincetown: a Story of the Theatre* (New York, 1931); and D. G. Paige, ed., *The Letters of Ezra Pound, 1907–1941* (New York, 1950).

Leaders of the youth movement include Max Eastman, whose *Heroes I Have Known* (New York, 1942) and *Great Companions* (New York, 1959) contain useful details, qualified by Eastman's tendency to be more personal than penetrating. Granville Hicks's *John Reed* (New York, 1936) emphasized the political Reed. Randolph Bourne has been better recalled as a war resister than litterateur, but John Moreau, *Randolph Bourne, Legend and Reality* (Washington, 1966) attempts to right the balance. Floyd Dell's *Homecoming* (New York, 1933) is more lightweight than it seemed, thanks to his more talented associates. Like Dell, Harry Kemp was picturesque rather than substantial, but his *Tramping through Life* (New York, 1922) was respected in its time.

Poetry and art were earnest concerns in the 1910's. Louis Untermeyer was a comrade of the avant garde and responsive to changing fashions. His own book of verse, *These Times* (New York, 1917), reflected current clichés, as in his scorn of "gentlemen-reformers." His most distinguished friendship was with Robert Frost, who wrote him valuable letters. Untermeyer's *From Another World* (New York, 1939) includes sidelights on the era. Two different anthologies bearing on the time are Genevieve Taggard, ed., *May Days: An Anthology of Verse from Masses-Liberator* (New York, 1925) and Margaret Anderson, ed., *The Little Review Anthology* (New York, 1953). See also Horace Gregory,

Amy Lowell (New York, 1958); Alfred Kreymborg, *Troubadour* (New York, 1925); and Orrick Johns, *Time of Our Lives* (New York, 1937).

An artist who brings the 1910's back with their insistence on a union of realism and romance is John Sloan. His diaries, notes, and correspondence form the heart of Bruce St. John, ed., *John Sloan's New York Scene* (New York, 1965). The radical component guides Art Young's hearty memoirs, *On My Way* (New York, 1928). See also William L. O'Neill, *Echoes of Revolt: The Masses 1911–1917* (Chicago, 1966).

The form of some of the women's memoirs and the contours of their work help define the influence of female youth in the period. There is a sharp contrast between Harriet Monroe's *A Poet's Life* (New York, 1935), a staid account by a central figure in *Poetry: a Magazine of Verse,* and, for example, Mabel Dodge Luhan's *Movers and Shakers* (New York, 1936), volume three of her "Intimate Memories." Of broad interest here is June Sochen, *The New Women: Feminism in Greenwich Village 1910–1920* (New York, 1972); see also Sochen, ed., *The New Feminism in Twentieth Century America* (Lexington, Mass., 1971). Revealing aspects of the new feminism are Emma Goldman, *Living My Life* (New York, 1931); Mary Desti, *The Unknown Story* (New York, 1929), an account of the dancer Isadora Duncan not to be fathomed from her own autobiography; Alyse Gregory, *The Day Is Done* (New York, 1948), by an editor and associate of the movers and shakers; and Margaret Anderson, *My Thirty Years War* (New York, 1930). See also Barbara Gelb, *So Short a Time* (New York, 1973), an effort to interest a current world in Reed and his wife Louise Bryant.

World War I put a temporary quietus on youth who, in their radical or Bohemian aspects, found it offensive or constraining. They expressed their resentment in such novels as John Dos Passos's *One Man's Initiation—1917*, first published in 1920 and reprinted with a new introduction (New York, 1945). Allan Seeger's *Poems* (New York, 1916) is almost startling as by a poet of youth. Norman Thomas's *The Conscientious Objector in America* (New York, 1923) is the author's finest book; Robert M. La Follette's introduction to it ties it to the larger subject of Progressive

America and the war. Randolph Bourne, the resistant's hero, is memorialized in Lillian Schlissel, ed., *The World of Randolph Bourne* (New York, 1965). Frank Harris, the buccaneer hero of wartime youth, has been accorded a number of derogatory books. He is conscientiously tracked down in A. I. Tobin and Elmer Gertz, *Frank Harris: A Study in Black and White* (Chicago, 1931). A bitter youthful denunciation of the country is by the pioneer expatriate Harold Stearns, who traced America's failures to racism and Puritanism in *Liberalism in America* (New York, 1919). Stearns's own odyssey is described in *The Street I Know* (New York, 1935).

Youth in Boom Times and in Depression. Roderick Nash, *The Nervous Generation: American Thought 1917–1930* (Chicago, 1970), despite its impressionistic title, usefully summarizes matters ranging from Mencken to Henry Ford. Caroline F. Ware's *Greenwich Village 1920–1930* (Boston, 1935) gives the reader pause; it sets aside only thirty pages out of 496 to "Villagers," the rest being concerned with the majority of ethnic groups, businesses, recreation outlets, and so forth. Ware noted the deterioration of social unity among the conventional groups in the area, but could not perceive that the weakness of the traditional community was the strength of the interlopers, the drinkers, and experimenters whom she despised.

Helpful to perspective because of its effort at realistic assessment is a publication of the Council of Christian Associations, Milton T. Staffer, ed., *Youth and Renaissance Movements* (New York, 1923). It attempts to cover conditions throughout the world and succeeds in showing striking variations, for example, between Communist and democratic nations.

Writing was conspicuous in the period, and is surveyed in John K. Hutchens, ed., *The American Twenties* (Philadelphia, 1952) and in Frederick J. Hoffman, *The Twenties* (New York, 1962). Charles Angoff, *The Tone of the Twenties* (New York, 1966) is from the pen of H. L. Mencken's aide on *The American Mercury*. Edmund Wilson's *Axel's Castle* (New York, 1931), his first and best book, successfully explains avant-garde thinking. Irene and Allen Cleaton, *Books and Battles* (Boston, 1937) is a swift and shallow review of censorship conflicts and vogues which declined in the 1930's. Allan Hunter's *Youth's Adventure* (New York, 1925) is wholly obsolete, but worth a glance because of its attempt to fathom war, morality, and religion from the viewpoint of youth and for its contemporary bibliography.

John Peale Bishop was the most distinguished critic of poetry in the 1920's. His *Collected Essays,* edited with an introduction by Edmund Wilson (New York, 1948), helps put questions of quality in the arts in perspective. H. L. Mencken's series of *Prejudices* (New York, 1919–1927) express much of the spirit of the times. See also his *Letters*, ed. Guy J. Forgue (New York, 1961). Louis Untermeyer's *Modern American Poetry* (New York, first published in 1919 and continued into the 1960's) shows changing tastes, some of which involve youthful preferences.

Published letters include Donald Gallup, ed., *The Flowers of Friendship. Letters Written to Gertrude Stein* (New York, 1953); F. W. Dupee and George Stade, *Selected Letters of E. E. Cummings* (New York, 1969); Ann N. Ridgeway, ed., *Selected Letters of Robinson Jeffers, 1897–1962* (Baltimore, 1968); Allan Ross Macdougall, ed., *Letters of Edna St. Vincent Millay* (New York, 1952); and Brom Weber, ed., *Letters of Hart Crane 1916–1932* (New York, 1952). The latter may be read along with Alan Trachtenberg's *Brooklyn Bridge* (New York, 1965), which explicates some of Crane's psychology and art. Among memoirs and biographies of the time are Burton Rascoe, *We Were Interrupted* (New York, 1947); William Carlos Williams, *Autobiography* (New York, 1951); Harold Loeb, *The Way It Was* (New York, 1959) Walker Gilmer, *Horace Liveright, Publisher of the Twenties* (New York, 1970); John Dos Passos, *The Best of Times* (New York, 1966). Ernest Boyd's *Portraits: Real and Imaginary* (New York, 1924) tells much of the literary temper of the time.

Expatriatism was a major symbol of the youth revolt of the 1920's, involving feelings of alienation from home ways. Malcolm Cowley's *Exile's Return* (New York, 1935) concerns his post-Paris days, but by way of the values he learned abroad. Ernest Hemingway more frankly enjoyed Paris in *A Moveable Feast* (New York, 1964), without cerebral elements. Samuel Putnam's *Paris Was Our Mistress* (New York, 1947) is less famous than

Hemingway's book, but includes observations which did not concern Hemingway. Gertrude Stein's *Autobiography of Alice B. Toklas* (New York, 1933) was her best book after *Three Lives*; see also Alice B. Toklas, *What Is Remembered* (New York, 1963). Eugene Jolas, ed., *Transition Workshop* (New York, 1949) refers to the most famous of expatriate publications. James Joyce was its spirit. Anthony Burgess, *Rejoyce* (New York, 1965) is a relatively popular study explicating the master's method.

Humanism arose in the 1910's, but was fought and destroyed in the 1920's. Several landmarks in the controversy include *Criticism in America: Its Function and Status* (New York, 1924); Gorham B. Munson's *Destinations* (New York, 1928); and Norman Foerster's *Humanism and America* (New York, 1930). A bitter, frustrated essay by Seward Collins, "Criticism in America," *Bookman*, LXXI (June-October, 1930) expresses the last recriminations of the dispersed Humanists.

Negro youth probed the social pattern for opportunities precisely as did white youth, and often in tandem, in stage productions, radical movements, and other vantage points. The great work embodying such materials is Nancy Cunard, ed., *Negro*, edited by Hugh Ford (New York, 1970). Cunard was the maverick daughter of the shipping magnate. Nathan I. Huggins seeks to integrate the literary aspects of the 1920's in *Harlem Renaissance* (New York, 1971). William C. Handy's *Father of the Blues* (New York, 1941) provides seminal materials on the jazz movement, so crucial to youth.

Stearns had already provided one symposium on American Civilization in 1921. In 1938 he edited another, *America Now* (New York): a somewhat less jaundiced survey. Malcolm Muggeridge's *The Thirties ... in Great Britain* (London, 1940) is worth careful reading for its high literacy and sense of values relevant to youth on both sides of the water. Daniel Aaron and Robert Bendiner, eds., thought of the time as *The Strenuous Decade* (New York, 1970). Louis Filler, ed., *The Anxious Years* (New York, 1963) focuses on the literary record. Louis Adamic, *My America, 1928–1938* (New York, 1938) is a fascinating one-man journey, and more successful than Waldo Frank's *In the American Jungle, 1925–1936* (New York, 1937), which is befuddled by egotism and a mystic inclination. More useful is Frank's posthumous *Memoirs,* ed., Alan Trachtenberg, with a compassionate introduction by Lewis Mumford (Amherst, Mass., 1973). See also Robert E. Spiller, ed., The *Van Wyck Brooks-Lewis Mumford Letters . . .1921–1963* (New York, 1970). Matthew Josephson, one of the more pliant literary radicals, in *Infidel in the Temple* (New York, 1967) moves "from commitment in the wars of art to engagement in the social action of our time" (p. 368), but he also labored in the stock market. Henry Miller's autobiographical novels carried over a 1920's attitude into the 1930's.

Hemingway did not so much display sex as indicate its presence: see, for example, his short story, "Up in Michigan." Miller displayed sex. During World War II he had no status of any sort, and begged for handouts. Following the war, he was esteemed a great master, soon to be superseded by greater displayers of sex. Several aspects of 1930's writing and art may be gleaned from William Saroyan's autobiographical *Here Comes There Goes You Know Who* (New York, 1961); Constance Webb, *Richard Wright: a Biography* (New York, 1968); and Woody Guthrie, *Bound for Glory* (New York, 1943). Guthrie is memorialized in Robert Sheldon, ed., *Born to Win* (New York, 1965), which includes essays, letters, and other matter.

Simply living was a serious issue to youth in the 1930's; see Kingsley Davis, *Youth in the Depression* (Chicago, 1935); Kenneth Holland and Frank Ernest Hill, *Youth in the CCC* (Washington, 1942); and Hill, *The School in the Camps* (New York, 1935). See also "Youth Movements in the United States," *Annals of the American Academy,* 194 (November, 1937). There is an interesting contrast in Philip G. Altbach and Patti Peterson, "Before Berkeley: Historical Perspectives on American Student Activism," *ibid.,* 395 (May, 1971), 214.

Conservatives were to a degree swept aside in the fears of the period and sustained their viewpoints mostly in terms of fascistic thinking, but not to the extent of being able to mobilize youth. Ronald Lora, *Conservative Minds in America* (Chicago, 1971) surveys conservative traditions from John Adams to William F. Buckley, and raises questions about its potential. Peter Viereck's *Conservatism Revisited: The Revolt against Revolt 1815–1949*

(London, 1950) interestingly equates Fascism with Communism, at a time when some deemed the latter a modern permutation of liberalism. James T. Farrell's *Tommy Gallagher's Crusade* (New York, 1939) portrays a youthful would-be Fascist. Some intellectuals expressed frustration through the *American Review* (1933–1937; formerly *Bookman*); see, for example, Stebelton H. Nulle, "America and the Coming Order," Summer, 1936, 272 ff.

Communism quickened many more youthful pulses than Fascism. Investigations of radical movements were bitterly fought from the 1930's onward. "Dies Lies!" was a slogan aimed at United States Representative Martin Dies who conducted such investigations, and whose effectiveness was destroyed by the Grand Alliance of World War II. Printed records of government interrogations involved youth movements and related personages; see Eric Bentley, ed., *Thirty Years of Treason: Excerpts from Hearings before the House Committee on Un-American Activities 1938–1968* (New York, 1971). For a monograph specifically on youth, see *The Communist International Youth and Student Apparatus, Printed for . . . the Committee on the Judiciary, 88th Cong., 1st Sess.* (Washington, 1963). David Caute, *The Fellow-Travellers* (New York, 1973) interestingly traces the role of those who supported Communist activities while evading the direct stigma of Communist Party membership. See also Richard Cornell, *Youth and Communism* (New York, 1965).

Joseph Freeman, *An American Testament* (New York, 1936) describes the odyssey of an East Side boy of New York who rose from humble origins to power on the cultural front of Soviet-American Communism. Alvah Bessie, *Men in Battle* (New York, 1939) is a Stalinist account of the "Children's Crusade" which took the Abraham Lincoln Brigade to Spain. Bessie's story differs widely from John Dos Passos's *Adventures of a Young Man* (New York, 1939) and George Orwell's *Homage to Catalonia* (London, 1939).

The transition from 1920's writing to 1930's writing was startling. Edmund Wilson's *The Shores of Light* (New York, 1952) puts the finger on qualities which he, a product of Twenties thinking, discerned in his own heyday and that which followed. Bernard Smith's *Forces in American Criticism* (New York, 1937) looked back at American writing from a Thirties' perspective. Elizabeth Howell, ed., *Thomas Wolfe's Letters* (New York, 1956) reveals another figure moving through drastically different eras. Albert Halper properly called his autobiography *Good-bye, Union Square* (Chicago, 1970), since his first and most successful novel had been *Union Square* (New York, 1933). Murray Kempton, *Part of Our Time* (New York, 1955) is an apologia for the Halper type of intellectual "activism."

Proletarian Literature in the United States, ed., Granville Hicks and others (New York, 1935) includes memorable and forgotten younger authors. Harold Clurman, *The Fervent Years— the Story of the Group Theater and the Thirties* (New York, 1957 ed.) contrasts well with the story of the earlier Provincetown. Young artists and writers substantially staffed government relief projects; their story is told in Jerry Mangione, *The Dream and the Deal: The Federal Writers Project 1935–1943* (New York, 1972) and Richard D. McKinzie, *The New Deal for Artists* (Princeton, N.J., 1973).

From Victory to the Beats. World War II did little for the youth—or, for that matter for their elders, who turned from the anxieties of the 1930's and the mixture of heroism and war prosperity to a flatulent postwar prosperity which did them little honor. In the general expansion of services there was a general expansion of educational services. Christopher Jencks and David Riesman surveyed one aspect of it in *The Academic Revolution* (New York, 1968); A. E. Bestor, Jr.'s *Educational Wastelands* (Urbana, Illinois, 1953) sparked a controversy as to whether the younger generation was being ruined by irresponsible educators. John W. Aldridge's *In Search of Heresy: American Literature in an Age of Conformity* (New York, 1956) curiously assumed that only a time of jutting voices could be a healthy time. Richard Hofstadter's campaign assumed the basic inadequacy of conservatism; it reached fulfillment in his *The Paranoid Style in American Politics* (New York, 1965), and was one of a number of such works; see Daniel Bell, ed., *The New American Right* (New York, 1955).

Harrison E. Salisbury's *The Shook-Up Generation* (New

York, 1958) gives an evocative view of aimless youthful delinquency which all but explains the adult malfeasance which gave
validity to Beats and justification to vandals seeking "kicks."

Erich Fromm, *Escape from Freedom* (New York, 1941),
suggested that the rulers of society were not free, having been
"freed" from traditional authority. Seen as isolated, powerless, and
alienated, the older generation received an image which encouraged youthful disrespect. David Riesman, *The Lonely Crowd*
(New Haven, 1950) was another work in the same genre which
sharpened the unattractive image. William F. Buckley, Jr., *God
and Man at Yale* (Chicago, 1951) was a conservative blast at
liberal and radical thinking by a young man who became a conservative leader. The looseness of the social fabric in the 1950's
could be seen in such a contrast as Henry D. Aiken's *The Age of
Ideology* (New York, 1956) which assessed such philosophers as
Kant, Marx, and Nietzsche with Daniel Bell's *The End of Ideology* (New York, 1960).

J. D. Salinger was a phenomenon of the 1950's and undoubtedly helped teach the young and some of their elders how to reject
reality and concentrate on self. His *Catcher in the Rye* (New
York, 1951) was blunt in its youthful egotism and ready contempt
for everything; but Anatole Grunwald, ed., *Salinger* (New York,
1962) indicates the astounding range of comments and analyses
which the author invoked.

The old radicalism, soon to be shelved, may be traced in Irving Howe, *The Radical Papers* (New York, 1966) and Marion K.
Sanders, *The Professional Radical: Conversations with Saul Alin-
sky* (New York, 1970). Its major lack was the component discernible in Richard King, *The Party of Eros* (Chapel Hill, 1972)
which discusses Paul Goodman, Marcuse, N. O. Brown, and
others. Alexander Klein, ed., *Natural Enemies? Youth and the
Clash of Generations* (Philadelphia, 1969) runs through a wide
variety of opinion encompassing much of the above. Harold Jaffe
and John Tytell, *The American Experience: A Radical Reader*
(New York, 1970) especially associates literary and activist perspectives. Henry J. Silverman, ed., *American Radical Thought*:
The Libertarian Tradition (Lexington, Mass., 1970) is a survey
from early national to recent times, within which youth movements

proliferated. *Youth in Ferment* (Munich, 1962), a Soviet publication, features Russian authors on such topics as "Conflict of the Generations," and "Longings for 'Bourgeois Liberties.'" Especially interesting is "The Communist Bid for the Youth of the World."

The Beats were to the 1950's what the Hippies became to the decade following. The key work is Jack Kerouac, *On the Road* (New York, 1957). It marked an era, defining it, as well as creating emulators. John Cohen, ed., *The Essential Lenny Bruce* (New York, 1967) describes the life and thought of another basic figure. Kenneth Keniston, *The Uncommitted: Alienated Youth in American Society* (New York, 1965) deals with personality types which fed the Beat growth. Edward Mitchell, ed., *Henry Miller: Three Decades of Criticism* (New York, 1971) runs from under-the-table circulation to apotheosis.

Two anthologies of the Beats are Thomas Parkinson, ed., *A Casebook on the Beats* (New York, 1961) and Gene Feldman and Max Gartenberg, eds., *The Beat Generation and the Angry Young Men* (New York, 1958), the latter selecting from British and American sources. Accounts of the development include Fred Darrah and Elias Wilentz, *The Beat Scene* (New York, 1960) and Bruce Cook, *The Beat Generation* (New York, 1959). Lawrence Lipton, *The Holy Barbarians* (New York, 1959) deals with Hippies and "Cats" as well as Beatniks. Nolan Miller, *Why I Am So Beat* (New York, 1954) is a novelistic effort to catch the Beat mood, though mild by later standards. Neil Cassady, a Beatnik saint—Dean Moriority in *On the Road*—set down his own account in *The First Third* (San Francisco, 1971).

The Presidential Papers of Norman Mailer (New York, 1964) marked Mailer's transformation from Beat to guru: a pompous act which sympathizers took seriously. It can be read along with Joe Flaherty's revealing *Managing Mailer* (New York, 1970) which deals with Mailer's "mayoralty campaign" of 1969, which also engaged such worthies as Gloria Steinem and Jerry Rubin. Mailer received 41,000 votes: enough to have changed the final results for other candidates.

Drugs pervaded the scene; see James T. Casey, *The College*

Drug Scene (Englewood Cliffs, New Jersey, 1968); Alan W. Watts, *The Joyous Cosmology* (New York, 1962); Timothy Leary, *High Priest* (New York, 1968); and Gunther M. Weil, Ralph Metzner, Timothy Leary, eds., *The Psychedelic Reader* (New York, 1965).

Music was indispensable to the youth movement. Relevant works include Nat Shapiro and Nat Hentoff, *Talkin' to Ya* (New York, 1955), reminiscences of jazz makers; A. B. Spellman, *Four Lives in the Bebop Business* (New York, 1966); Jonathan Eisen, ed., *The Age of Rock* (New York, 1969); Paul Williams, *Outlaw Blues* (New York, 1969); Hughes Panassié and Madelaine Gautier, *Guide to Jazz,* ed., A. A. Gurwitch, trans. Desmond Flower (Cambridge, Mass., 1956); and Tom Glazer, *Songs of Peace, Freedom & Protest* (Greenwich, Conn., 1972). An oddity of the book—one not shared by the author of *La Marseillaise*—was that it could not use Dylan's "The Times They Are A-Changin' " because of copyright problems.

A valuable collection of essays, Greil Marcus, ed., *Rock and Roll Will Stand* (Boston, 1969), explicates songs and singers, and provides a wide discography of the time. R. Serge Denisoff and Richard A. Peterson, ed., *The Sounds of Social Change* (Chicago, 1972) gives an overview of music as protest, in social movements and in relations with the music industry.

Worth separate mention is *The Threepenny Opera,* adapted by Marc Blitzstein from Bertolt Brecht's and Kurt Weill's 1928 German success. It became a dramatic hit in the United States in 1954 and fed anti-Establishment opinion throughout the youth revolt.

The impact of conservative opinion on dissident youth is difficult to judge. Certainly the conservatives had grassroots support and could affect the vistas the youth explored; see Seymour Martin Lipset and Earl Raab, *The Politics of Unreason* (New York, 1970). Leonard Freedman, ed., *Issues of the Seventies* (Belmont, Calif., 1970) shows interesting variations in its selections. Overviews are also provided in Herbert E. Robb and Raymond Sobel, *From Left to Right: Readings on the Socio-Political Spectrum* (New York, 1968); *Youth in Turmoil, Adapted from a Special*

Issue of Fortune (New York, 1969); and Irwin Unger, *The Movement: A History of the American New Left 1959–1972* (New York, 1974).

Highly regarded by conservatives was Richard M. Weaver, *Ideas Have Consequences* (Chicago, 1948), which deplored the effect of radical rhetoric on society. It contrasts with Max Lerner, *Ideas Are Weapons* (New York, 1939). William F. Buckley, Jr., *Rumbles Left and Right* (New York, 1965) are selections from his writings. Frederick Wilhelmsen, ed., *Seeds of Anarchy: A Study of Campus Revolution* (Dallas, 1969) includes essays by Ronald Reagan, Jeffrey Hart, and others. So thorough a review of modern conservatives as George H. Nash, *The Conservative Movement in America since 1945* (New York, 1976) covers older partisans as well as younger, but in doing so gives a clear sense of their personnel and direction.

The Youth Uprising. It is instructive to observe various intellectual influences draw together to inspire and direct actions of the era. Some have already been noted. C. Wright Mills began his career with the Establishment. He moved on in his classic—and corrosive—*White Collar: The American Middle Classes* (New York, 1951) and *The Power Elite* (New York, 1956) which, in effect, saw a group repressive in its unity. His *Listen Yankee* (New York, 1960) opened Mills's arms to the Cuban revolution. His own revolutionary implications are spelled out in I. L. Horowitz, ed., *Power, Politics and People* (New York, 1963), which collects Mills's essays.

Michael Harrington, *The Other America: Poverty in the United States* (New York, 1962) was one of a number of works which fed opinion that the nation was in need of fundamental change. Kenneth Keniston, *Radicals and Militants: An Annotated Bibliography of Empirical Research on Campus Unrest* (Lexington, Mass., 1973) adds further materials relative to these topics.

See also Edward E. Ericson, Jr., *Radicals in the University* (Stanford, Calif., 1975).

Alexander De Conde, ed., *Student Activism* (New York, 1971) consists of historical reviews by various hands. Roderick Aya and Norman Miller, eds., *The New American Revolution*

(New York, 1971) presents quasi-academic essays empathetic to radical developments. Allen Katzman, comp. and ed., *Our Time* (New York, 1972) is an anthology of interviews with Leary, Alan Watts, Abbie Hoffman, and others. *The Critical Spirit: Essays in Honor of Herbert Marcuse,* eds., Kurt H. Wolff and Barrington Moore (Boston, 1967) sets Marcuse's work in the academic context of his time. See also his *One-Dimensional Man* (Boston, 1964), one of the bibles of the New Left. George F. Kennan, *Democracy and the Student Left* (New York, 1968) contrasts older and student generation views.

Marshall McLuhan's *Understanding Media: The Extensions of Man* (New York, 1964) almost certainly influenced Hippie thinking. The blurb writer for the book's jacket suggested that the book constituted a "Good-Bye to Gutenberg," in evident anticipation of a change in his firm's manufacturing processes. Clifford Adelman, *Generations: A Collage on Youthcult* (New York, 1972) emphasized McLuhan's influence, in a hard, skeptical effort to assess results.

Edward Quin and Paul J. Dolan, eds., *The Sense of the Sixties* (New York, 1968) covers personalities, the Negro, antiwar attitudes, and other areas. Ronald Berman, *America in the Sixties: An Intellectual History* (New York, 1968) was a strong effort. Norman O. Brown's *Love's Body* (New York, 1966) was another of the comforts and supports of venturing children. Theodore Roszak, *The Making of a Counter Culture* (New York, 1969) gave their moment in time a phrase. Bruce Douglas, ed., *Reflections on Protest* (Richmond, Va., 1967) viewed it from a religious perspective. J. Anthony Lukas, *Don't Shoot—We are Your Children!* (New York, 1971) consists of youthful portraits, including one on Jerry Rubin. See also, Arthur Lothstein, ed., *"All We Are Saying . . ." The Philosophy of the New Left* (New York, 1970).

A unique commentator was Tom Lehrer, a satirist in song; see his record *That Was the Year That Was* (Reprise, 1965) with its musical comments on National Brotherhood Week and the Folk Song Army, among others.

A sense of youth as a problem affecting adults permeated educational, psychological, and popular writings. Examples out of such fields would include Clark E. Moustakas, *Psychotherapy with*

Children (New York, 1959); Erik H. Erikson, *Identity: Youth and Crisis* (New York, 1968); and Philip Slater, *The Pursuit of Loneliness: American Culture at the Breaking Point* (New York, 1970). See also Arthur Daigon and Ronald T. LaConte, *Dig USA: This Generation* (New York, 1970), the latter culling news items for evidence of a "generation gap."

Embattled youth were conscious that they were part of a social upheaval. Marjorie Hope, *Youth Against the World* (Boston, 1970) surveyed unrest internationally. E. Wight Bakke and Mary S. Bakke, eds., pursued the same goal in *Campus Challenge* (Hamden, Conn., 1971). Other scholarly efforts included Seymour Martin Lipset and Philip G. Altbach, eds., *Students in Revolt* (Boston, 1969); Kenneth Keniston, *The Young Radicals* (New York, 1968); Lewis S. Feuer, *The Conflict of Generations* (New York, 1969); Mitchell Cohen and Dennis Hale, *The New Student Left* (Boston, 1966); Julian Foster and Durward Long, *Protest!* (New York, 1970); Anthony Esler, *Bombs, Beards, and Barricades* (New York, 1972). Marc Liberle and Tom Seligson, eds., *The High School Revolutionaries* (New York, 1970) make it evident that the unrest which swept the universities often began in precollege experiences. See also Steven Kelman, *Push Comes to Shove, The Escalation of Student Protest* (Boston, 1970), an account of the Harvard uprising. A fellow student of Kelman's, Mark Gerzon, attempted a broader explanation of youth's "alienation" in his *The Whole World Is Watching* (New York, 1970) which ran the gauntlet of references from Simon and Garfunkel to Albert Camus and drugs.

There was an efflorescence of publications, filled with news of strikes and demonstrations, vivid illustrations, pen-portraits, and personals of every sort. Lawrence Leamer, *The Paper Revolutionaries* (New York, 1972) surveys this marvel of publicity. See also Raymond Mungo, *Famous Long Ago: My Life and Hard Times with Liberation News Service* (Boston, 1970); Daniel Wolf and Edwin Francher, eds., *The Village Voice Reader* (New York, 1962).

Teach-ins began at the University of Michigan in 1965, and were intended to create a "dialogue" between professors and students. The wave of teach-ins brought students together, but for action, not words. Louis Menashe and Ronald Radosh, eds., *Teach-Ins: U.S.A.* (New York, 1967) caught authors and contributors in a positive mood. Alienated attitudes may be found in Jerry Farber, *The Student as Nigger* (North Hollywood, Calif., 1969).

The greatest of all revolts took place at the Berkeley campus. Books about it include David Horowitz, *Student* (New York, 1962); Hal Draper, *Berkeley: The New Student Revolt* (New York, 1965); Seymour Martin Lipset and Sheldon S. Wolin, eds., *The Berkeley Student Revolt* (Garden City, 1965); Christopher G. Katope and Paul G. Zolbrod, *Beyond Berkeley* (New York, 1966); Michael V. Miller and Susan Gilmore, eds., *Revolution at Berkeley: The Crisis in American Education* (New York, 1965); and the detailed Max Heinrich, *The Spirit of Conflict, Berkeley 1964* (New York, 1971), which seeks a theory to implement experience. George Napper, *The Struggle for Campus Unity* (Grand Rapids, Mich., 1973) deals with "the politics practiced by black college students" at Berkeley.

Works dealing with other confrontations include Jerry L. Avorn, *Up Against the Ivy Wall: A History of the Columbia Crisis* (New York, 1968); Jack N. Porter, *Student Protest and the Technocratic Society: The Case of ROTC* (Milwaukee, Wis., 1973), a shorter version of a doctoral thesis, emphasizing Northwestern University; and Roger Rapoport and Laurence J. Kirshbaum, *Is the Library Burning?* (New York, 1969), a personal tour of troubled campuses.

Hippies were more than a symptom of unrest; they were a flying wedge of the intense militant drive of the late 1960's. Leonard Wolf, ed., *Voices from the Love Generation* (New York, 1968) was a literate work "affectionately dedicated to the entire Haight Ashbury community." Nicholas von Hoffman's *We Are the People Our Parents Warned Us Against* (Greenwich, Conn., 1968) and Burton H. Wolfe, *The Hippies* (New York, 1968) were less shiny-eyed, but strove to reflect the Hippie viewpoint. Sherri Cavan, *Hippies of the Haight* (St. Louis, Mo., 1972) and Lewis Yablonsky, *The Hippie Trip* (New York, 1968) applied techniques for assessing Hippies. J. L. Simmons and Barry Winegrad, *It's Happening* (Santa Barbara, 1967), like other writings, could not credit how swiftly the dream was collapsing.

Michael Rossman, *The Wedding within the War* (New York, 1971) bestrides Hippie ideals and revolutionary dreams. Richard Neville, *Play Power* (New York, 1971), from another vantage point, treats the youth movement as fun. Ed Sanders, *The Family* (New York, 1971) and Vincent Bugliosi, *Helter Skelter* (New York, 1974) are the best books on the Charles Manson prodigy.

Tom Wolfe was not so much a student of youth as of the temper of the time which gave them options. His *The Kandy-Kolored Tangerine-Flake Streamline Baby* (New York, 1965), a product of "new journalism," reflected a mood rather than a permanent change in reporting. There is a wide range of publications, some all but unreadable in psychedelic colors and unconsidered prose. One example would be *Chamisa Road, with Paul & Meredith Doin' the Dog in Taos* (New York, 1971) which tried to reflect the euphoria of the young male and female from New York who experienced "ecstatic earth visions" in New Mexico. The distance from this book to David Horowitz, Michael Lerner, Craig Pyes, *Counterculture and Perdition* (New York, 1972), with a wide range of selections, is less far than appears at first glance. The combination of unprincipled attitudes and action is well expressed in Dotson Rader, *I Ain't Marchin' Anymore* (New York, 1969) whom *Newsweek* called "the Eldridge Cleaver of the white new left," perhaps accurately, and who moved from "militancy" to fashionable New York journalism almost without breaking step.

Michael Useem, *Conscription: Protest and Social Conflict* (New York, 1973) is a sociological analysis. Unrelated, and probably not so much as a halfway house for some aspiring youth, was the Peace Corps, which gave travel opportunities to a variety of youth and was a secondary movement of sorts; see *The Peace Corps Reader* (Washington, 1967), a collection of articles explaining the Corps' mission, by David Riesman and Frank Mankiewicz, among others.

Several novels bearing on the youth theme include: Rudolph Wurlitzer, *Nog* (New York, 1970); Ray Mungo and Peter Simon, *Moving On* (New York, 1973); Robert Stone, *Dog Soldiers* (Boston, 1974); Tom Robbins, *Another Roadside Attraction* (New York, 1975).

Ideology built on the unstanched passion and free movement

of the young. The academics contributed important rationales for their deeds. Tom Christoffel, et al., *Up against the American Myth* (New York, 1970) in essays traced the failure of American capitalism. Irwin Ungar, ed., *Beyond Liberalism: The New Left Views American History* (Waltham, Mass., 1971) tried to institutionalize the youth uprising. William Appleman Williams, *The United States, Cuba, and Castro* (New York, 1962), a pioneer in this field, is oddly dedicated to John Quincy Adams, apparently as a defensive measure.

The rise and crystallization of youth revolt can be traced in Jack Newfield, *A Prophetic Minority* (New York, 1970), with a new introduction interpreting post-1966 events; Allan Brownfeld, *The New Left: Memorandum* (Washington, 1968), a congressional document; Richard E. Peterson, *May 1970: The Campus Aftermath of Cambodia and Kent State* (Berkeley, 1971); Alan E. Bayer and Alexander W. Astin, *Campus Disruption during 1968-1969* (Washington, 1969); George Lavan, ed., *Che Guevara Speaks* (New York, 1967); Burton M. Atkins, comp. *Prisons, Protest, and Politics* (New York, 1972), one of a number of books showing the ramifications of issues fueling student attitudes; James S. Kunen, *The Strawberry Statement, Notes of a College Revolutionary* (New York, 1969), to be read alongside of John R. Coyne, Jr., *The Kumquat Statement* (New York, 1970), a conservative retort.

Stephen Spender, *The Year of the Young Rebels* (New York, 1969 ed.) is by a distinguished poet of the 1930's Left. Massimo Teodori, *The New Left: A Documentary History* (Indianapolis, 1969) is compendious, much of it obsolete; see also Mitchell Goodman, ed., *The Movement toward a New America* (Philadelphia, 1970), an oversized collage. Greg Calvert and Carol Neiman, *A Disrupted History: The New Left and the New Capitalism* (New York, 1971) utilizes the movement's jargon. Better written is Alan Adelman, *SDS* (New York, 1972). See also Kilpatrick Sal, *SDS* (New York, 1973). Phillip A. Luce, *The New Left,* (New York, 1966) and *The New Left Today: America's Trojan Horse* (Washington, 1971) trace the author's progress from New Left to Anti-New Left. The "Trojan horse" metaphor has appeared before in unsympathetic views of "left" movements. See also *Hear-*

ings before the Committee on Un-American Activities, House of Representatives. Nineteenth Congress, second Session. 3 Parts (Washington, 1968). James A. Michener, *Kent State: What Happened and Why* (New York, 1971) is definitive. Bruce Franklin, ed., *From the Movement toward Revolution* (New York, 1971) is by an activist and former academic. Desperate facets of the movement are present in Harold Jacobs, ed., *Weatherman* (N.p., 1970), and Thomas Powers, *Diana: The Making of a Terrorist* (New York, 1971).

The Berrigan brothers, as Catholics and as war resisters, were representative of dissent which came from various directions to feed the youth revolt; see William VanEtten Casey and Philip Nobile, eds., *The Berrigans* (New York, 1971); also Daniel Berrigan, *They Call Us Dead Men* (New York, 1968).

The Vietnam War created its torrent of books, and their influence may be found in many of the above works. The youth factor can be discerned in such a sample of writings as Willard Gaylin, *In the Service of Their Country: War Resisters in Prison* (New York, 1970); Arlo Tatum and Joseph S. Tuchinsky, *Guide to the Draft* (Boston, 1967); Abbie Hoffman, Bobby Seale, and others, *The Conspiracy* (New York, 1967), with an introduction by Noam Chomsky; I. F. Stone, *Polemics and Prophecies, 1967–1970* (New York, 1970); Staughton Lynd and Thomas Hayden, *The Other Side* (New York, 1966), an account of a North Vietnam visit; Alice Lynd, ed., *We Won't Go* (Boston, 1968); and Roger N. Williams, *The New Exiles: American War Resisters in Canada* (New York, 1971).

There was some, but not much, overlap from youth revolt to national concerns. Sidney Hyman, *Youth in Politics* (New York, 1972) strikes as fair an equation as is possible. See also Richard T. Stout, *People: The ... Grass-Roots Movement That Found Eugene McCarthy* (New York, 1970), and Gary Warren Hart, *Right from the Start: A Chronicle of the McGovern Campaign* (New York, 1973). Ralph Nader's numerous projects enlisted youth at the beginning, but seems to have leveled off in this respect. See Ralph Nader and Donald Ross et al., *Action for Change: A Student's Manual for Organizing* (New York, 1971).

Blacks. Norman Mailer's *The White Negro* (San Francisco, 1969 ed.) was an early empathetic statement which influenced many intellectuals. Among other books of 1960's interest here are Frank Hercules, *American Society and Black Revolution* (New York, 1972); Benjamin Muse, *The American Negro Revolution from Nonviolence to Black Power* (New York, 1968); August Meier and Elliott Rudwick, eds., *Black Protest in the Sixties* (Chicago, 1970), and *CORE* (New York, 1973); Lerone Bennett, Jr., *Before the Mayflower* (Baltimore, 1964 ed.), an influential work; Floyd B. Barbour, ed., *The Black Power Revolt* (Boston, 1968). For one of a number of the tragedies accompanying city change and unrest, largely led by youth, Van Gordon Sauter and Burleigh Hines, *Nightmare in Detroit* (Chicago, 1968), an account of the 1967 riot which left forty-three persons dead and the city measurably damaged.

Peter Geismar, *Fanon* (New York, 1971) discusses a foreign revolutionary influential on Americans; *The Autobiography of Malcolm X* (New York, 1964) ranks with Fanon in this respect. Numerous Negroes were individualized and made centers and inspirations for actions; for example, Regina Nadelson, *Who Is Angela Davis?* (New York, 1972); James Baldwin, *Nobody Knows My Name* (New York, 1961); Ethel N. Minor, ed., *Stokely Speaks* (New York, 1967); Dick Gregory, *Nigger* (New York, 1964). Gregory's *No More Lies* (New York, 1971) is a bold attempt to create revisionist American history, which impressed academics and therefore their students, as well as sympathetic readers. Bobby Seale, *Seize the Time: The Story of the Black Panther Party and Huey P. Newton* (New York, 1970) is one of a canon of books which probably added up to a greater number than the party's adherents. For one of the lingering incidents attending police-Black Panther confrontations, Roy Wilkins and Ramsey Clark, chairmen, *Search and Destroy: A Report by the Commission of Inquiry into the Black Panthers and the Police* (New York, 1973), an investigation into the deaths in Chicago of Fred Hampton and Mark Clark, allegedly by police firearms.

Blacks in the student movement created a smaller library.

Howard Zinn, SNCC (Boston, 1964) treated the organization as composed of "New Abolitionists." Broad views of the problem of campus rationales are in David C. Nichols and Olive Mills, *The Campus and the Racial Crisis* (Washington, 1970), James Mc-Avoy and Abraham Miller, *Black Power and Student Rebellion* (Belmont, Calif., 1969). The San Francisco State College (now University) uprising was notable as being led by blacks; see William H. Orricks, Jr., *College in Crisis* (Nashville, 1970), and De Vere E. Pentony, et al., *Unfinished Rebellions* (San Francisco, 1971).

The Symbionese Liberation Army of San Francisco was one of many exotic by-products of the era's efforts, made famous by the "kidnaping" of heiress Patricia Hearst and subsequent sensations. A starting point for those interested would be Marilyn Baker, with Sally Brompton, *Exclusive! The Inside Story of Patricia Hearst and the SLA* (New York, 1974).

Writing was not urgently pursued as a goal in itself. See Theodore Solotaroff, *The Red Hot Vacuum and Other Pieces on Writing of the Sixties* (New York, 1970); Harry J. Cargas, *Daniel Berrigan and Contemporary Protest Poetry* (New Haven, Conn., 1972); Seymour Krim, *Shake It for the World, Smartass* (New York, 1970), by an avant-garde writer, as in his essay, "Who's Afraid of the *New Yorker* Now?" LeRoi Jones (Imamu Amuri Baraka) was hailed as an original writer, as in his *Tales* (New York, 1967). He mixed impressionistic prose with activism in the Newark, New Jersey, area. See his essay, "Heroes Are Gang Leaders." See also Walter Lowenfels, ed., *In a Time of Revolution: Poems from Our Third World* (New York, 1969).

Sylvia Plath was vaguely perceived as a victim of "sexism" and as a poet; see Eileen M. Aird, *Sylvia Plath* (New York, 1973).

Also related to culture, as well as "counterculture," were Daniel Foss, *Freak Culture* (New York, 1972), and Michael Horowitz, comp., *A Freak's Anthology: Golden Hits from Buddha to Kubrick* (Los Angeles, 1972).

Other Causes attracted youth. A scattering of writings suggests the areas and approaches taken toward them: Merle Miller,

On Being Different: What It Means to Be a Homosexual (New York, 1971); Kay Tobin and Randy Wicker, *The Gay Crusaders* (New York, 1972); Michael E. Adelstein and Jean G. Pival, eds., *Perspective: Women's Liberation* (New York, 1972); Keith Melville, *Communes in the Counter Culture* (New York, 1972); Ray Ald, *The Youth Communes* (New York, 1970); Richard Fairfield, *Communes USA: A Personal Tour* (Baltimore, 1972); Justus J. Schiffires, *The Older People in Your Life* (New York, 1962).

Robert Houriet, *Getting Back Together* (New York, 1971) was a tour of communes from Oregon to New England, describing the variety of experimenters and "kooks" who sought everything from inner peace to outer euphoria. Briefly popular was "Stephen's" *Monday Night Class* (Santa Rosa, Calif., 1970), a lengthy, carelessly phrased monologue responding to questions on the virtues of being "stoned," on Karma, on Zen Buddhism, and on getting it all together. See also Ronald M. Euroth, Edward E. Ericson, and Breckinridge Peters, *The Jesus People: Old Time Religion in the Age of Aquarius* (Grand Rapids, Mich., 1972).

Though not a critical issue for youth, "environment" furnished one of its complaints against the status quo. Fred Carvell and Max Tadlock, *It's Not Too Late* (Beverly Hills, Cal., 1971) is a semiacademic anthology on the issue.

Courtroom injustices were linked with other offenses imputed to capitalism, and so served embattled youth, as in Leonard Downie, Jr., *Justice Denied* (New York, 1972).

Index